PHOTOGRAPHIC
FIELD GUIDE

BIRDS

OF BRITAIN AND EUROPE

PHOTOGRAPHIC FIELD GUIDE

BIRDS

OF BRITAIN AND EUROPE

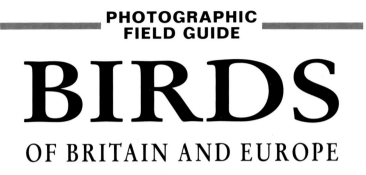

Text by Jim Flegg
Photographs by David Hosking

NEW
HOLLAND

Acknowledgements

The publishers, author and principal photographers gratefully acknowledge the assistance of all those involved in the compilation of this book, with special thanks to Caroline Flegg and Jean Lane. All the photographs were taken by Eric or David Hosking with the exception of those listed below:

Kevin Carlson 147br, 175br, 177br, 189br, 197bl, 221bl; R.J. Chandler 43tr, 135tr, 139bl, 173tr, 175mr; Richard Coomber 47bl; Dennis Coutts 49tl, 115bl, 159bl, 183br, 193m, 195bl; Paul Doherty 47m, 111tr, 131m, 193t, 195t, 197tr, 201tr; Yossi Eshbol 51br; Jim Flegg 87bl, 159br; Hannu Hautala 101ml, 151tr, 153br, 161br, 163br, 167br, 215tr, 229br, 235tr, 239bl, br; John Hawkins 45br, 101bl, 123br, 157tr, 163bl, 177tr, 201br, 205br, 215bl, br, 219m, 237mr, 239tl; Roger Hosking 99bl, 205bl; Chris Knights 129bl; Dr I. Vatev 53b; Steve Young 133tl.

Frank Lane Picture Agency: Ron Austing 89tr, 231tl, tr, ml, mr; Leo Batten 51tr; B. Borrell 195br, 209tl; B.B. Casals 189tl, 197tl; Tom & Pam Gardner 127bl; Gosta Hakansson 205m; A. Johnson 115mr; S. Jonasson 49tr; Frank Lane 69br; F. Merlet 73ml; Mark Newman 45m, 101tl; D.A. Robinson 189m; Heinz Schrempp 93tr, 211bl, 225br, 229m; Roger Tidman 121tl, 133ml, 189tr, 205tr, 233br; L. West 231bl, br; Roger Wilmshurst 115tl; D. Zingel 197br.

Silvestris: Hansgeorg Arndt 43br, 105tr, 179m; Hans-Dieter Brandl 153tr, 163ml, 211tr, br, 217tr, 241bl; Claudio Chini 191tl; A. Christiansen 83tr, 89br, 121bl; Rudolph Höfels 163mr; Eugen Hottenmosser 211ml; Gerhard Kriso 177bl, 189bl; Werner Layer 93br; Stefan Meyers 101br; Günter Moosrainer 201tl; Manfred Pforr 99tl; Norbert Rosing 91m; Silvestris 51mr; Konrad Wothe 107bl, 155br, 165tl, 169tr, 185tl, 223bl, 225bl.

(t = top; tl = top left; tr = top right; m = middle; ml = middle left; mr = middle right; b = bottom; bl = bottom left; br = bottom right.)

This edition first published in 1993 by
New Holland (Publishers) Ltd
37 Connaught Street, London W2 2AZ

Copyright © 1990 New Holland (Publishers) Ltd
Copyright © 1990 photographs as credited above

All rights reserved. No part of this publication may be reproduced, stored in a retrieval system, or transmitted in any form or by any means, electronic, mechanical, photocopying, recording, or otherwise, without the prior written permission of the copyright owners.

ISBN 1 85368 244 6 (hbk)
ISBN 1 85368 263 2 (pbk)

Commissioning Editor: Charlotte Parry-Crooke
Editors: Ann Hill, Alison Copland
Assistant Editor: Tracey Williams
Design: ML Design, London
Cartography/diagrams: ML Design, London
Artwork: Martin Woodcock

7 4 4

Typeset by ML Design, London
Reproduction by Scantrans Pte Ltd, Singapore
Printed and bound in Singapore by Kyodo Printing Co (Singapore) Pte Ltd

CONTENTS

SOUTHERN EDUCATION
AND LIBRARY BOARD

Acc. No.
2049005

CLASS No. OR AUTHOR
598·294

INTRODUCTION

One major attraction of birdwatching is that, no matter where you are, or when, there will always be birds to watch. More than that, birdwatching can be as casual or as detailed as you wish. There are plenty of sheer bird spectacles: wild geese in flight over the marshes, or starlings wheeling in the dusk sky over a city square.

The enjoyment of such scenes can be increased by learning how to watch more closely and by being able to answer the challenge of identifying the birds correctly. This book aims to help you do that – and to increase the fascination of birds still further by providing a background knowledge of their habits and lifestyles.

The book covers most of the species that you are likely to encounter in

The spectactular sight of starlings in roosting flight seen against the setting sun

Britain and Europe – even in a lifetime of birdwatching. Included are more than 430 individual species – the majority of birds which breed in, or regularly visit, or pass through some part of Europe. Since birds do not observe political boundaries, by 'Europe' we mean an area north to the Arctic Circle and south to the Mediterranean Sea. Eastwards the area extends to 30° longitude (a line which joins Leningrad to Alexandria) and westwards to the Atlantic coast of Ireland. Iceland is also included. Omitted here are birds that visit Europe only extremely rarely. Some of these rarities have been seen only once or twice, others just a handful of times. Others that, while still very rare, do occur with some regularity are featured on pages 50-1, 114-15, 158-9 and 230-1.

The main guide, which runs from page 42 to page 241, contains the photographs and descriptions of the birds. Each species is shown in its characteristic habitat and described – on the opposite page – in detail. Extra photographs of many species are also included; these depict plumage variations and birds in flight or at the nest. How to use the guide, and in particular how to interpret the maps, diagrams and symbols, is described in the section which follows.

6

The other introductory sections provide background information on the birds. *Bird Biology* identifies, with the aid of diagrams, the distinctive physical features of birds and of their plumage, and summarizes the biology of the birds. *Bird Habitats*, a major feature not usually found in field guides, will assist the birdwatcher in identifications by describing, in general terms, which bird families favour which type of terrain. *Bird Names and Classification* examines the system of classification in current use and according to which the birds in this book are arranged. Finally, in *Family Characteristics* there is a description of each of the orders and families into which the European birds included here are divided and the characteristics which they share.

The sections at the end of the book concentrate not so much on the birds as on the birdwatcher. In *Fieldcraft*, the reader is advised on the best birdwatching methods and how to prepare for an expedition in the various habitats described earlier, while *Field Equipment* gives information on the choice of binoculars and telescopes. *Conservation* explains the need for habitats to be defended and preserved and suggests how the birdwatcher can help; *Clubs and Societies* lists many ornithological organizations committed to the cause of conservation. Lastly, the *Bibliography* recommends a selection of books – from amongst the enormous number now in print – which are of real use to the birdwatcher.

How to Use the Guide

The species included in the guide are arranged according to the widely accepted order described on page 25 under *Bird Names and Classification*. The guide begins in the conventional way with the divers (family Gaviidae) and ends with the buntings (family Emberizidae). There are some pages, however, which interrupt this sequence to make other specific points. These are pages 50-1, 68-9, 114-15, 158-9, 174-5 and 230-1. Further details of these 'special pages' are given on pages 25-6.

Each species included in the guide is illustrated with one or more photographs and described in a detailed text. Each text is accompanied by a distribution map, a seasonal abundance diagram and a range of habitat symbols. All the elements relating to each species are displayed together for ease of use.

Detailed texts provide full descriptions of the birds, their lifestyles, habits, voices and distribution

Symbols give instant reference to the habitats frequented by the birds

Maps show the birds' winter, summer and year-round distribution

Seasonal abundance diagrams indicate the likelihood of seeing the birds in each month of the year

Captions identify, where relevant, male and female, adult and immature, winter and summer plumage

Photographs show the birds in typical stance and habitat, as well as plumage variations, in flight or at the nest

8

The Photographs and Captions

Each species is illustrated with at least one photograph. Where plumage varies between males, females and immatures, and between summer and winter, additional photographs are included. The variations are identified in the photograph captions. Species which are almost always seen in flight are depicted thus. Very occasionally, a photograph of perhaps not the highest quality is included: some birds, because of the nature of their lifestyles, are extremely difficult to photograph so any photograph that is available is of immense identification value to the birdwatcher.

The Maps

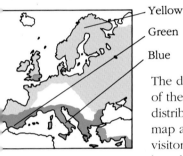

Yellow	Summer migrants' breeding range
Green	Year-round presence
Blue	Winter visitors

The distribution maps included in the left-hand columns of the text pages show winter, summer and year-round distribution for each of the species in the guide. The map areas coloured blue indicate the presence of winter visitors, the yellow areas summer migrants and their breeding range and those shown in green a year-round presence. Birds are unlikely to be found in the areas which are left white.

The Diagrams

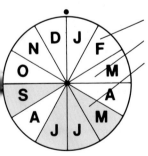

White	Not seen
Light blue	Fairly frequent
Dark blue	Most abundant

The abundance diagrams included in the right-hand columns of the text pages indicate, for each species in the guide, year-round abundance – from January (J) to December (D). The dark blue segments indicate the months in which the birds are most abundant, the light blue segments the months in which the birds are fairly frequently seen. The segments left white indicate months in which the birds are unlikely to be seen. The diagram should be read clockwise from January (at twelve o'clock) through to December (at eleven o'clock).

The Descriptions

The descriptions provide detailed information on each species included in the guide. The popular, or common, name is printed in **bold** type. The scientific name is given in *italics*. Then comes the measurement – the length from beak-tip to tail-tip. The general description covers relative size, physical appearance and flight pattern, followed by a note of any special behavioural characteristics. Calls and songs are described phonetically. Habitat information is followed by an abundance description. Habitat symbol(s) come last.

Scientific name — Length

Common name —— **Common Sandpiper** *Actitis hypoleucos* 20cm Small wader with distinctive flight. Summer adult sandy brown above, flecked with white; white below, with brown

Physical appearance — streaking on throat and on sides of breast forming half-collar. Winter adult and immature duller, less spotted. Beak dark, short and straight. Legs greenish. Flight low

Flight pattern — over water and fast, with characteristic, rapid, shallow wingbeats and downcurved wings. In flight, shows white wingbar, brown rump, brown tail with brown-barred white outer feathers. Bobs incessantly. *Voice:* distinctive, trilling

Behavioural characteristics — 'twee-wee-wee...' call; song high-pitched 'tittyweety-tittyweety'. *Habitat:* breeds beside lakes, rivers and — Voice (call and song)

Habitat — streams. On migration and in winter on fresh and salt marshes; sheltered coasts. Widespread. 🐦 ⛲ 🦆

Abundance — Habitat symbols

As shown above, each species is identified by a vernacular name – its 'popular' name – and also by its scientific name. The latter is important, as to a French birdwatcher, the British 'Robin' is a 'Rouge-gorge' – but to all birdwatchers, not just European but world-wide, there can be no confusing *Erithacus rubecula*. Thus it is well worth becoming familiar with the birds' scientific names.

Across a group as diverse as birds there are obviously going to be some problems in setting common standards, particularly with regard to size and abundance. Thus the size gradings of tiny, small, medium, large and huge are augmented by a measurement of overall length. When it comes to abundance, natural differences make things more complex. The Kestrel is the most abundant bird of prey, but as predators (hunting and catching live prey) are naturally much less numerous than their prey, the description 'common' applied to the Kestrel does not quite mean the same, numerically, as the same word applied to the House Sparrow.

Consequently, the abundance indications that fall at the end of each description reflect more than anything the likelihood of seeing that particular bird.

In each description, information has been given as to the likely habitats in which the species may be found, and of the likely chances of seeing it. But birds are mobile creatures, whose movements may be long-range and regular (like warblers migrating to and from Africa for the winter); or minimal (like garden Robins in the British Isles, though not in all parts of Europe); or erratic, like Crossbills and Waxwings, which may be common one year and then absent for several. So it is difficult to lay down any 'rules' – and the birds would surely break them if we did. The only answer is an ever-alert approach – not just with eyes and ears, but with the mind open to an unusual occurrence. Blue Tits *are* seen in reedbeds, and Reed Buntings can and do come into gardens for food in winter. Despite this caution, there *are* typical habitats and these are mentioned in the descriptions and shown in symbol form.

The Habitat Symbols

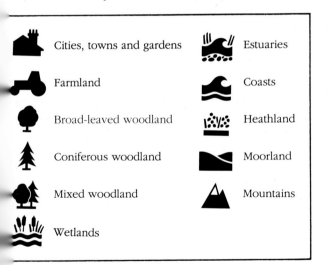

	Cities, towns and gardens		Estuaries
	Farmland		Coasts
	Broad-leaved woodland		Heathland
	Coniferous woodland		Moorland
	Mixed woodland		Mountains
	Wetlands		

As mentioned above, symbols which represent the major types of habitat are included at the end of each species description. For easy cross-reference to and from the background information on habitats, the same symbols are used in the *Bird Habitats* and *Fieldcraft* sections of the book.

Bird Biology

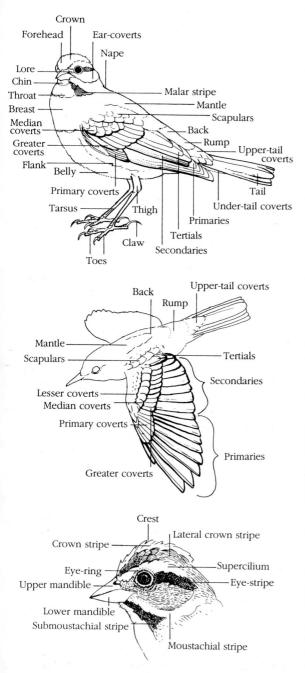

The birds branched off from their ancestral reptile stock around 130 million years ago – at much the same time as did the mammals.
Although both birds and mammals are highly evolved, very efficient animals, they have achieved their success by different routes. Both are warm-blooded and maintain their body warmth by an insulating coat – of fur or hair in the mammals, of feathers in the birds. In some ways, the birds have departed (in the process of evolution) rather less than the mammals from the structure of their reptilian ancestors, and indeed the newly-hatched naked young of many birds closely resemble reptiles in appearance. The shelled egg itself is a reptilian feature, abandoned by all but the most primitive of mammals, and perhaps birds can best be regarded as extremely well-tuned, high-performance reptiles.

The basic skeletal structure of a bird consists of a strong central 'box' of backbone, ribs and breastbone, in which the vital organs are grouped, both for protection and to place their weight between the wings – a centre of gravity making effective flight much more easily achieved. The breastbone, or sternum, is usually keeled, and carries the powerful flight muscles. To this central box are attached the wings – such a distinctive feature of birds. Yet although flight is often regarded as being typical of birds, it is not an action which is unique to them.

The outline of the wings may vary greatly, but the basic skeletal structure is uniform between birds, and can easily be related to the human (or any other) arm and hand. The 'shoulder' of a wing – the forward-protruding joint – is in fact the wrist, beyond which is a much-reduced hand. Differences in wing outline reflect wing function: game

Wing Shapes

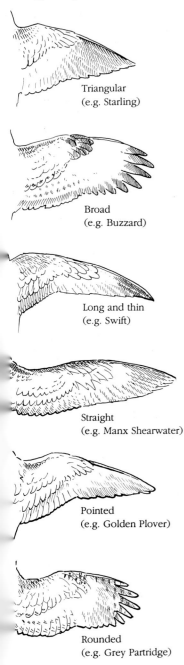

Triangular
(e.g. Starling)

Broad
(e.g. Buzzard)

Long and thin
(e.g. Swift)

Straight
(e.g. Manx Shearwater)

Pointed
(e.g. Golden Plover)

Rounded
(e.g. Grey Partridge)

birds have rounded wings for quick take-off, oceanic gliders like the Fulmar have long, straight and narrow wings, while the soaring birds of prey have long, broad wings with heavily 'fingered' tips. Each outline is adapted to the life of the bird concerned, and these wing shapes are often of great value in field identification.

If flight is not unique to birds, feathers certainly are. Made of the protein keralin, and possibly derived from reptilian scales, they wind- and water-proof birds, give thermal insulation, and above all provide the 'variable geometry' flexibility that make the birds so much more successful in flight than any device yet invented by human beings. Often coloured, they give birds plumages that allow them to recognize one another, that can provide amazing camouflage, that can be useful in display or for sending contact or warning signals through a flock. Although their flexibility is an asset, it does mean that feathers wear out over the year, and must regularly be changed in the process called moult. Thus although feathers create the plumages that we use as key identification features, wear and moult, by altering these familiar plumages, (which may also differ according to the age or sex of the bird), can add a further layer of complexity to bird recognition.

Attached to the body of the bird is a tail, of major use in flight for steering, but also used in display, which again by shape or colour, or in the way that it is held, offers useful identification aids. At the other end is the neck and head. Interestingly, compared with the mammals which all have seven neck vertebrae (even giraffes), birds have vertebral numbers ranging up to twenty-five in the case of the Mute Swan. Beak adaptations are legion, and most are valuable field guides, even if they only direct the observer to a family or group. Many, like those of the ducks, or the waders, or the birds of prey, or the finches are most usefully characteristic. The range of adaptation is not only vast, but fascinating, and more easily explained when it is realized that in order to take up flight with such superlative skill, the birds 'abandoned' the 'hands' which would otherwise have been of such use in food gathering.

Last of the sets of appendages to the body are the legs and feet. Once again, the range of adaptations is enormous, and most useful to the field ornithologist. Leg length, colour, and the nature of the feet may all be of value – the long legs of the herons and waders, the talons of the birds of prey and owls, the webbed toes so different between the divers and the ducks. In the bird, although the leg bones (like the wing) closely relate to the mammal hind limb, their proportions differ markedly.

Tail Shapes

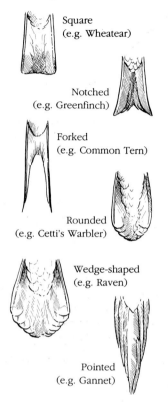

Square
(e.g. Wheatear)

Notched
(e.g. Greenfinch)

Forked
(e.g. Common Tern)

Rounded
(e.g. Cetti's Warbler)

Wedge-shaped
(e.g. Raven)

Pointed
(e.g. Gannet)

The true thigh is short, and normally hidden beneath the body feathers. What looks like the thigh is actually the shin (tibio-fibula), and what looks like the knee, only the 'wrong' way round, is actually the ankle. The long horny-covered bone below the ankle, called the tarsus, is derived from parts of the ankle and the upper ends of the toes.

Finally, a note about the bird's year, which so heavily governs its movements and plumages. In *winter*, summer migrants have departed south; residents and winter visitors are in dense winter plumage, often different in colour from the summer. Some larger birds may start displaying. In *spring*, summer plumages begin to appear, usually quite quickly and often through feather wear rather than moult. Singing and display begin in earnest, as does nest-building and egg-laying. The winter visitors depart and summer migrants appear, in increasing numbers as summer draws nearer. In *summer*, the breeding season is in full swing, though song diminishes as the year progresses. Increasing numbers of young birds appear, in drab, immature plumages. In late summer, adults moult into fresh plumage, while juveniles moult into feathers almost if not quite as bright as those of their parents. In *autumn*, summer migrants gradually depart, and winter visitors begin to trickle in, the flow increasing as the months pass, until the annual kaleidoscope of birdlife, with all its attractions and fascinations, begins once again.

Beak Shapes

Tiny
(e.g. Swallow)

Conical
(e.g. Tree Sparrow)

Long and thin
(e.g. Dunlin)

Fairly thin and pointed
(e.g. Whinchat)

Hooked
(e.g. Peregrine)

Decurved
(e.g. Mallard)

Bird Habitats

The power of flight has enabled birds to become perhaps the most widely distributed of all groups of living creatures. Insects may be more widely dispersed on land, but are poorly represented at sea, while fish, though unquestionably masters of the waters are of course absent from terrestrial habitats. Yet there is virtually no area of the world where some bird cannot be found, from mountain top to mid-ocean.

Although many birds are catholic in their choice of habitat, and although these same powers of flight mean that a travelling bird may turn up just about anywhere (especially during the migration seasons or immediately after periods of stormy weather) a knowledge of bird habitats – how they are structured and what kinds of bird may be expected there – can be of tremendous assistance. Such information allows for a better planning of birdwatching excursions, as well as easing a surprising number of potential identification problems.

Cities, Towns and Gardens

Contrary to popular belief, interesting bird life does not necessarily cease at the approach to a village, town, or even city. A number of bird species (some of them quite surprising) have managed to penetrate these predominantly human preserves, and despite the many hazards, adapted successfully to their new habitat.

The unusual hazards of urban or suburban life include a shortage of natural foods and an abundance of alien predators like cats, rats and dogs. Perhaps the motor car, should also be placed in this category. But there are benefits too: the plants that gardeners grow, for example, being cultivated rather than wild, often have larger fruits or seeds, and seem to be perfectly palatable and nutritious. Furthermore many householders feed birds with kitchen scraps, especially in bad weather. And the temperature on a cold winter's night may well be 3° C higher within a city than in the surrounding countryside, which makes the long hours of chilly darkness appreciably easier to survive.

In strictly urban surroundings the House Sparrow and Starling may well be the most numerous birds, but there can be few householders or flat dwellers that do not see the occasional Jackdaw, Greenfinch or Blackbird. A well-stocked bird table can be a great attraction, tempting Blue and Great Tits. With the larger gardens and more extensive open spaces of suburbia, the number and variety of birds increases. Robins, Song Thrushes and Mistle Thrushes may appear, as well as Dunnocks and Wrens. Municipal parks, even those in city centres, can attract a great variety of species like Woodpigeons, Scops or Tawny Owls, with, on the lakes, waterbirds like Moorhen, Coot, Canada Goose, Mute Swan and several species of duck besides the ubiquitous Mallard. Feral pigeons, those escaped from pigeon-fanciers' lofts, are plentiful enough to be a nuisance in many areas and the Collared Dove (a recent newcomer to the European bird list after an impressive invasion from the Middle East over the last fifty years) is already extremely common. Winter playing fields are an ideal location for various thrushes and gulls, the latter resting between bouts of feeding at nearby refuse tips, where they are joined by members of the crow family.

In Mediterranean towns and cities the variety of bird life is extraordinary. Splendid birds like White Storks nest in the rooftops and there may be colonies of Lesser Kestrels in tall church towers. Unexpected, supposedly mountain-loving birds like the Crag Martin, Alpine Swift and Black Redstart fly around quite unconcerned by the bustle of people and traffic.

Country gardens, of course, see a far greater variety of birds, as they can draw upon nearby farmland and woodland. Indeed, with no disrespect to the gardener, many neighbouring birds will look upon gardens as scrubland to be foraged in, enjoying them all the year round.

Farmland

On farmland, as in no other rural habitat, a human hand shapes the environment. Changes to the landscape may be sudden and sweeping – and often of annual occurrence as crop succeeds crop. It is all too easy nowadays to be critical of farmers for the destruction of the landscape, for creating prairie farms, and for the over-use of pesticides, herbicides and fertilizers. There are undoubtedly instances where such criticism is valid, but many others where it is not, particularly when one considers that today's consumers demand high-yielding, cheap crops with little or nothing in the way of pest or disease blemishes.

It should be remembered, too, that it is the farmers who have created the landscape as we know it, and that, in general, they have respected it. Two thousand years ago, much of Europe would have been clad in dense forest – largely unbroken except by rivers – and it is tempting to assume that the bird life would then have been much richer. A moment's serious thought, though, of the numbers of birds to be seen today in huge tracts of mature timber, compared with those to be found in a similar area of farmland with a good hedgerow network and plenty of small woods and spinneys, will reveal that farmland is richer by far both in numbers of bird species and in the total number of individuals. Many of the birds – thrushes, finches, buntings, for example – that we consider typical of 'the countryside' are in fact birds of woodland edges or clearings, and for them the matrix of hedge, wood and field that the farmers have created over the centuries has provided much extra habitat.

Relatively few species favour the really open spaces of huge areas of grass or cereal: the Skylark is the ubiquitous example of one that does, year-round, while over much of Europe the partridges do so too, while the related Quail is a summer visitor, particularly to southern areas. Over much of Europe, perhaps more commonly in winter than in summer, the Lapwing which is a wader, but encountered more commonly inland than on the coast, is to be found on damp pasture and plough. In eastern Europe, these open expanses are home to the huge and exciting Great Bustard, as they are in southern Europe to its smaller relative, the Little Bustard.

But it is the hedges, copses and spinneys that are most valuable to farmland birds. They offer food and shelter at every season, and, during the summer months, while continuing to house the seed-eating birds like Linnets and Yellowhammers, they support sufficient insect life for migrant warblers like the Whitethroat and Lesser Whitethroat to flourish. They tend to be rich in autumn fruits, too, and at this time of year may be full of Blackbirds and Song Thrushes squabbling with recently-arrived migrant Fieldfares, Redwings and Starlings over an abundance of hawthorn berries.

The farm buildings themselves are used by a variety of species prepared to tolerate close proximity to human beings: among the nesting species to be expected are Spotted Flycatchers, Swallows, Pied Wagtails, Little Owls and the ever-present House Sparrow. Perhaps the typical bird of this habitat is the Barn Owl – a normally silent nocturnal hunter which offers effective 'biological control' of rats and mice to the farmer. Floating white and silent through the night, it will occasionally produce a shriek sufficient to make even the best-controlled hair stand on end.

Despite weedkiller usage, the field headlands – as well as the stubble fields themselves – are a rich source of autumn and winter food for the seed eaters. At this time of year most of them are drably plumaged (even the male Yellowhammer has brown feather fringes masking its canary-like summer plumage) and well-camouflaged as they feed upon the ground. Flocking seems to be rule: Starlings, Lapwings and the Golden Plover (that winter on wet meadows in some areas) all seem to keep to themselves, while thrushes flock in a variety that may include five or six species, as do the finches.

'oodland

any of the birds of farmland and gardens are basically woodland species and will thus be
et on woodland walks. The type of woodland, though, can make a very considerable differ-
ice and most of the farm and garden species are naturally associated with broad-leaved (or
ciduous) woodlands. These consist mainly of trees such as oak and elm (sadly now disap-
aring from some areas), ash and beech (on chalky soils), birch (on acid soils), alder (in
imp areas) and the introduced sycamore. They tend, too, to have a fair amount of under-
owth, bramble, hawthorn, elder and so on, mixed with plenty of herbaceous wildflowers
id grasses, which provides good feeding and nesting areas for small birds. This picture is
obably far more typical of the woodland of today, all of it 'secondary' in forestry terms and
uch influenced over the centuries by human activity. It seems likely that today's woods, with
earings and glades, differ appreciably from the ancient ancestral closed-canopy forest, which
ould have had much less undergrowth because so much light was excluded by the trees. It
ands to reason that the amount of insect and plant food available is greater in these gladed
oods than it is in an area with little or no undergrowth, and this is the main reason why de-
duous woodland holds more birds than mature stands of conifers. Because different types of
oodland support differing bird species, they are considered here under separate headings.

Broad-leaved Woodland

Mature deciduous woodland is usually the home of some members of the
owl family. To the south, Little and Scops Owls hold sway, but over much
of Europe it is the Tawny Owl that is most familiar. Several of the owls join
with the Sparrowhawk and Goshawk as the major predators on other birds
in woodland habitats, but partly because of their scarcity, speed of movement (the hawks) or nocturnal habits (the owls), they are not easy to find.
Listening for the concentrated scolding chatter of a group of small birds
ay often lead you to the daytime roost of the owl that has aroused their wrath.

In summer, the often huge insect population in the woodland canopy will support both
e year-round residents, including several members of the tit family, and a number of
igrants ranging in size from the bee and wasp-eating Honey Buzzard, the Turtle Dove with
 all-pervading purring song, to a range of warblers. Ample nest sites are available in the
es themselves and in the undergrowth. Attractive though summer may be, it is during the
inter months that woodlands may be of greatest benefit to their bird populations because of
e food and shelter that they provide during climatically hard times.

Coniferous Woodland

Long-established, widely-spaced coniferous forests offer a fascinating
habitat, with, depending on location, birds as diverse as Crested Tits,
Redstarts, various crossbills and the spectacular Capercaillie flourishing,
together with several woodpecker species and birds of prey like the Hobby.
In the coniferous forests of northern Europe are to be found some of the
more exciting members of the owl family, such as the Hawk Owl, Tengmalm's Owl and the Great Grey Owl.

Where conifers, sometimes pine, but more often spruce or other imported trees, are
own commercially they are planted close together to encourage rapid, straight growth with
w side branches. The close growth cuts down light penetration so that side branches hardly
evelop, but neither does any undergrowth. Furthermore, the seeds of conifers are available

only to a handful of specialist species like the various crossbills, whose scissor-like, overlapping, parrot-shaped beak can reach between the segments of the cones to extract them.

This does not mean that coniferous woodland, or even mature conifer plantations, are destitute of birds. In summer, many coniferous woods buzz with the activity of birds like Crested Tits, Coal Tits, Goldcrests and Chaffinches, and at the larger end of the size scale, Woodpigeons and Sparrowhawks are not uncommon. However, it is during the first ten to fifteen years after the planting of conifers that the richest birdwatching opportunities occur. The trees are not tall enough to shade out smaller plants; food abounds and shelter is plentiful as the trees are so close-planted. Thus the despair with which country-lovers tend to greet the prospect of a new plantation must be tempered with an eager expectation of the benefits arising from these early years, and with the knowledge that the gloomy conditions of maturity will not last long, as the forests will be regularly felled for timber and then replanted.

There are some species – the Tree Pipit and the Nightjar, for example – to be expected in areas of freshly cleared woodland and in the first couple of years after planting. Other scrubland species soon begin to appear: finches, thrushes, Wrens, Dunnocks and so on, with summer visitors like Whitethroats and Willow Warblers. As the cover continues to develop, other rather unexpected birds may appear – the Reed Bunting and Grasshopper Warbler for example, both birds more often associated with wetland areas. In wilder places, where forestry is reappearing on moorland, Hen Harriers have quickly adapted to the new habitat and may be seen patrolling their hunting beats on stiffly-held wings. Long-eared Owls may also exploit what for them seems an improbable habitat.

♣ Mixed Woodland

Predictably, mixed woodland shares most of the features of both conifers and broad-leaved timber areas. True, a number of 'specialities' may be missing, but in general terms the bird population benefits, rather than suffers, from the mixing of tree species.

Old woodland with mixed coniferous and deciduous trees, acquires additional character once branches start to break off, timber to soften and rot, trees to fall, all of these providing new 'niches' for fresh species to exploit. Elderly timber in woodland that is not managed with the hygiene unfortunately still popular with many commercial foresters, shelters more insect life, and falling trees leave gaps in the canopy so that patches of undergrowth (rich in bird food plants) can develop. Holes can be hacked into the softer timber by woodpeckers and other birds seeking insect larvae or excavating a nest. Woodpecker holes tend to be used once by their constructors, but are then 'passed on' as potential homes to other species like Starlings, tits and the Redstart and Pied Flycatcher. Other natural holes, larger in size, resulting from old age and falling branches are potential nesting sites for various owls, Jackdaws and Stock Doves.

♒ Wetlands

Of all bird habitats, 'wetlands' must form the broadest category. Covering streams from their sources high in the hills until they discharge as rivers into the sea, it also includes ponds, lake marshes and swamps, as well as fabricated water areas, like reservoirs and gravel pits. And even this list begins to sub-divide, for upland streams clattering down a hillside differ greatly in nature and in bird life from the sluggish, turbid waters of the lowlands.

Upland streams, descending rapidly over a rocky landscape, are naturally fast-moving and clear. The small plant and animal life that they support is characteristic: it must thrive on the abundant oxygen and must not get swept away by the speed of the current. On these smaller life-forms the larger animals of the streams, the fishes and the birds, depend and, because of the rather specialized nature of the stream, the birds, too, tend to be characteristic. The higher reaches of many such streams may well be inhospitable during the winter months, and the avian inhabitants not infrequently migrate to lower altitudes, so this is predominantly a summer birdwatching site. On the pebbly banks and spate beds will nest Common Sandpipers, forever bobbing their tails, as are the Dippers, perched on mid-stream boulders before plunging into the torrent in search of food.

Other birds are characteristic of clear waters both near the source and as they mature into rivers: the electric-blue, arrow-like passing Kingfisher, for example, or the again ever-bobbing but supremely elegant Grey Wagtail. (Why, one wonders, are so many birds of sparkling watersides endowed with this habit?) The fish population will be pursued under water by two specialist fish-eating ducks, called 'sawbills' because of the fish-gripping serrated edges to their long slim beaks. Streamlined and speedily propelled by webbed feet which are set back near the tail, both the Red-breasted Merganser and the Goosander are effective hunters.

Lowland streams may hold more birds year-round, but they too are richer during the summer months because the plethora of insect life supports migrants like the Reed and Sedge Warblers. On the water, vegetarian ducks, both surface-feeding and diving, find plenty to eat, as do Coot and Moorhen, while fish-eaters like the Little Grebe find food, sheltering marginal vegetation in which to vanish should danger threaten, and still waters on which to build their floating raft of a nest, made of reed and sedge leaves and often 'moored' to nearby vegetation, rising and falling with the changes in the water level. Other fish-eaters – the herons, egrets and, once again, the Kingfisher – find ample sustenance in size ranges to suit their hunting abilities, and where the slow flowing water is broken by rapids or by a weir or mill sluice, the Grey Wagtail will often reappear on the scene.

Where the flow of these lowland rivers is impeded, swamps and marshes tend to occur. In many cases these may support just a few more river-bank birds, with the addition of fresh-marsh waders like Ruff, Black-tailed Godwit, Redshank and Snipe. When an extensive reedbed proper develops (formed largely of the common reed *Phragmites*), then a more specialist bird community gathers, which is well worth seeking out.

Again, reedbeds in summer are richer than in winter. Among the summer migrant reedbed specialists are the Reed, Great Reed and Savi's Warblers, while the Bearded Tit (which eats much *Phragmites* seed in autumn and winter) is a colourful and acrobatic addition. This is, not surprisingly, the habitat of the Marsh Harrier, and extensive areas of reed seem to be required by the Bittern (which, in its alarm posture, bolt upright, uses its streaked plumage to mimic the reed stems for camouflage) and various rails. The Water Rail is typical with long spidery toes to support it across mud and floating vegetation, and a body flattened from side to side in order to pass easily through the reeds. Many of the denizens of reedbeds are often heard than seen: the distant foghorn boom of the Bittern and the pig-like squealing of the Water Rail are cases in point.

Over the last few centuries, human intervention has wrought havoc in the wetlands of Europe by draining them to improve their agricultural performance. In consequence, the few large semi-natural wetlands that do remain (or have been re-created by conservation bodies) such as the Camargue, the Coto Doñana, the Nadermeer, Lake Neusiedl and Minsmere are of immense interest to naturalists because of the numbers and rich variety of birds and other creatures that they support. Some, indeed, would feature prominently on a list of the world's top areas for birdwatching.

On the credit side, though, has been man's creative role in the wetland story, which revolves around the creation of reservoirs and mineral extraction workings, usually sand or gravel pits. These are of course associated with building programmes, urban sprawls and industrialization, but they, and the even more unprepossessing (but fast becoming extinct) sewage farm, often make extremely good birdwatching sites. Huge numbers of a variety of wintering waterfowl depend on reservoirs for food and shelter, and many migrant waders use inland gravel pits and sewage farms as resting points where they may feed up for the next stage of their journey. In many such areas, industry and conservation now work hand in hand to design and manage these new wetlands, so that, far from being scars on the landscape once their industrial use is over, they become a most beneficial addition.

![] Estuaries

Estuaries are broad, shallow, sheltered areas, often of considerable size, where a slow-moving river joins the sea. They have a number of attribute that make them superb bird habitats. As it winds through the landscape, the river collects run-off water rich in various nutrients: in the estuary, sheltered and relatively warm, these terrestrial nutrients mingle with thos brought in by the sea, and the combination produces salt or brackish water and mud or sand flats extremely rich in minute (often microscopic plant and animal life. On these tiny life forms and on the detritus in the settling silt flourish countless millions of larger creatures – shellfish, shrimps and the like. It is these, and the specialist estuary plants and seaweeds, that support a considerable fish population and often a huge number of birds.

Although scenically attractive in summer, most estuaries are not at their ornithological prim at that time of year. The mudflats and islands are relatively quiet, except for the odd pair or two of breeding waders (Oystercatcher, Ringed Plover, Redshank) or duck (particularly Shelduck), and for the colonies of gulls and terns. Ecologically speaking, it is in autumn, winte and spring that most estuaries are of greatest value to birds – especially wildfowl, gulls and waders. Many of these breed in the far north of Europe and overwinter from western Europe southwards to the southern tip of Africa. For the long-haul migrants, anxious to get back to their breeding grounds quickly and in good condition, but with several thousand kilometres to fly, estuaries serve in spring as vital staging-posts, where, in sheltered surroundings, the birds - waders in particular – may enjoy the rich feeding and prepare rapidly for the next northward stage of their journeys. Moving southwards in autumn is a more leisurely affair, but the staging posts and the food they offer are, of course, just as necessary as in spring. Many waders will pause on western European estuaries to moult, a process that the brief Arctic summer does no allow time for, and many remain in their shelter over winter.

Clearly, therefore, the best rewards will come from visiting the estuaries in the spring, whe the range of birds to be seen will be at its greatest. There can be no better way of getting to grips with the problems of identifying waders, or ducks, than watching an array of species close together. To this can be added the sheer thrill of watching smoke-like mobs of waders twisting and turning with perfect timing across the open estuary sky.

By their very nature, estuaries are a scarce type of habitat, but nevertheless of extreme importance to many birds. Thus it is that conservation bodies must view with great alarm the increasing demands to industrialize these (in land developers' eyes) barren and useless feature of our landscape.

Coasts

The coasts of Europe are very varied, and in consequence provide varied birdwatching. In the north and north-west, rocky coasts predominate, often with extremely spectacular cliffs and rock stacks. Further south, the land is lower-lying, giving rise to extensive sweeps of mud or sand flats. By their nature, coasts of all types are exposed habitats, particularly those bearing the brunt of frequent Atlantic storms, and it should come as little surprise that many are relatively bare of birds through the winter months. During the winter, a number of coastal-breeding birds (like the auk family) will feed on the sea, often quite close inshore, and many gulls (despite the large numbers also to be seen inland) share this habit. In spring (and in the reverse direction in autumn) these may be joined by migrant seabirds and also by waders and wildfowl whose migratory routes commonly follow coastlines.

For most birdwatchers, though, the coasts and islands are at their best during the summer months. Particularly in those areas where precipitous cliffs offer both nesting sites and some protection from predators, breeding seabirds will gather in huge numbers. In some cases the sheer spectacle must be difficult to equal – for example the huge Gannet colony on the Bass Rock in the North Sea, not far distant from the Scottish border.

For practical reasons, the great majority of seabird colonies are situated in fish-rich seas. A boat trip will provide ample opportunity to watch the differing fishing techniques of the birds, ranging from Gannets spectacularly plunge-driving from twenty or thirty metres above the waves, to terns gently plopping into the surface waters from a couple of metres, to auks like the Razorbill, Guillemot and Puffin, swimming on the surface and then slipping beneath it, leaving hardly a ripple, as they set off in pursuit of fish. By selecting different sizes of fish and by hunting them at different depths by differing techniques, the broad spectrum of seabirds share their habitat and food supply without competing for its resources.

Equally fascinating can be the inspection of seabird colonies themselves. These seabird cities are crowded places where each species chooses a different type of nest site. Guillemots prefer flat ledges and stack tops, no matter how exposed or how long the drop beneath, while Puffins nest in cavities in boulder tumbles or excavate their own burrows in the cliff-top turf. Herring Gulls nest on substantial ledges, while the similar Lesser Black-backed Gull usually selects the grassy slopes. The Kittiwake, most maritime of gulls, cements its nest with mud and guano to the smallest of rocky projections, even under an overhang, and its young cannot stray from the nest itself until the day they fly.

Smaller birds are relatively scarce in these towering surroundings, but Rock Pipits, Jackdaws, Choughs and Rock Doves are characteristic. These are preyed on by the occasional Peregrine Falcon, and in the far north by the majestic Sea (or White-tailed) Eagle. At migration times, and often during the winter months, rocky shores are home for waders like the Turnstone, Purple Sandpiper and limpet-feeding Oystercatcher which are able to exploit this rather specialist and rough habitat.

Sandy lowland shores lack the cliff-nesting birds, but remote areas can be the location of substantial colonies of gulls (Black-headed, Herring and Lesser Black-backed) and terns (Sandwich, Common, Arctic and Little). Sadly, pressure from holidaymakers, quite innocently enjoying themselves on the beaches, is one of the major threats to the confiding Little Tern's continued survival. Wheatears, Eider and Shelduck also relish sand-dunes as a nesting habitat. During migration, and in the winter months, the expanses of sandy beach hold much less food than estuaries, but again specialists like the Sanderling, a small silver-grey wader, seek them out and scamper in and out between the waves in search of morsels of food.

Heathland

Within the broad category of heathland fall various structurally similar habitats which differ in various ways, including their names. Thus scrub, a feature of more northerly and westerly regions, often with hawthorn, blackthorn or gorse as the major bush component, is included, as are areas of 'waste-land' (in the farmer's eyes), which may be very temporary in location and life-span. The 'true' heathland often merges imperceptibly with rough grassland on the one hand, or with low-lying moors on the other. Its normal characteristics include a sandy, rather acid soil, with birch, gorse and heather as major vegetation components in varying degrees. In southern Europe, thorny, often evergreen, scrub develops on rocky, arid hillsides and close to the coast, and this rich but often near-impenetrable habitat is usually known by its French name maquis. Much sandy heathland, particularly further south, tends to be better for summer birdwatching, as many of its avian inhabitants are summer-visiting migrants: various warblers, pipits, shrikes, the Nightjar, Hoopoe, Bee-eater and Woodlark are good examples. Nearby birds of prey naturally tend to exploit the summer situation, but in addition a migrant falcon, the Hobby (one of the fastest-flying of birds), is very typical of the heathland scene, feeding on birds and large insects. Perhaps because heathland is a relatively exposed habitat, most of the smaller birds tend to be skulking and extremely difficult to see. Most of the warblers, for example, churr harshly at intruders from the depths of the bushes, and only in spring, when they sing from exposed perches or in a parachuting song-flight, are they at all obvious. The Stonechat, perched on top of a gorse bush, 'chacking' loudly, is a conspicuous exception to this rule.

Scrub – once described by the early writer on agriculture, Cobbett, as 'the most villainous country God ever made' ◄ can often be rich birdwatching habitat. A prime reason for this is that scrub is an intermediate vegetation stage – part-way between bare ground and forest – and in consequence it tends to be rich in plant species as, while some are fading out, others are just emerging in the natural succession of vegetation. Plants adapted to such transitional habitats tend (for their own safety, as it were) to set a lot of fruit or seed: the numbers of berries on hawthorn bushes, or seeds in a thistle-head, illustrate this well. This variety and abundance of plants and their seeds tends also to encourage large numbers of insects, and other small invertebrate animals, the whole making a rich feeding ground for a considerable variety of birds.

Most of the families of the order Passeriformes (the song or perching birds) are represented at least at some stage during the year. Bushes and brambles provide abundant nest sites, well protected by thorns, and the insects, seeds and fruit are enjoyed in season by a wide variety of birds. Many will be present year-round, but thrushes and the Starling will show up in abundance to feed particularly on autumn berries; finches and buntings exploit the seed crops, some (like the Goldfinches on thistle and teazel seed-heads) being especially obvious in autumn and early winter. Summer migrants like the Whitethroat exploit insect stocks for much of their stay, but turn readily to berry-eating in late summer when the sugars in the fruit are the easiest way for them to acquire stored body fat, which will shortly be used to fuel their long migration south.

During the winter, the dense thorny bushes provide shelter from the wind for flocks of finches, thrushes and other small birds, and protection from the scrub predators like the Barn Owl (not at all averse to the occasional bird in its diet) and the Kestrel. Best known for its hovering capability and acute eyesight when seeking insect or small rodent prey passing on the ground beneath its aerial vantage point, the Kestrel is a falcon and will readily behave like one in pursuit of unwary birds.

Maquis, the southern European scrub, shares many of the attributes and disadvantages of both heath and scrub. Most of it fringes the Mediterranean basin, and so endures very hot, late summer temperatures. The warblers of the genus *Sylvia* are all lovers of dense cover, and hey reach their peak in the maquis, with many species distributed throughout the region and others restricted to a series of very small geographical areas. Drab larks and colourful birds like the Hoopoe, Bee-eater and Woodchat Shrike often favour the maquis or its fringes: it is a habitat not to be missed.

Moorland

Moorland is predominantly a feature of northern and north-western Europe, for the most part associated with remote upland areas. In the most northerly regions, however, far from being upland, the moors descend to sea level. From about the latitude of the Arctic Circle northwards, these vast treeless expanses are more properly called tundra.

In high summer, as any walker will know, the moors are rich in insect life. It is the fantastically abundant larval stages of the insects that support many of the moorland's summer visitors. These – commonly from the wader and pipit families – tend to arrive on the uplands late in spring, but then transform them with their songs or plumages. Meadow Pipits are to be seen everywhere, drab in plumage but with an attractive song delivered during a parachuting display flight. Much larger, the Curlew is also undistinguished in plumage but it has a thrillingly wild bubbling song, with much repetition of its own name included. On the plumage side, Golden Plover and Dunlin adorn the moor, and brilliantly colourful though their plumage appears at close range, it still camouflages them effectively against heathers, mosses and lichens.

Here, on the summer moors, are to be found spectacular birds like the Greenshank, while further north, where moor and tundra merge, many long-haul migrant waders and ducks breed, feeding themselves and their young largely on insect larvae. The huge summer population brings with it, naturally enough, a range of predators from mammals, like foxes and stoats, to a variety of birds. There being few if any trees, birds must nest on the ground, relying on camouflage or choosing an inaccessible crag for safety.

Predatory birds on moorland range from the ferocious skuas, ready and willing to attack by dive-bombing even the birdwatcher entering their breeding territories, to the Merlin, a fast-flying falcon, and the Hen Harrier, which hunts by stealth in a leisurely low-level glide. Even the eagles will venture away from the mountains to hunt over these areas. Over most moors, the owls are represented by the daytime-hunting Short-eared Owl, but further north the huge all-white Snowy Owl (camouflaged well against the residual snow) can sometimes be seen hunting lemmings and birds across the tundra.

Year-round residents of the moors must be capable of surviving for all or part of the year on plant food. Prime amongst these are the grouse: the elegant Blackcock and the commoner Red Grouse in Britain, and the Willow Grouse in continental Europe. These birds feed largely on heather shoots. During the spring, groups of grouse (especially Blackcock) gather at traditional sites on the moors – their lekking grounds – where the males perform spectacular and noisy mock-fighting communal displays, or leks.

Mountains

The upland areas of Europe are widely dispersed, with mountains of considerable height and grandeur (and plentiful snow cover through all or most of the year) even in the most southerly regions. Here, where the sea-level climate is Mediterranean, the mountain ranges form 'ecological islands' of arctic-alpine habitats.

Evolution and adaptation over millions of years have gradually suited birds to this harsh environment. They are nevertheless scarce among the mountains in winter, while in the

summer months the high tops are transformed. Choughs swirl around in the upcurrents of air, their calls echoing off the rocks. Another member of the crow family, the Raven, indulges in aerial sparring matches of great skill with nearby Peregrines, Buzzards and even Golden Eagles. The bigger birds of prey, because of their food demands, require huge territories to keep adequately fed: Golden Eagle home ranges may approach a hundred square kilometres in extent, so it is to be expected that unless you are reasonably close to a nesting crag, sightings will be few and far between. Hardiest of all mountain birds is a member of the grouse family, the Ptarmigan. Protected by heather-coloured plumage in summer and snow-white feathers in winter, it ranges far up the mountains, continuing to feed in cavities and tunnels beneath the snow, where its dense plumage, with feathering extending even to the underside of its toes, insulates it from the cold.

Small birds are not entirely absent, either, from these rooftops of the world: in the north, it is often the Ring Ouzel, or the well-camouflaged Snow Bunting that make an appearance. Further south, in the Alps, Pyrenees and Sierras, other birds like the Alpine Swift, Crag Martin, Rock Bunting and Alpine Accentor appear, with strikingly colourful birds like the Wall Creeper, Black Wheatear and the two Rock Thrushes making for really memorable days.

Bird Names and Classification

The placing of bird species within groups and the gathering of these groups together at progressively higher levels is a scientific exercise undertaken by specialist ornithologists called taxonomists. The established classification system operates as follows: closely-related species are placed in the same genus. Related genera are grouped together in families and families, in turn, combine to form orders, the largest grouping of all. (Some orders, like the Phoenicopteriformes – the flamingos – contain only a handful of species. At the other extreme, the Passeriformes, world-wide, contains several thousand species.) Thus the Black Tern *Chlidonias niger* (*niger* = black) joins the White-winged Black Tern *Chlidonias leucopterus* (*leuco* = white, *pterus* = wing) in the genus *Chlidonias*. The first part of the scientific name is always the genus (plural genera), the second refers to the species. Related genera are grouped in families – so *Chlidonias* (marsh terns) joints *Sterna* (sea terns) and *Larus* (gulls) in the family Laridae, which contains about eighty different species. Laridae belong, together with fourteen other families, to the order Charadriiformes.

Technically, a species is defined as a group of animals that breed with others similar, but not with different animal groups. Thus Chaffinches and Goldfinches though obviously related to each other as finches, with broadly similar beaks, feet and habits, never interbreed in the wild. We can recognize them as distinct from each other, and so can they. Several factors prevent interbreeding, including song and plumage. A Chaffinch only recognizes the song, and plumage colours and patterns of another Chaffinch when selecting a mate. The courtship display reinforces this. A displaying male Goldfinch would mean nothing to a female Chaffinch, which reacts to a completely different display programme. There are ecological barriers too. Goldfinches are birds of heath and scrub, while Chaffinches are essentially woodland species. Thus there are two distinct groups of birds, Chaffinches and Goldfinches, which for a variety of reasons do not interbreed: each of these groups is a species.

If a species occurs over a wide geographical range, some variations in plumage, and song, can occur. Each of these variants may be called a subspecies, or a race. Usually there will be a barrier of some sort separating them from others of their kind: often a mountain range, or a substantial stretch of sea. Thus there are detectable differences, subtle in plumage, greater in song, between the Chaffinches of the British Isles, of northern Europe, and of the Mediterranean basin. This is because of the barriers of the Channel and the Alps.

The birds in this book are arranged following the widely accepted order published by the eminent Dutch ornithologist, Dr Karel Voous, in two parts in 1973 and 1977. Each family is treated separately, starting with the divers, which are thought to be the oldest in terms of evolution and ending with the order Passeriformes, or perching birds, which contains more recent and more advanced birds.

Some pages, however, interrupt this orderly sequence to make other, particular points. These are as follows:

Ocean Wanderers (*see* pages 50-1)

By their very nature, ocean birds are pelagic, spending much of their life often well out to sea, and coming ashore only in the breeding season, when they need dry land to nest. Many rover prodigious distances, and in consequence may get caught up in storms or other unusual weather conditions, coming within sight of land far from their natural homes. The six ocean birds illustrated come from as far afield as the American marshlands and the Indian Ocean, yet all are seen in European waters sufficiently frequently to merit inclusion in a European field guide.

Escapes (*see* pages 68-9)

Since the dawn of human history, birds have been kept as 'pets'. In more recent centuries, particularly ornamental birds have been captured all over the world and kept in collections -

the pheasants and ducks are excellent examples. Often individuals may escape from these collections, greatly puzzling even expert local ornithologists.

Transatlantic Wanderers (*see* pages 114-15)

With their greater powers of flight increasing their chances of survival if blown far off course, larger birds like ducks and waders feature more frequently as vagrants from North America, as the journey across the Atlantic is well within their capabilities.

Oriental Accidentals (*see* pages 158-9)

Europe is linked, without major physical interruption, to the eastern extremes of China and South-east Asia. So, given suitable (if freak) weather conditions, occasional arrivals of birds of all sizes from the Near and Far East should perhaps be expected, no matter how amazing their journey.

The 'Yellow' Wagtails (*see* pages 174-5)

These races or subspecies of the Yellow Wagtail span Eurasia. Although in summer plumage the males seem so distinct, where the various races touch, or overlap, interbreeding can occur and hybrids (with a mixture of characters from both parents) are produced, confusing the issue still further. Females and immatures of the various races are usually impossible to separate.

Smaller Transatlantic Vagrants (*see* pages 230-1)

Not all the vagrants that survive the journey across the Atlantic are large ones. Some small birds may have a 'ship-assisted' crossing, but others simply get caught up in the high-speed winds of the jet stream, arriving exhausted, often on the island bird observatories that dot the west coast of Europe.

Family Characteristics

The features isolated by researchers to form the basis of a grouping are sometimes quite obvious and useful to the birdwatcher in the field. But often they are minute details, even of internal anatomy and thus of little field use. However there *are* family likenesses that, once memorized, can be of immense value in field identification. The webbed feet of the ducks and geese help you to place a bird in the right family quickly: then you can scan the finer details to achieve the final identification. But beware – there are some pitfalls: closely similar though the Swallow and the Swift may appear in shape and behaviour, they are only very distantly related. Their similarity is a result of ages of evolution shaping each to much the same way of life, and is purely superficial.

The family likenesses given below are all ones which can readily be recognized by birdwatchers in the field. For the non-Passerines, where most orders are small, the families are either mentioned in the heading or in more detail in the text which follows the heading. For the Passerines, or perching birds, their order (Passeriformes) is so massive that many of the families within it themselves contain numerous species. Here, each family has its own descriptive paragraph(s).

Divers – order Gaviiformes, family Gaviidae (*see* pages 42-3)

Specialized fish-eating, diving waterbirds, with elongated, streamlined bodies, short necks and dagger-shaped beaks. To assist fast movement under water, the wings are comparatively small and the feet (with characteristic lobed toes) large, powerful and set back near the stumpy tail. Divers rarely land except near the nest, and walk very clumsily. With such short wings, they are not expert in flight, lacking manoeuvrability and requiring a long, pattering take-off run. Outstretched beak, neck and feet, slim cigar-shaped silhouette and rapidly beating wings are good flight characteristics. They nest on the ground, always close to water, laying one or two strikingly elongated olive eggs. Noisy, often spectacularly so, during courtship, the male and female are similar in plumage.

Grebes – order Podicipediformes, family Podicipedidae (*see* pages 44-5)

Specialized diving waterbirds, smaller and plumper than the divers and appreciably longer-necked. All have medium or short dagger-shaped beaks and small wings. They often swim with bodies almost submerged, using powerful feet with lobed toes, set back near the stumpy, fluffy tail. They dive frequently. Although many migrate, they fly relatively infrequently once settled on breeding or wintering waters, requiring a long take-off run. The nest is a characteristic floating raft of waterweeds, moored to nearby reeds. Spherical chalky white eggs quickly become stained brown and are always covered with weed when the adult leaves the nest. They indulge in elaborate and noisy courtship display. Male and female differ only slightly in plumage, the male being brighter in colour.

Tubenoses (or petrels) – order Procellariiformes (*see* pages 46-51)

Oceanic seabirds with characteristic beaks, showing distinct outward signs of segmentation and prominent paired tubular nostrils on the ridge of the beak. Shearwaters and Fulmars – family Procellariidae – are master gliders, sweeping low over the sea on wings held stiffly at right angles to the body. They dive shallowly, often from the surface, to reach food. The smaller European petrels – family Hydrobatidae – are sooty black, and tend to flutter low over the waves, dipping down to pick small food items off the surface. They come to land only to breed in summer or when storm-driven, otherwise they are mostly pelagic, although many Fulmars remain in inshore waters year-round. Shearwaters and petrels normally visit breeding grounds (nests are in burrows) only at night. Weirdly noisy display songs. Male and female are indistinguishable in plumage.

Gannets, cormorants, pelicans – order Pelecaniformes

(*see* pages 48-9, 52-3)

A diverse order of large to enormous waterbirds, usually easy to place in their family, more difficult to identify as species (cormorants, pelicans). The Gannet – family Sulidae – is maritime, breeding in a few ancestral and usually vast colonies. It is a spectacular black and white seabird, with slim, pointed wings normally held at right angles to the body. It plunge-dives into the sea from considerable heights, pursuing its fish prey under water. Cormorants – family Phalacrocoracidae – are dark, slim-bodied seabirds often fishing by diving in inshore waters. They can be seen standing on rocks with wings outstretched to dry. Pelicans – family Pelecanidae – are huge and ungainly, with an unmistakable beak. European species feed by sweeping up fish in their beak pouch while swimming. They fly on broad, heavily-fingered wings with heads retracted between the shoulders. All Pelecaniformes have huge feet, with all four toes joined by webbing for effective swimming propulsion. Normally breeding colonially, they lay comparatively large clutches of rather small eggs. Their young are perhaps the most reptilian in appearance of all bird chicks. Male and female are very similar in plumage.

Herons, bitterns, storks, spoonbills, ibises – order Ciconiiformes

(*see* pages 54-9)

Medium to large-sized, long-legged, long-necked wading birds, usually of marshes or coasts, occasionally adapted to drier habitats. Most stab or seize their prey – fish and other aquatic animals – with a powerful dagger-like beak, and then swallow it whole. The Spoonbill and Glossy Ibis – family Threskiornithidae – have clearly evolved specialized beaks to suit their feeding techniques. All have long broad wings, usually heavily fingered at the tips, and fly with slow, steady wingbeats but making surprising speed. All have long slender toes, many with one claw on each foot adapted as a comb to assist in preening. As a family, the herons and egrets (Ardeidae) are a magnificent example of how variations in size and feeding strategy allow several similar species to exist, without excessive competition, in the same habitat. Some (bitterns, some herons and egrets) are excellently camouflaged for reedbed life, while others (White Stork, Spoonbill, Little Egret) are strikingly conspicuous birds. Most are noisy, with harsh, goose-like calls and beak-clatterings during the breeding season, but are rarely vocal at other times. Most breed colonially, in trees or reedbeds, building bulky nests, often in company with several other members of the order. Storks – family Ciconiidae – ibises and Spoonbills fly with both head and neck and legs extended, while herons, bitterns and egrets carry their necks hunched back between their shoulders in flight. On the ground, the larger species walk and hunt with necks erect; the smaller species carry their necks hunched, extending them only to stab prey. Male and female are usually very similar in plumage.

Flamingos – order Phoenicopteriformes, family Phoenicopteridae
(*see* pages 58-9)
A family with uncertain relationships, possibly linked to the herons, or to the geese, depending on which anatomical features are given most weight. Unmistakable in almost all circumstances, with characteristically long legs and neck and specialized banana-shaped filter-feeding beak, they fly with neck and legs extended. Flamingos breed and normally feed colonially. Male and female are very similar in plumage.

Waterfowl – swans, geese and ducks – order Anseriformes, family Anatidae (*see* pages 60-81, 114-15)
One of the more uniform groups of birds, characterized in particular by their webbed feet (joining the three forward-pointing toes) and beaks that can only be described as 'duck-like'. Within the order are a series of easily recognized groups. The swans are the largest in size – huge, with broad, heavily-fingered wings, characterized by their very long necks and all-white adult plumage. Long necks allow them to feed by 'upending' in deep water, but they also graze by the water's edge. They build huge nests of reeds and are aggressive in defence of eggs or young. Take-off usually follows a long pattering run across the water, and considerable space is required for a long 'water-skiing' landing. The 'wild' swans (Whooper and Bewick's) have wonderful trumpeting calls. Male and female are similar in plumage.

The geese, although also long-necked, are rather smaller. They may roost on water, but often feed by grazing on fields, marshes or mudflats. Most fly in characteristic straggling V-shaped skeins, and most are vocal in flight and when feeding, using various honking or barking cries. The geese are further subdivided into grey species (genus *Anser*) and black (genus *Branta*), the black geese being in general small and more coastal in habitat. Male and female are similar in plumage.

The third group is the ducks. Only one, the Shelduck, has a neck anywhere near as long as the geese – most are characterized by short necks and comparatively elongated bodies, floating buoyantly on the water. Their feet are often set well back on the body, effective for swimming but giving them a clumsy waddling walk on land. Their wings tend to be relatively small, fast-beating and pointed at the tips. The ducks, too, fall into several natural groups. The surface-feeding (or dabbling) ducks graze close to the water's edge, or dabble for seeds in soft mud or shallow water, sometimes 'upending'. These are birds of freshwater marshes and lakes, lagoons and sheltered estuaries, less often seen on the open coast.

'Diving' ducks (sometimes called 'bay' ducks) are found more often out on deep freshwater lakes, in open estuaries and off the coast. Usually these are dumpier in build than the dabbling ducks, and dive neatly and frequently for their food. Related, but easily distinguished by the birdwatcher, are the sea ducks. These, too, dive for food, but are large and heavily built, often with a heavy beak. They are usually to be found in coastal waters, often tolerating very rough conditions. All the diving ducks have comparatively small wings, with legs set well back towards the tail. This gives a good underwater swimming performance, but necessitates a long take-off run pattering across the surface. The stiff-tails are dumpy diving ducks with long, stiff tails and large heads. The sawbills (or mergansers), with slim, streamlined, cigar-shaped bodies, are expert underwater swimmers, catching their prey (often fish) with long slender beaks with serrated edges.

Apart from the Shelduck, the ducks differ from other waterfowl in having distinctive male and female plumages. The female is normally dull and well-camouflaged (she does all the incubation and rears the family), the male brightly-coloured and at his best in late winter, the time of display. In mid-summer, he moults into an 'eclipse' plumage, dull and similar to his female, to moult again in autumn into his full breeding plumage. Females of related species can be difficult to separate, and males moulting into, or out of, eclipse plumage can be most confusing.

Birds of Prey – orders Accipitriformes and Falconiformes
(*see* pages 82-99)

These flesh-eating predators, often called 'raptors', are characterized first and foremost by powerful, hooked beaks for tearing flesh. Comparatively large eyes (with superb powers of resolution, many times more efficient than that of a human being) help pinpoint prey, and the kill is achieved through long legs ending in powerful talons tipped with dagger-sharp claws. Over the base of the beak is a fleshy pad, called the 'cere', containing the nostrils and often golden in colour in adults. Many birds of prey have the tarsus section of the leg unfeathered (but not the eagles or the Rough-legged Buzzard): this, and the talons, are also usually golden. In almost all birds of prey, the female is larger than the male (sometimes substantially so, weighing thirty percent heavier): thus many males will be smaller than the average measurement given, and many females larger. Most birds of prey take three or four years to reach maturity – or at least to reach fully adult plumage. Unlike smaller birds, their pattern of moult is irregular, and in consequence the variability of their plumage over the years between juvenile and adult is considerable, and often extremely confusing. (We are still gathering data on how best to identify raptors in these difficult immature plumages: some are easier than others, but it should be expected that not all raptors seen, especially briefly or in the distance, will be identified.)

The order Accipitriformes is divided into two families. One, the Pandionidae, contains only the Osprey. The other, the Accipitridae, is much larger, and from the viewpoint of the field birdwatcher, astonishingly diverse, containing the kites, eagles, vultures, harriers, hawks, and buzzards.

The kites usually feed by scavenging, and have small beaks. They are medium-sized for raptors, with strikingly long tails and long wings normally held bent at the 'wrist' (or carpal joint), soaring frequently but very agile in low-altitude, low-speed flight. The sexes of the Red Kite have differing plumages; in the Black they are similar.

Eagles pose more field identification problems even than other raptors because of their varied immature plumages. They range in size from medium to very large, and soar frequently on wings that are usually broad and long, heavily fingered at the tips, and held at right angles to the body. Their beaks are usually large and powerful. Helpful features to note are the size of the head, the length of the tail, and whether the wings are held flat or in a 'V' when soaring, as well as details of plumage coloration. Sexes are similar in plumage.

Vultures are scavengers, with powerful beaks but comparatively small, ineffectual talons. The Egyptian Vulture is atypically small, with slim wings and a wedge-shaped tail; the Lammergeyer has a similar long-winged flight silhouette but is much larger. The other vultures are huge, with immense, broad, heavily-fingered wings. They soar effortlessly, often at a great height, with head and tail protruding little beyond the wings. Sexes are similar in plumage.

In some ways similar to the kites, the harriers are medium-sized raptors with small beaks and long legs. They have long slender tails and long, fingered wings carried straight at right angles to the body. Characteristically they hunt by gliding low on wings held in a shallow 'V', pouncing on prey taken by surprise. Sexes are strikingly distinct in plumage.

The hawks range from small to medium size for raptors, and are characterized by their rounded, fingered wings and long tails. They have comparatively long beaks. They are woodland birds, dashing after prey and flying between the trees with great agility. In spring, they may soar high above the trees. Sexes have differing plumages.

Buzzards are medium sized, and characterized by broad, heavily fingered wings, a broad tail (often fanned), and circling soaring flight. At a distance, care is needed to separate buzzards and small eagles. Buzzards are notoriously variable in plumage, and have smaller beaks than most eagles. Rough-legged Buzzards sometimes hover clumsily. The Honey Buzzard – not a true buzzard – has a strikingly long narrow tail, and a comparatively small head. Sexes are similar in plumage.

The Osprey is a large raptor, a specialist fish-eater catching its prey by spectacular dives, carrying its catch torpedo-fashion, head forwards. Its wings are long and broad, heavily fingered and characteristically held in an 'M'. Sexes are similar in plumage.

The other order, the Falconiformes, contains only one family – Falconidae, the falcons. These have pointed, rather than rounded or fingered wingtips, and relatively long, narrow tails. Small to medium in size, with relatively small beaks, they are characterized by their fast, purposeful flight in pursuit of prey, usually in open country. The Kestrel is unusual in hunting mostly by hovering. Sexes have differing plumages.

Because of their predatory life-style, raptors are comparatively scarce in any habitat because they need large territories. Thus it is to be expected that raptor sightings (except of Kestrel and Buzzard) will be relatively infrequent. Vultures may gather at a kill, but are otherwise solitary; only the Red-footed Falcon and Lesser Kestrel are gregarious, living and hunting in groups. On migration, however, large gatherings (often of several species) can be expected, especially at sea crossings like Falsterbo in Sweden, Gibraltar and the Bosphorus in the Mediterranean.

Game birds – order Galliformes (*see* pages 68-9, 100-3)

The game birds are all comparatively heavy-bodied, with small heads and chicken-like beaks well able to tackle tough seeds and invertebrates like beetles and snails. Their wings are markedly rounded and fingered, giving almost vertical take-off in emergencies. Even half-grown young are able to fly. In flight, they characteristically travel low and swift, with spells of whirring wing beats interspersed with long glides with the wings held stiffly downcurved.

Grouse – family Tetraonidae – are medium sized, stocky, with an upright stance. Their nostrils are shielded by feathers, and their legs and toes are feather-clad as an adaptation to upland exposed environments. Partridges which, along with Quails and Pheasants, belong to the family Phasianidae, are similarly stocky but rather smaller in size, and shorter tailed than grouse. Legs and toes are covered in the usual horny scales, more suited to their habitat of dry grassland or rocky areas, often in warm climates. The Quail is the smallest of ie group, surprisingly (as the others are sedentary) a long-haul migrant. The Pheasant is the argest and most striking. Initially introduced to Europe from the Far East, it is now widespread, though its numbers are often dependent on artificially reared birds. Apart from the handsome, brightly-coloured male Pheasant, game-bird males tend to be only slightly better marked or more colourful than the females, which are well camouflaged to protect them during the long weeks of solo incubation on a ground nest. Large clutches of eggs (up to fifteen) are normal.

Rails, bustards and cranes – order Gruiformes *(see pages 104-7)*

On outward appearance, comparatively long legs are the only common character in this very diverse group of birds. Rails – family Rallidae – are dumpy-bodied, small to medium-sized, generally wetland birds, with bodies markedly flattened from side to side to ease their passage through the reeds. Long spidery toes support them on mud and floating vegetation, and are effective in swimming. The Coot has lobed toes to increase swimming and diving efficiency, and it and the Moorhen swim frequently, the others much less often. Coot and Moorhen are often to be seen in the open: the other rails are secretive, often extremely so. All walk sedately, with frequent tail flicking (the tail colour is often a useful feature) and swim jerkily, also with tail flicking. All fly infrequently, and often feebly, low over the water. Most have strident voices, particularly during the breeding season. The majority of rails have short stout beaks, the Water Rail being an exception. The sexes are generally similar in plumage.

Bustards – family Otididae – are extremely wary birds, perhaps an adaptation to avoid hunters who since the Stone Age have pursued them for their flesh. They are large to huge in size, with long legs, a long neck and long broad wings. The larger and brighter male has a complex display before the well-camouflaged female.

The Crane – family Gruidae – large and stork-like on the ground and in flight, (when it carries its head and neck and legs extended) is the European representative of a family renowned for their whooping calls and dancing display rituals. The male is only slightly more colourful than the female.

Waders or shorebirds – part of the order Charadriiformes

(see pages 50-1, 108-29, 158-9)

The Charadriiformes is another complex and diverse order of birds containing, besides the waders, the skuas, gulls and terns, and the auks, all related by common but inconspicuous anatomical features, despite external appearances apparently quite to the contrary.

Within the wader section lie six families. Four are small, and their members are quite distinctive: these are the Haematopodidae – Oystercatcher; Recurvirostridae – Avocet and Stilt; Burhinidae – Stone Curlew; and Glareolidae – pratincoles. The first three show the typical wader features of long legs, body held horizontal, and a relatively long neck, and behave as waders usually do in a wetland or coastal environment (although the Stone Curlew breeds on arid plains). The pratincoles can be best characterized by the statement that they look like terns but behave like swallows. The Charadriidae contains the plovers, small to medium in size, long-legged but with characteristically short stubby beaks. The Scolopacidae, the last family is diverse. Its members range from small to medium-large, and include the *Calidris* sandpipers; the snipes and Woodcock, long-beaked and well-camouflaged; the godwits and curlews, also long-beaked; the *Tringa* shanks and sandpipers, slim-beaked and noisily vocal; the harlequin-like Turnstone and the pelagic phalaropes.

Wader identification, because of the waders' coastal or marshland habitats and natural wariness, is often a longish-range task. Important features to note – besides size and plumage colour – are the patterns visible on the wings and tail in flight; the length and particularly the colour of the legs; any calls given; and the length and shape of the beak. Waders hunt the various food items (usually small animals like worms, shrimps and shellfish) with a fascinating variety of techniques, using beaks ranging from short and stubby (plovers) to needle-fine and upturned (Avocet) or extremely long and downcurved (Curlew). This range of structural adaptation enables them to share the food available without undue competition, but provides a most useful identification feature at the same time.

Most waders are ground-nesters, laying commonly four sharply-pointed, well-camouflaged eggs. Male and female are normally similar in plumage, the male in some cases brighter. In the phalaropes, unusually, the female is larger and brighter. While many have bright breeding-season colours, almost all in winter are drab and grey-brown, well-suited to the mudflats on which they feed. Immatures, too, although often brighter than winter adults, fall short of the adults' spectacular summer plumage.

Skuas – part of the order Charadriiformes (*see* pages 130-1)

The skuas – family Stercorariidae – are medium-sized seabirds resembling dark gulls, with similar flight patterns. Some have two plumage phases – light and dark, plus intermediates – but all have the characteristic white flashes in the centre of the wings, conspicuous in flight. Adults of all species except the Great Skua have elongated central tail feathers, but these not in frequently may get broken. Unlike gulls, skuas rarely venture inland. Expert fliers, they get much of their food by piracy, harrassing other seabirds until they drop their catch. The sexes are similar in plumage; immatures are dark brown.

Gulls – part of the order Charadriiformes (*see* pages 50-1,132-7)

The gulls – family Laridae – are a uniform group of medium to large species among the best-known of birds. They are comparatively long-winged, hold their bodies horizontally when standing, and have longish legs with webbed feet. They fly effortlessly and swim buoyantly. Essentially coastal birds with some inland breeding grounds, many gulls have now adapted to a year-round inland existence, scavenging on fields and refuse tips for food. Most are gregarious and vocal year-round, often breeding in huge colonies. Adult birds are generally white-bodied, with back and wings white, grey or black. Immatures are normally brown, becoming paler with age. Larger species may take four years to reach maturity, and intermediate stages can often be confusing. Black-or brown-hooded species lose their hoods in winter. The sexes are similar in plumage.

Terns – part of the order Charadriiformes (*see* pages 50-1, 138-41)

The terns – family Sternidae – are aptly called sea-swallows. They are amongst the most graceful of sea-and-marsh birds. Generally smaller and slimmer than gulls, with shorter necks, slimmer wings and shorter legs, they have webbed feet but swim less often than gulls. Most obtain food by diving, or dipping to the water surface, from flight. There are two groups. The 'sea terns' are largely white-plumaged, with a black cap (reduced in size in winter) and often with long tail streamers. Many are predominantly maritime. The 'marsh terns' are shorter-winged and plumper-bodied, and hunt largely over freshwater habitats. Grey and black colourings feature in their plumage, and their feeding technique of dipping down to the water surface to pick off food is characteristic. The sexes are similar in plumage, with immatures greyer or browner versions of winter adults.

Auks – part of the order Charadriiformes (*see* pages 50-1, 142-3)

The auks – family Alcidae – are quite unlike the fellow members of their order. Essentially they appear like a cross between the divers and the ducks. All are seabirds, long-bodied and expert underwater, with small wings and whirring flight, often low over the sea. They swim buoyantly diving frequently. Most are colonial breeders, coming to land only during the summer months.

he sexes have similar plumages, but in some species, summer and winter plumages are markedly different.

Pigeons and doves – order Columbiformes, family Columbidae
(see pages 144-5)

A uniform family of medium or medium-small birds, relatively heavy-bodied, with small heads and beaks carried on a longish neck. Their wings are usually pointed, their tails relatively long (some are noticeably falcon-like in silhouette) and their flight swift and direct. Most are gregarious during the winter, feeding and roosting together. Of the European species, soft cooing calls are characteristic of all except the Turtle Dove, which has a distinctive extended purr. Rock and Stock Doves are hole-nesters, laying characteristically rounded white eggs on a twig nest. Tree-nesting species build characteristic flat flimsy platform nests of twigs. The sexes are similar.

Sandgrouse – order Pteroclidiformes, family Pteroclididae
(see pages 146-7)

Sandgrouse are similar in appearance and in their fast direct flight to the pigeons and doves, with which some taxonomic authorities link them. Heavy-bodied, with long, pointed wings and comparatively small heads with tiny beaks, they have extremely short legs, giving them a odd 'leg-less' appearance on the ground. They have pointed tail feathers. Males are brighter plumaged than females.

Cuckoos – order Cuculiformes, family Cuculidae (see pages 146-7)

Medium-sized, long-tailed birds with short pointed wings, giving them a characteristically falcon-like flight silhouette. The sexes are similar.

Owls – order Strigiformes, families Tytonidae and Strigidae
(see pages 148-53)

Few groups of birds are as well known as the owls, popular but at the same time instilling some fear because of their strange calls and nocturnal habits. Owls range in size from medium-small to very large, and characteristically are stockily built, with very large heads and a neck-less appearance. All have very long legs (often concealed in the body plumage) armed with powerful feet with feathered toes and strong sharp talons. Most have soft grey or brown, speckled plumage, and have a facial disc of stiffer feathers that is both characteristic and serves to focus the slightest of sounds on the huge (but hidden) ears. Wing silhouettes vary from rounded to long, but are usually heavily fingered. All have powerful, hooked, flesh-tearing beaks, which are not particularly conspicuous. Owls make no nest, laying in a natural cavity or in the disused nest of another bird. The characteristic spherical white eggs are quickly surrounded by pellets – the castings of indigestible fur, feathers and bones of their prey. The sexes have similar plumage.

Nightjars – order Caprimulgiformes, family Caprimulgidae
(see pages 154-5)

Medium-small, long-tailed hawk-like birds, with tiny legs. Magnificently camouflaged with flecked brown plumage, they nest for much of the day, perching horizontally, hunting insects in the evening or at night. Externally the beak appears tiny, but it gapes hugely to aid insect-catching in flight. Extended purring song and wing-clapping display flight are useful features. They are ground-nesters. The sexes are superficially similar, but the males have white wing and tail markings.

Swifts – order Apodiformes, family Apodidae (*see* pages 154-5)

Visually very similar to the swallows and martins, but in fact very different, the swift's nearest relatives surprisingly are the hummingbirds. Distinctively long, sickle-shaped wings indicate the swift's high-speed, largely aerial life. The body is torpedo-shaped, the tail short and shallowly forked. The legs are tiny, and rarely do swifts come to ground except to the nest, which is in an elevated crevice from which, outgoing, they can drop to gain sufficient speed for flight. The beak is the outwardly small evidence of a huge gape, evolved for catching insect prey in flight. The sexes are similar in plumage.

Rollers and their allies – order Coraciiformes (*see* pages 156-9)

This is a poorly-defined grouping of birds so colourful in plumage that individually they pose few identification problems. In Europe, basically it gathers simple representatives of four families: the Alcedinidae (Kingfisher), Meropidae (Bee-eater), Coraciidae (Roller) and Upupidae (Hoopoe). Apart from colourful plumage, common features are scarce, the most obvious being that all the hole-nesters lay near-spherical white eggs in unbelievably smelly nest chambers. Kingfishers dive for their fish prey in streams and lakes. Bee-eaters hawk like giant, rainbow-coloured swallows agilely chasing flying insects. Rollers hunt larger terrestrial insects and small animals from a perch, displaying the full beauty of their electric-blue wings only when they fly. They favour roadside telephone and power cables. Hoopoes, with pied heavily-fingered rounded wings and a long, often fanned crest frequently feed on the ground, seeking insects with their long downcurved beaks.

Woodpeckers – order Piciformes, family Picidae (*see* pages 160-3)

Apart from the Wryneck, the woodpeckers form a characteristic and well-defined group. All have stout dagger-shaped beaks; all climb trees in a head-uppermost position, using stiffened tail feathers as an additional support; and all have powerful feet with toes arranged two pointing forwards, two back, which with the long claws gives an excellent grip. All excavate cavity nests, in living or dead timber, into conspicuous and characteristic nest entrance holes. These may subsequently be used by other birds. Most use their beaks to excavate grubs, catching their prey on the barbed tip of an immensely long tongue. Most are strikingly plumaged, with loud harsh calls. The sexes differ, but often only slightly in plumage.

Larks – order Passeriformes, family Alaudidae (*see* pages 164-7)

Most larks are small, generally with relatively featureless plumage of mottled browns, giving excellent camouflage for their largely terrestrial lives, often in dry (thus brown) habitats. Most have comparatively long, strong legs with big claws (an adaptation to terrestrial life). Most have evolved a song-flight, where display song is produced at a considerable height over terrain lacking suitable song-posts. Song is a valuable aid to identification. Care is necessary to avoid confusion with some similar pipit species. (Study of song and plumage details is recommended.) Beak shape varies from comparatively slender to short, stout and finch-like, depending on the amount and nature of the vegetable matter in the diet. Nests are on the ground and always well concealed, the young frequently scattering into hiding nearby before they fledge. The sexes have similar plumage.

Swallows and martins – order Passeriformes, family Hirundinidae (*see* pages 168-9)

Often called 'hirundines' this family is characterized by a largely aerial life, well-streamlined, torpedo-shaped body and by relatively long, slim, curved wings. The tail is forked, slightly in some species, very markedly in the case of the swallows. Though similar in build and flight habits to the swifts, swallows and martins come to land occasionally, and perch frequently and conspicuously on wires. Most (except the hole-nesting Sand Martin) build characteristic nests of mud pellets, often fixed in the shelter of houses and outbuildings. Legs and beaks are small. Songs are markedly twittering. They are often gregarious when breeding, feeding and migrating. The sexes have similar plumage.

Pipits and wagtails – order Passeriformes, family Motacillidae
see pages 158-9, 170-5)

Pipits and wagtails are largely terrestrial in behaviour, running swiftly and agilely in pursuit of insect and other invertebrate prey. Although related, the two form easily distinguished groupings. The wagtails are small, slim-bodied and comparatively long-legged, with a characteristically long, white-bordered tail incessantly wagged up and down. Their flight is deeply undulating. Their plumages are boldly patterned, often colourful, and males are appreciably brighter than females. These are conspicuous birds, but build well-hidden nests.

The 'Yellow Wagtail' complex needs special mention, (*see* page 174-5). Over the course of evolution, males of the various geographical races have developed often quite strikingly distinctive plumages, and the colours and patterns of the male head are diagnostic. The females and immatures are indistinguishable one race from another, and where race distributions abut, interbreeding takes place producing hybrid offspring whose plumages further complicate identification.

In contrast to the wagtails, the pipits are inconspicuous, even secretive. Their plumage is generally brownish and well streaked (except for males of a few species in spring), their tails of medium length with white or grey edges. They are open-land birds, tending to be terrestrial. Identification is often difficult, but habitat and song or call can usefully augment plumage detail, especially in seasons other than spring. Flight is shallowly undulating, and several species have a song-flight. The sexes are generally similar, again except for the brighter males of a few species in spring.

Waxwing – order Passeriformes, family Bombycillidae
(*see* pages 176-7)

There is just one species, easily identified at close range. At a distance, the Waxwing is Starling-like in flight, with a trilling call. Creatures of habit, in winter they return daily to the same berry-bearing bushes. They are gregarious. Sexes are similar in plumage.

Dipper – order Passeriformes, family Cinclidae (*see* pages 176-7)

Again there is just one species. Looking like giant wrens, and with a large white 'bib', Dippers have the habit of bobbing on boulders before plunging into rivers. Sexes are similar in plumage, and, unusually, both sing at the start of the breeding season.

Wren – order Passeriformes, family Troglodytidae (*see* pages 176-7)

There is one species (in contrast to many in North America). Their tiny cocked tail, chestnut coloration and low, short-range whirring flight are all useful features, as is the powerful, melodious song. Races from the far north and west are often slightly larger and grey, especially from remote islands. Sexes are similar in plumage.

Accentors – order Passeriformes, family Prunellidae (*see* pages 176-7)

Small, retiring and inconspicuous birds with comparatively drab plumages. The leaden-grey head and breast of the Dunnock are distinctive, and the Alpine Accentor is one of the very few slim-beaked insectivorous birds in its mountain habitat. Knowledge of their songs can be helpful. Sexes are similar in plumage.

Thrushes and chats – order Passeriformes, family Turdidae
(*see* pages 176-87)
A large but coherent grouping of small to medium-sized birds, relatively plump, relatively strong-legged, and recognizably 'thrush-shaped' with a medium-length, medium-thickness beak suitable for eating fruit and various invertebrate animals such as worms. There are several natural sub-groups, varying appreciably in plumage characteristics. All fly in a gently or deeply undulating manner.

The Robin and the two nightingales are clearly related, small, with very similar speckled immature plumages. Basically they are secretive birds of dense undergrowth, spending much time on the ground. The long, rufous tails of the nightingales are a useful identification feature, but song is the most useful guide. The sexes are similar in plumage.

The redstarts are rather slimmer but similar in size. The Redstart and Black Redstart both have comparatively long chestnut tails, which they flick frequently. The former is a woodland bird, the latter a bird of mountain or (strangely) urban or industrial habitats. The sexes have markedly differing plumages, the male being much brighter.

The chats are characteristically 'spherical bodied', with long slim legs and short wings and tail, which flick incessantly. They are often seen on prominent perches or overhead wires in their relatively open or scrub habitats. They have scratchy songs and a distinctive 'chat' alarm call (similar to two pebbles being knocked together). The sexes have different plumages, the male being brighter.

The wheatears have a similar alarm call, but are longer and slimmer in the body, spending much time on the ground. They are characterized by white rump and tail markings, often in the shape of an inverted 'V' contrasting with a black or dark-brown tail. Males are brighter than females, but both sexes and the immatures have the rump pattern. Close attention to plumage features allows males to be identified reasonably easily, but females and immatures of the various wheatear species may be extremely difficult to separate.

The rock thrushes are larger, but similar in build to the well-known Song Thrush, and distinctively brightly coloured. The largest sub-group, the genus *Turdus*, contains the larger thrushes, often familiar birds like the Blackbird and Song Thrush. Drabber in plumage than most of their smaller relatives, they spend part of their lives on the ground, part in the trees, feeding on a wide variety of fruit and animal matter with a 'general purpose' beak. In most, the sexes are similarly plumaged. Those thrushes with typical speckled breasts can be usefully separated by their songs, and in flight by the colour of their underwings. They are often gregarious when feeding or roosting outside the breeding season.

Warblers and crests – order Passeriformes, family Sylviidae
(*see* pages 158-9, 188-203)
Another coherent group of tiny to small birds, with an overall similarity but readily separated into several sub-groups. The majority are migrants – summering in Europe, wintering in Africa. All are largely insectivorous for much of the year, with finely pointed, often slim needle-like beaks, but turn readily to fruit-eating in autumn. All build well-concealed nests, in dense vegetation, often close to, or on, the ground. The character that does not conform to expectation is their voice: although some produce a melodious warble, in many the song is rudimentary, or scratchy, or metallic. Nevertheless, a knowledge of songs is of great value in separating species within the groups and indeed in locating warblers in the field, as many are either skulking or frequently concealed in the vegetation canopy.

The *Acrocephalus* warblers favour wetland habitats, are slim, and tend to be brownish above (sometimes streaked, sometimes plain) and paler fawn below. *Cettia*, with its single European species, is similar, but rufous, with a long rounded tail. The *Locustella* warblers are often found in damp areas, and although brown, are darker and duller, heavily streaked, with wedge-shaped tail. They are secretive in the extreme but have distinctive long-drawn-out churring songs. Superficially similar to them is the tiny, wren-like Fan-tailed Warbler (*Cistiola*), the sole European representative of a large and confusing African genus. In all, the sexes are similar in plumage.

The *Hippolais* warblers are more upright in stance, favour trees or shrubs, and are greenish or brownish above with yellow or white underparts. They have unusually large beaks, and flat-topped heads, though in excitement the crown feathers can be raised. They all have melodious songs. The sexes are similar in plumage.

The genus *Sylvia* is the largest, and contains the most distinctive and colourfully-plumaged warblers. They are birds of woodland, or, more commonly, scrub. The woodland species have melodious songs, the scrub species tend to be secretive, and have scratchy songs often delivered in a vertical song-flight. The scrub species tend to have domed crowns and comparatively long tails, often with white edges. Several are remarkably local in their occurrence. In almost all, males are appreciably brighter plumaged than females.

The 'leaf warblers' of the genus *Phylloscopus* also form a large group but its members are mostly tiny and drab, brownish, olive or greenish above, buff, yellowish, or white below. Crown, rump and wingbar patterns are useful identification aids, and a knowledge of songs is particularly helpful. The sexes are similar in plumage.

The genus *Regulus* – 'the crests' – contains two tiny species (Europe's smallest birds) closely allied to the warblers, and similar in anatomy and behaviour to the *Phylloscopus* warblers. Strikingly characteristic head patterns aid identification, and their songs are distinctive. The sexes differ only slightly in plumage.

Flycatchers – order Passeriformes, family Muscicapidae (*see* pages 204-5)

A small family, close-knit, and broadly similar to the warblers. All are migrants, wintering in Africa and Asia. Viewed from the side, their insectivorous beaks appear slim, but seen from above or below they are broad at the base, with prominent bristles surrounding the gape. They are arboreal birds, hunting insect prey on the wing from a prominent perch, and catching it with an audible 'snap'. They are slim, with a rather horizontal perching posture caused by their relatively long wings and comparatively very short legs. Their songs are brief and inconspicuous, but their plumages are reasonably distinctive. Except for the Spotted Flycatcher, males are brighter plumaged than females.

Tits and their allies – order Passeriformes, families Timaliidae, Aegithalidae, Paridae (*see* pages 206-9)

Both the Bearded Tit or Reedling (Timaliidae) and Long-tailed Tit (Aegithalidae) are very distinctive in appearance. They are probably closely related to each other, and though similar in behaviour, probably only distantly related to the true tits, the Paridae. As a family, the Paridae are familiar, both in plumage and for their stubby but sharply-pointed beaks, and in their agile behaviour and inquisitiveness. Most are arboreal and nest in holes, favouring nest-boxes. They can be identified with reasonable ease by their plumage characteristics, but at a distance their apparently rather weak flight, with bursts of fluttering wingbeats, can be a help, while up in the woodland canopy, a knowledge of their songs and calls is a great asset – although the Great Tit produces over ninety different calls! The sexes are fairly similar in plumage, except with the Bearded Tit.

Nuthatches – order Passeriformes, family Sittidae (*see* pages 210-11)

In many ways these resemble small woodpeckers, with stout dagger-shaped beaks. Although they spend much time climbing on trunks and branches, they move with equal facility head-up or head-down, as the tail feathers are soft and do not serve as a prop. Their toes, too, are arranged in typical Passerine format, three forward, and one back. Both plumage and calls are distinctive. Males are slightly brighter plumaged than females.

Creepers – order Passeriformes, family Certhiidae (*see* pages 210-11)
This small family behaves as its name suggests. The mouse-like Treecreepers move (always head-up - they have stiffened tail feathers) woodpecker-like on tree trunks, the much more colourful Wall Creeper on rocks. They have comparatively large eyes under beetling eyebrows, and a long, finely-pointed downcurved beak. They have a deeply undulating flight, showing rounded, fingered wings and an unexpectedly prominent wingbar pattern. The sexes are similar in plumage.

Penduline Tit – order Passeriformes, family Remizidae (*see* pages 210-11)
Tit-like in appearance, but with a longer, more pointed beak. The call and plumage of this bird are both distinctive, but the nest is even more so, and unusual in being made of cobwebs and willow down. Shaped like an alchemist's retort, with a nesting 'flask' and an entrance tube pointing downwards, it is suspended from the end of a branch, often over water. The male is more brightly plumaged than the female.

Shrikes – order Passeriformes, family Laniidae (*see* pages 212-13)
A group of long-tailed, fairly small to medium-sized passerines, boldly plumaged, which have evolved a predatory life-style. In consequence, they have hawk-like hooked beaks, and well-developed toes and claws. Characteristically they hunt from an exposed perch, dropping onto prey as it passes. Excess prey is stored in a 'larder' impaled on thorns or barbed wire. Their wings are comparatively short and rounded, often with striking wingbars. Plumage, colours and details of head and wing markings are useful in identification. Most have attractive songs. The sexes are similar in the two grey species, but males are more brightly plumaged in the others.

Crows – order Passeriformes, family Corvidae (*see* pages 214-19)
Medium to large birds, usually gregarious in habit and normally omnivorous in diet. Their beaks are stout, heavy and relatively long, suited to life as a scavenger and predator on other birds' eggs or young. True crows (genus *Corvus*) are black or black and grey, usually with a metallic sheen. They fly easily on broad, fingered wings, and on the ground walk or hop with equal ease. The related genera, the choughs, jays, Nutcracker and magpies, are more strikingly plumaged but are similar in habits, except for the slim-billed Chough, which specializes in eating ants. All otherwise share a very mixed diet. Crows build bulky twig nests, usually high in trees or on inaccessible crags. Their calls are characteristically harsh and brief, though some occasionally produce a warbling song. The sexes are similar in plumage.

Golden Oriole – order Passeriformes, family Oriolidae (*see* pages 220-1)
Starling-like in size, build and flight, the Golden Oriole is the sole European representative of a brightly-coloured tropical family. Despite the bright plumage, it is often inconspicuous in a sunlit canopy, when its distinctive fluting call becomes a useful guide. The male is much more brightly plumaged than the female.

Starlings – order Passeriformes, family Sturnidae (*see* pages 220-1)
Universal and familiar, the Starling needs little introduction, and nor does its spotless close relative or the colourful Rose-coloured species. All starlings are vocal, most being excellent mimics. Swift, direct flight on characteristic equilateral-triangle wings, and gregarious habits

re useful aids to distant identification. Sexes are similar except in the case of the Rose-coloured Starling.

Sparrows – order Passeriformes, family Passeridae (*see* pages 222-3)

Small, stocky, relatively short-legged seed-eating birds with a robust wedge-shaped beak. They are often gregarious in the breeding season and in winter. All build untidy, bulky nests of straw or grass lined with feathers, often domed in structure, and often associated with domestic buildings. Three genera are involved: *Passer* are the most familiar, however drab in plumage, with fairly long beaks and only a series of harsh chirrups for a song. They have an undulating flight and in most species the male is more strongly plumaged than the very dull female, (but not in the case of the Tree Sparrows). With the genus *Petronia*, the sexes are similarly drab. In the third, *Montifringilla* (Snow Finch), outward appearances are more suggestive of a finch than a sparrow. The male is slightly brighter, and has a twittering song.

Finches – order Passeriformes, family Fringillidae (*see* pages 224-9, 232-5)

Small, occasionally tiny birds of comparatively uniform appearance. Their characteristic feature, a short, fairly heavy, triangular or wedge-shaped beak, is well suited to a seed-eating diet. In the course of evolution, the basic format has been modified to suit a range of feeding adaptations, and these variations in shape (ranging from small and stubby in the redpolls, through 'normality' in the Greenfinch, to elongated in the Goldfinch and scissor-like in the crossbills) provide a useful guide to identification. Songs and flight calls are also often distinctive and helpful. Finch flight is undulating, often deeply so, and some species have noticeably forked tails.

In most finches, the males' well-developed song is associated with a colourful plumage, serving him well in both courtship and territorial displays. The females are duller, often fawn or brown, but retain conspicuous markings like rump patches and wingbars, and characteristic beak shapes, which are often a useful guide to their identity. Immatures, too, retain these characteristics, but otherwise resemble the females, though often with a streaked plumage. All construct very neat cup-shaped nests in bushes or trees.

Buntings – order Passeriformes, family Emberizidae
see pages 230-1, 236-41)

Outwardly resembling rather large, elongated and colourful sparrows, the buntings, too, have thickish wedge-shaped beaks. On closer inspection, the lower mandible can be seen to be appreciably larger than the upper, giving a characteristic 'whale-jaw' appearance. In summer, males of almost all species have distinctive plumages and songs, and are comparatively easy to identify. However, most females and immatures have heavily-streaked, well-camouflaged plumages and the differences between species can be extremely subtle, demanding close observation of plumage detail if positive identification is to be achieved. Males in winter also have much of their summer colour obscured by buff feather fringes, and can be difficult to identify. At a distance, deeply undulating flight is a helpful guide, as is a knowledge of their harsh but distinctive songs, and their characteristic flight calls. The Corn Bunting is the exception to the rule that males are more brightly plumaged than females.

BIRDS
OF BRITAIN AND EUROPE

Red-throated Diver *Gavia stellata* 55cm Smallest of the divers. Summer adult has white underparts and grey-brown back with sparse, pale markings. Head grey-brown; neck white with dark brown streaks. Central, dark red throat patch often looks almost black. Beak pale, dagger-shaped and slightly upturned, usually held pointing at an angle upwards. Winter adult greyish above, with bold, white flecking; white below. Immature resembles winter adult. In flight, looks slimmer and paler than other diver species, with deeper, more rapid wingbeats. *Voice:* in breeding season, various cackling and barking calls; silent in winter. *Habitat:* breeds beside small pools in moorland areas of northern Europe (occasionally by sea inlets); often flies out to sea to feed. In winter and on migration, occurs inshore along the west European coast; occasionally seen on inland fresh waters. Widespread; rarely numerous. ⚓🦅🌊

Black-throated Diver *Gavia arctica* 62cm Bulkier and heavier-headed than Red-throated. Summer adult has white underparts and black back with bold white markings. Head and nape grey; throat streaked black with central black patch. Beak dark, straight and dagger-shaped. Winter adult grey-brown above; whitish below, with clear line between white throat and grey nape. Immature resembles winter adult but has pale, scaly markings on back. Wingbeats slower and shallower than Red-throated. *Voice:* on breeding grounds, rhythmic, eerie, wailing song; in flight, gruff, quacking calls; silent in winter. *Habitat:* breeds on islands in large, northern European lakes. In winter and on migration, occurs on coastal seas; occasionally seen on inland fresh waters. Scarce. ⚓🦅🌊

Great Northern Diver *Gavia immer* 75cm Much bulkier-looking than Black-throated. Summer adult has white underparts and black back with bold, white chequer markings. Neck black and heavy; head angular and greenish-black. Beak dark, dagger-shaped and massive. Winter adult grey-brown above with diffuse pale markings on neck; whitish below. Immature resembles winter adult with pale, scaly back markings. Slow, shallow wingbeats. *Voice:* on breeding grounds, amazingly evocative, yodel-like wailing; in flight, harsh quacks; silent in winter. *Habitat:* breeds beside remote, large lakes in northern Europe. In winter and on migration, occurs on coastal seas; occasionally seen on inland fresh waters. Rare.(Similar **White-billed Diver** *Gavia adamsii*, from far north, is occasional vagrant; closely resembles Great Northern, but with upturned, pale beak.) ⚓🦅🌊

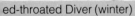
Red-throated Diver (winter)

Red-throated Diver (summer)

Black-throated Diver (summer)

Great Northern Diver (summer)

Little Grebe *Tachybaptus ruficollis* 25cm Smallest and dumpiest of the grebes, with short-necked and characteristically tailless appearance. Summer adult dark brown; chin and upper throat rich chestnut; small yellow patch at base of beak. Winter adult drab brown above; paler below. Immature resembles winter adult. *Voice:* far-carrying, shrill, whinnying song. *Habitat:* slow-moving rivers, canals, ditches, lakes and reservoirs, usually with ample marginal vegetation, year-round. Widespread; common.

Great Crested Grebe *Podiceps cristatus* 45cm Largest grebe, with long, slender neck. Summer adult grey-brown above; white below. Neck white; head conspicuously crested, tufted in chestnut and black. Beak orange and dagger-like. Winter adult generally greyer, only slight indication of crest. Immature resembles winter adult. In flight, appears hump-backed, showing conspicuous white patches on whirring wings. *Voice:* various guttural honks and croaks. *Habitat:* larger, reed-fringed fresh waters year-round; some winter on sheltered coastal waters. Widespread; fairly common.

Red-necked Grebe *Podiceps grisegena* 42cm Slightly smaller, stockier and thicker-necked than Great Crested. Summer adult grey above; whitish below. Neck richly rufous; crown dark brown, contrasting with conspicuous white cheek patches. Beak yellow and black-tipped. Winter adult paler and greyer overall, but with whitish cheek patches still discernible. Lacks white stripe above eye of Great Crested. Immature resembles winter adult, but with pale russet neck. *Voice:* high-pitched 'keck' call. *Habitat:* breeds on heavily vegetated fresh waters. Usually winters on coastal waters, less often inland. Widespread; scarcer in west.

Slavonian Grebe *Podiceps auritus* 32cm Small, dumpy-bodied grebe, with longish, slender neck. Summer adult underparts and neck chestnut; back dark brown. Head black, large and crested, with conspicuous, long, orange tuft over each eye. Winter adult black above; white below. Crown black, clearly demarcated from white cheeks. Beak dark, small, straight and dagger-shaped. Immature resembles pale brownish winter adult. *Voice:* in breeding season, low, rippling trill. *Habitat:* breeds on small, vegetated lakes. Winters on sheltered, coastal seas and large fresh waters inland. Scarce.

Black-necked Grebe *Podiceps nigricollis* 30cm Small, dumpy-bodied, with high forehead and rounded head profile. Summer adult back, neck and head black; flanks chestnut. Golden, fan-shaped crest on sides of head. Winter adult greyish above; whiter below; gradual shading between. Shading, head profile and Black-necked's short, noticeably uptilted beak are good distinguishing features. Immature resembles winter adult. *Voice:* piping 'peep' call, like young Great Crested. *Habitat:* breeds on densely vegetated lakes. Winters on estuaries, lakes and reservoirs. Very variable in occurrence; rarely common.

Little Grebe (summer)

Great Crested Grebe (summer)

Red-necked Grebe (summer)

Slavonian Grebe (summer)

Black-necked Grebe (summer)

Fulmar *Fulmarus glacialis* 45cm Heavy-bodied, well-streamlined seabird, flying on short, straight wings, often held downcurved. Glides extensively, with few wingbeats except close to cliffs. Adult and immature superficially gull-like in plumage; pale grey above, shading to white below. Wings have no black. Beak yellowish, with tubular nostrils on ridge. *Voice:* on breeding ledges, various cackling and crooning calls; silent elsewhere. *Habitat:* breeds colonially, on coastal cliff ledges or on ground along remote coastlines; sometimes on buildings. Some remain in coastal waters all year; in winter, others disperse to mid-ocean. Widespread; locally numerous.

Manx Shearwater *Puffinus puffinus* 35cm Readily recognized seabird in flight, with frequent changes in direction, flashing black and white alternately, skimming on stiff wings low over the waves with minimal wingbeats. Adult and immature completely black above; strikingly white below. Beak black. Mediterranean race *P.p. mauretanicus* (**Balearic Shearwater**) browner above; sooty grey below; can be confused with Sooty Shearwater. *Voice:* on breeding grounds, amazing nocturnal cacophony of bubbling and crowing calls; silent elsewhere. *Habitat:* breeds colonially on remote rocky coasts or islands. In winter, disperses widely at sea, many reaching Brazilian waters. Locally numerous.

Cory's Shearwater *Calonectris diomedea* 45cm Heavy shearwater, with long, relatively broad wings held stiffly at right angles to the body. Distinctive, effortless shearwater flight, with long spells of gliding and banking interspersed with deep, slow wingflaps. Adult and immature similar in plumage; greyish-brown above; head paler; white below. Tail blackish. Beak yellow, with tubular nostrils; legs pale pinkish-yellow. *Voice:* on breeding grounds, raucous 'kaa-oof' and drawn-out wail; silent elsewhere. *Habitat:* breeds colonially in crevices on remote Mediterranean islands; otherwise scarce visitor to coastal waters.

Great Shearwater *Puffinus gravis* 50cm Typical large shearwater in flight and shape, best identified by dark brown cap. Adult and immature grey-brown above, darker on wings; tail often near-black. Whitish rump band often visible; neck white emphasizing capped appearance. White below. Glides on stiffly held wings. In calm weather, wingbeats faster than Cory's. In flight, white wing underside is bounded by dark leading and trailing edges, unlike all-white Cory's. Beak dark and slender; legs and feet greyish-pink. *Voice:* raucous squawks, rarely heard. *Habitat:* offshore seas. Rare.

Sooty Shearwater *Puffinus griseus* 45cm Heavily built shearwater with relatively long, narrow wings. Adult and immature uniformly sooty brown above; uniformly slightly paler grey-brown below. Beak black, long and slender. In windy conditions, glides like other shearwaters; on calm days, alternates brief glides with bursts of 'wristy' wingbeats. Underside of wing shows pale central stripe, unlike Balearic form of Manx. *Voice:* rarely heard in North Atlantic. *Habitat:* offshore seas.

Fulmar

Manx Shearwater

Cory's Shearwater

Great Shearwater

Sooty Shearwater

Storm Petrel *Hydrobates pelagicus* 15cm Tiny, dark seabird with weak, butterfly-like flight low over the waves. Adult and immature sooty black above and below. In flight, bold white, rectangular rump patch clearly visible; wing also shows faint, greyish, diagonal bar on upperside, and bolder white bar on underside. Tail black, often held in rounded fan in flight. Beak dark, tiny, with tubular nostrils. *Voice:* on breeding grounds, sustained, penetrating, high-pitched purring, interrupted sporadically with clicks, produced nocturnally. *Habitat:* breeds colonially on remote rocky islands and coasts. Winters far offshore. In summer, locally numerous; at other times, scarce wanderer. ◄

Leach's Storm Petrel *Oceanodroma leucorhoa* 20cm Larger than Storm Petrel, longer-winged and with more resolute characteristic bounding flight. Adult and immature sooty black above and below. Beak small, dark, with tubular nostrils. In flight, black tail held slightly forked (not rounded as in Storm Petrel). White rump patch usually divided by dark central streak. Underside of wing appears all-dark in flight; upperside has conspicuous grey patches on innermost section. *Voice:* on breeding grounds, very vocal nocturnally with extended, crooning calls broken by shrill, whistling cackles. *Habitat:* breeds colonially on a handful of remote islands; oceanic at other times. Rare, except close to colonies. ◄

Gannet *Sula bassana* 90cm Huge seabird with long-necked, long-tailed, cigar-shaped body, and long, straight, slender wings. Adult largely white above and below; wings sharply pointed with black tips; head and neck have yellow tinge. Beak steel grey, long and dagger-shaped. In first year immature grey-brown flecked with white; gradually shows more white as adult plumage is acquired over following three years. Flight characterized by slow, stiff wingbeats, interspersed with frequent glides. Plunges spectacularly when hunting fish. *Voice:* on breeding grounds, raucous honks and grating calls; silent elsewhere. *Habitat:* breeds in few (often huge) colonies on remote islands or headlands. Winters in coastal and offshore waters. Widespread; locally numerous. ◄

orm Petrel

Leach's Storm Petrel

annet (adult)

Gannet (immature)

Black-browed Albatross *Diomedea melanophris* 85cm Gigantic seabird, with long, narrow wings reaching 230cm span. Adult predominantly white; wings and tail black; dark mark through eye. Flight characteristic, gliding on wings outstretched at right angles to body. Legs pinkish; feet blue-grey. Beak yellowish, long, stout. *Voice:* in colonies, weird honkings; silent elsewhere. *Habitat:* islands in southern oceans. Rare wanderers north may stay with Gannet colonies for years. ◣

Wilson's Phalarope *Phalaropus tricolor* 25cm Slim pelagic wader, large for a phalarope. Summer adult largely grey above, with chestnut bands on neck, back and wings. Crown grey; white stripe over eye; black stripe through eye and down neck. White below; pinkish-buff on sides of breast. Beak long, fine; legs grey, long. Winter adult pale grey above; white below. Shows no wingbar in flight. *Voice:* various 'chip' calls. *Habitat:* breeds on North American marshlands; migrates to South American seas; occasionally wanders east. ◣

Brünnich's Guillemot *Uria lomvia* 35cm Similar to Guillemot. Summer adult head, neck, back and wings almost black; strikingly white below. Beak black, shorter and stouter than Guillemot; narrow grey line along edges of beak. Winter plumage greyer; dark cap, extending below eye; no dark stripe through and behind eye. *Voice:* as Guillemot. *Habitat:* breeds colonially on northern cliffs; winters in Arctic seas. Occasionally wanders south. ◣

Ivory Gull *Pagophila eburnea* 42cm Plump, pigeon-like gull. Adult pure white above and below; legs distinctively black and short; beak yellow, with black base and tip, stubby. At close range, red ring visible round large, dark eye. Wings all-white. Rarely lands on water. Immature has grey smudges on head and neck, black spots on back and flanks. *Voice:* tern-like 'kreer'. *Habitat:* breeds on Arctic islands; occasionally wanders south in winter. ◣

Lesser Crested Tern *Sterna bengalensis* 40cm Medium-sized tern. Adult back, tail and wings grey, with dark grey flight feathers; white below. Shaggy black crest on crown of head; forehead black. Winter adult has grey-flecked crest and white forehead; beak yellow (not orange). *Voice:* harsh 'kreer' *Habitat:* breeds on islands and beaches from Indian Ocean to Australasia; occasionally wanders north. ◣

Great Black-headed Gull *Larus ichthyaetus* 70cm Largest of the dark-hooded gulls. Summer adult predominantly white; wings grey, with black and white tips; hood black; legs yellow; beak yellow, with black band near red tip. In winter, hood reduced to densely flecked nape. Immature mottled brown; beak and legs grey. *Voice:* harsh 'kow'. *Habitat:* breeds colonially beside Asian inland lakes and seas. Winters coastally; occasionally strays west. ◣

Black-browed Albatross

Wilson's Phalarope

Brünnich's Guillemot

Ivory Gull

Lesser Crested Tern

Great Black-headed Gull

Cormorant *Phalacrocorax carbo* 90cm Large, long-necked, broad-winged seabird, swimming low in the water, diving frequently. Adult blackish with metallic sheen; in summer, white patches on face and sometimes thighs. Southern European breeding birds may also have head and neck white. Facial skin yellow; beak yellow, hooked. Winter adult lacks white patches. Immature dark brown above; paler on throat and underparts. *Voice:* on breeding grounds, deep guttural grunts. *Habitat:* breeds colonially on islands and cliffs beside shallow seas or estuaries, or in trees beside large inland fresh waters. Winters in same habitats. Widespread. ◢ ▨ ▧

Shag *Phalacrocorax aristotelis* 75cm Large, dark seabird, similar to Cormorant but smaller and slimmer. Summer adult blackish, with green iridescent sheen. Shags never show white patches. Beak yellow, slim and hooked at tip. Curled crest in early spring, traces of which persist into summer. Immature brown above and below, appreciably darker-bellied than young Cormorant. In flight, slighter build, slimmer neck and smaller head help separation from Cormorant. *Voice:* on breeding grounds, harsh croaks. *Habitat:* year-round resident on rocky coasts and nearby clear seas. Semi-colonial or solitary breeding bird. Locally common. ◢ ▨

White Pelican *Pelecanus onocrotalus* 160cm Huge pelican, with broad wings spanning 250cm. Adult largely white; in breeding season has short drooping crest, yellow patch on breast, and sometimes overall pinkish flush. Huge beak pinkish-grey with yellow pouch; legs and feet flesh pink. In flight, small amount of black shows on upper wing, but broad black band stretches entire length of trailing edge on underside (*see* Dalmatian). Immature buff with brown wings; pale, often almost white, below. *Voice:* in breeding season, guttural croaks. *Habitat:* freshwater swamps and lakes; occasionally sheltered coastal seas. Breeds colonially. Scarce. ◢ ▨ ▧

Dalmatian Pelican *Pelecanus crispus* 160cm Huge pelican, with 250cm wingspan. Adult pale, streaky grey, with slight curly-crested crown for much of the year. Huge beak grey, with brownish-orange pouch. Bare facial skin pinkish. Legs and feet grey (*see* White). In flight, black on wings is restricted to wingtips and narrow trailing edge both above and below (*see* White). Immature brownish, paler below; often difficult to separate from White. *Voice:* in breeding season, guttural croaks. *Habitat:* breeds colonially on freshwater swamps. Often winters on sheltered coastal seas. Scarce. ◢ ▨ ▧

ormorant

Shag (summer)

White Pelican

almatian Pelican (adults and immatures)

Bittern *Botaurus stellaris* 75cm Large and heron-like, but long neck is concealed in normal stance, with head held low between shoulders. Adult and immature brown; copiously streaked and barred with black, chestnut and buff, forming perfect camouflage in reedbeds. Throat whitish. Beak yellowish, long and dagger-like; legs greenish and long. Flight slow, broad-winged, with head retracted. Inconspicuous and shy. *Voice:* in breeding season, foghorn-like booming. *Habitat:* extensive reedbeds year-round. Northerly populations move south-west in winter. Widespread; restricted by habitat.

Little Bittern *Ixobrychus minutus* 35cm Small, secretive, rather dumpy heron. Adult rich buff below; brownish-black above. In flight, pale buff patches on inner section of upperside of wing are conspicuous; also resembles black and buff Moorhen, with trailing green legs. Immature brown, streaked black like miniature Bittern, but with clearly visible buff patch on wing. *Voice:* in breeding season, deep croaking call at intervals day and night. *Habitat:* densely vegetated swamps. Widespread; rarely seen.

Night Heron *Nycticorax nycticorax* 60cm Medium-sized heron, mostly active during the evening, roosting during the day. Adult white below; wings pale grey; crown and back dark greenish-grey. In breeding season has white crest plumes, long, slim and trailing. Beak and legs yellowish. Immature buffish-brown, with darker streaks; characteristic large pale patches visible in rows on closed wings. Flight moth-like; groups often in irregular V-formation. *Voice:* in breeding season, harsh, heron-like cries; usually silent at other times. *Habitat:* fresh and salt marshes, streams and ditches. Nests in mixed egret colonies in waterside trees. Locally fairly common.

Squacco Heron *Ardeola ralloides* 45cm Small, stocky heron. Summer adult predominantly rich golden buff; wings white, concealed at rest but startlingly character-istic in flight. Crest plumes brown and white, long and drooping. Beak yellow with black tip; legs greenish. Winter adult drabber, lacking plumes. Immature buff, streaked dark brown; wings off-white. *Voice:* in breeding season, harsh, heron-like honks and shrieks. *Habitat:* fresh and saline swamps and lagoons. Breeds colonially, often with other egrets, in trees or reedbeds. Locally common.

Cattle Egret *Bubulcus ibis* 50cm Small, stocky, predominantly white heron. Summer adult white with crown, throat and plumes on back (during breeding season) ginger-buff. Winter adult white, tinged buff. Beak pinkish-yellow; legs pink. Immature dull white; legs grey. Heavy, underhung 'chin' characteristic. *Voice:* in breeding colonies, harsh calls. *Habitat:* nests colonially with other egrets in trees or reedbeds. Feeds on drier areas than other egrets, amongst cattle or following plough. Local.

Bittern

Little Bittern

Night Heron (adult)

Night Heron (immature)

Squacco Heron (summer)

Cattle Egret (summer)

Little Egret *Egretta garzetta* 55cm Slender, medium-sized heron. Adult white; neck long, slender, usually held extended. In breeding season, has long white crest and fine white plumes on back. Beak black, long and dagger-shaped. Legs black and long; feet golden, striking and characteristic. Immature whitish, lacking plumes and crest. In flight, head withdrawn between shoulders, but legs extended. *Voice:* various harsh honks and shrieks, usually confined to breeding season. *Habitat:* marshland of all types with open water; rivers, saline lagoons. Breeds colonially in mixed egretries in trees nearby. Locally quite common. 🦩 🌊

Great White Egret *Egretta alba* 90cm Huge, pure white heron, much larger than Little Egret. Adult glossy white, with fine white plumes on back during breeding season. Neck long, usually held in angular kinks. Beak in breeding season yellow, at other times yellow and black (*see* Little). Legs and feet blackish. Immature less strikingly white; beak blackish. Flight stately, head withdrawn between shoulders, legs extended. *Voice:* harsh 'aark', but rarely vocal. *Habitat:* extensive marshlands, reed-fringed lakes and saline lagoons. Usually solitary breeder in reedbeds. Scarce. 🦩 🌊

Grey Heron *Ardea cinerea* 90cm Huge – the typical heron. Adult blue-grey above, white below. Neck white, with dark streaks down throat, slender. Head white with black line through eye; beak yellow, heavy and dagger-shaped. Breeding adult has drooping black and white crest, long silver grey plumes on back and pinkish flush to beak. Legs yellowish and long. Immature resembles adult, but lacks crest and plumes. In flight, head retracted, legs extended. Flight stately on broad, heavily fingered wings, blackish primaries contrasting with otherwise grey wings. *Voice:* various harsh honks and shrieks, especially 'fraank', mostly used during breeding season. *Habitat:* wetlands of all descriptions from garden ponds upwards, estuaries and sheltered sea coasts. Breeds colonially in reedbeds or trees. Widespread. 🐟 🦩 🌊

Purple Heron *Ardea purpurea* 78cm Large, slim, dark heron. Adult dark grey-brown above; chestnut to black below. Neck very slender, long; nape chestnut; throat white, with dark streaks. In breeding season, dark purplish crown extends into drooping crest; back carries fine pale-edged chestnut plumes. Beak yellowish, long and dagger-shaped. Legs yellow or greenish-yellow and long. Immature rich brown above, paler below. In flight, head retracted, legs extended with hind toe character-istically carried prominently erect. Appears very dark. *Voice:* harsh 'aark', rarely heard. *Habitat:* freshwater marshes, lakes and rivers with abundant fringing vegeta-tion. Nests colonially in reedbeds. Locally fairly common. 🦩 🌊

Little Egret

Great White Egret

Grey Heron

Purple Heron (summer)

Black Stork *Ciconia nigra* 97cm Huge and heron-like, but head and neck characteristically held extended in flight. Back and wings of adult black, with iridescent sheen; largely white below. Head and neck glossy black; beak red, long and stout. Long legs and feet pink. Immature resembles adult, but drabber and browner. Flight slow and ponderous on broad, heavily fingered wings, but on migration soars effortlessly. *Voice:* vocal, with various rasping noises and nasal honks. *Habitat:* rivers, lakes and swamps set in forests. Usually solitary. Local; uncommon or rare.

White Stork *Ciconia ciconia* 100cm Huge and similar to Black in flight silhouette. Adult white (often dirty white) above and below; much black visible on wings. Head and neck white; in breeding season, throat feathers shaggy. Beak red and short; legs red and long. Immature resembles drab adult with brownish beak and legs. Wings white; flight feathers black. Flight slow and stately on broad, heavily fingered wings; head and neck carried outstretched. Soars effortlessly. *Voice:* hisses and grunts, but rarely vocal; much beak clattering at nest. *Habitat:* marshes, swamps and plains, sometimes arid. Nests in trees or on buildings. Sociable. Locally regular.

Glossy Ibis *Plegadis falcinellus* 55cm Resembles medium-sized egret, but in flight head and neck are outstretched more like giant Curlew because of long, downcurved beak. Adult distinctive dark copper brown above and below, with iridescent sheen. Wings narrow, dark brown, pointed rather than fingered in flight. Beak and legs blackish. Immature dark drab brown above; paler below. *Voice:* extended croak, but rarely vocal. *Habitat:* marshes, shallow lakes and lagoons, mudflats. Local; uncommon or rare.

Spoonbill *Platalea leucorodia* 82cm Large and heron-like, but in flight head and neck are outstretched. Beak long and spoon-shaped, characteristic at close range. Adult all-white, with yellow at base of neck, and drooping yellow-tinged crest in summer. Beak black with yellow tip; legs brownish. Wings white and narrow, pointed rather than fingered in flight. Immature dull white, lacks crest; beak and legs pinkish-grey. Black wingtips visible in flight. *Voice:* grunts, but rarely vocal. *Habitat:* extensive areas of open shallow water, fresh, brackish or saline. Social. Local; rarely numerous.

Greater Flamingo *Phoenicopterus ruber* 125cm Huge, slim and unmistakable on the ground or in flight. Adult body pale pink and small. Neck whiter, enormously long; head small; beak banana-like, pink and black, strange and downcurved. Legs bright pink and equally long. Wings startlingly scarlet and black in flight. Immature greyer, paler and smaller. In flight, neck and legs outstretched, often in loose V-formation, wings pointed rather than fingered. Feeds with head down. *Voice:* goose-like honks and cackles. *Habitat:* extensive, usually shallow, brackish or saline lagoons; occasionally fresh waters. Sociable. Locally common.

Black Stork

White Stork

Glossy Ibis

Spoonbill

Greater Flamingo

Mute Swan *Cygnus olor* 150cm Huge and unmistakable. Adult all-white year-round; long neck carried in graceful 'S' curve. Beak dark orange; black knob on forehead larger in male than female. Adult raises wings like sails high over back in defence of territory or young. Immature pale grey-buff; beak pinkish-grey. In flight, long, broad, heavily fingered wings creak loudly. *Voice:* rarely vocal; hisses or grunts when annoyed. *Habitat:* all types of fresh water larger than ponds, including town-park lakes; occasionally on sheltered seas. Widespread. 🦆 〰️

Bewick's Swan *Cygnus columbianus* 120cm Appreciably smaller than other swans. Adult all-white year-round; neck short, straight and goose-like. Beak short, wedge-shaped, largely black with irregularly shaped lemon yellow patches at base, pattern varying between individuals. Immature pale grey; basal patches on beak greyish- or pinkish-yellow. In flight, more buoyant and faster wingbeats than its larger relatives. Wingbeats silent. *Voice:* frequent, musical, goose-like honks and chatterings. *Habitat:* breeds on swampy tundra. Winters on sheltered seas, large freshwater areas and grazing marshes. Scarce; locally numerous on regular wintering grounds. 🦆 〰️

Whooper Swan *Cygnus cygnus* 150cm Huge swan. Adult all-white year-round; neck long and straight, carried vertical except when feeding. Beak black with large yellow triangles at base, large, wedge-shaped. No basal knob. Immature pale greyish; pinkish-grey markings on beak. Flight steady and powerful on broad, heavily fingered wings. Wingbeats silent. *Voice:* wild, bugle-like, whooping calls uttered frequently in flight and on ground or water. *Habitat:* breeds on swampy tundra. Winters on sheltered seas, grazing marshes and large fresh waters. Scarce; locally regular; rarely numerous. 🦆 〰️

Bean Goose *Anser fabalis* 75cm Large grey goose. Adult dark brownish-grey above; only slightly paler below. White beneath tail. Neck relatively long, very dark brown. Beak long, wedge-shaped, black with variable pattern of small orange-yellow markings. Legs orange-yellow. Immature similar, but legs pale yellowish. In flight, wings appear uniformly dark brown. *Voice:* rarely vocal, but low, gruff 'ung-unk' call is distinctive. *Habitat:* breeds in open boreal forest near water. Winters on damp meadows and marshes, occasionally on arable fields. Uncommon and local. 🦆🦆🦆🌾🦆

Pink-footed Goose *Anser brachyrhynchus* 65cm One of the smaller grey geese. Adult back blue-grey; breast and flanks dark brown; white beneath tail. Neck relatively short, appearing almost black. Head dark, small. Beak mostly black with pink markings, short and stubby. Legs pink. In flight, grey back and forewings contrast with dark head and neck. Immature similar or slightly paler. *Voice:* vociferous; characteristic 'wink-wink-wink' call. *Habitat:* breeds on rocky outcrops in tundra. Winters on fresh and salt marshes, large lakes, and arable fields nearby. Locally common; numerous. 🦆🦆🦆🌾

Mute Swan

Bewick's Swan

Whooper Swan

Bean Goose

Pink-footed Goose

White-fronted Goose *Anser albifrons* 70cm

Medium-sized grey goose. Adult grey-brown above and below; white beneath tail. Breast has heavy, black barring. Head and neck darker brown, with large white face patch at base of beak. Beak pink (eastern or Russian race), or orange-yellow (western or Greenland race). Legs orange. Immature similar, but lacks white face and breast barring. *Voice:* noisy; gabbling, yapping call. *Habitat:* breeds on tundra. Winters on rough grassland, fresh and salt marshes, fields. Widespread; locally numerous.

Lesser White-fronted Goose *Anser erythropus* 60cm

Small grey goose, similar in appearance to (but noticeably smaller than) White-fronted. Adult brown above; paler below, with dark bars on breast. Undertail white. Head and neck dark brown; steep forehead emphasized by extensive white face patch. Yellow ring round eye conspicuous at close range. Beak pale pink, small. Legs orange. Immature similar, but lacks breast barring and white face. Yellow eye-ring may help separation from immature White-fronted. *Voice:* detectably higher-pitched than White-fronted; yapping 'kyu-yu'. *Habitat:* breeds on high moorland and tundra, normally close to water. Rare.

Greylag Goose *Anser anser* 80cm

Largest of the grey geese, and most heavily built. Adult dark grey-brown above, with faint, paler feather fringes; pale grey-brown below. Undertail white. Head and neck dark brown, stout; beak pink in eastern race, orange in western race, and large. Legs pink. Wingbeats powerful and steady, with pale blue-grey forewing patches conspicuous in flight. Immature similar, but duller. *Voice:* vocal; nasal gabbling and honking, similar to farmyard geese. *Habitat:* colonial breeder on moorland and tundra, often close to water. Winters on marshes, farmland and estuaries. Widespread; locally numerous.

Snow Goose *Anser caerulescens hyperboreus* 65cm

Small goose, white or whitish in colour, but behaving as grey goose. Adult pure white with black wingtips, distinctive. Relatively short, stout neck and heavily built head white, often stained yellow or rust; beak pink and stout; Legs pink. Immature pale grey; beak and legs greyish. 'Blue Goose' colour-phase adult has grey body, contrasting with white head and neck. Immature sooty grey, with white throat. *Voice:* short, harsh 'kaark' and deep, chattering gabble. *Habitat:* breeds colonially on tundra, normally close to water. Winters on marshland. Rare.

White-fronted Goose

Lesser White-fronted Goose

Greylag Goose

Snow Goose

Canada Goose *Branta canadensis* 75cm Largest of the 'black' geese, almost swan-sized. Adult body dark brown above, paler below; white patch below tail. Head and long neck black; characteristic white face patch on cheeks and under chin. Beak black; legs dark grey. In flight, black rump and white band on black tail are conspicuous. Wingbeats powerful; wings dark brown. Immature similar to adult, but duller. *Voice:* hoarse, disyllabic 'aah-honk'. *Habitat:* vagrant North American birds winter with grey geese on coastal marshes. Most European birds are descendants of introduced stock and resident on large fresh waters, including park lakes and nearby grassland.

Barnacle Goose *Branta leucopsis* 62cm Small black goose, characterized by distinctive pied plumage. Adult back grey with black and white barring; rump white and tail black. Wholly white below. Head and neck black; face and throat white. Beak dark grey, stubby; legs blackish. Immature similar to adult. *Voice:* vocal; series of puppy-like, yapping calls. *Habitat:* gregarious; breeds on rocky outcrops in tundra. Winter flocks on coastal grassland and salt marshes. Rare; locally numerous.

Brent Goose *Branta bernicla* 60cm Small, very dark black goose, with very short-necked appearance. Adult back blackish-brown; rump black. Tail white with black terminal band. Head and neck sooty black, with small white collar mark. Breast and belly grey (pale-bellied race *hrota*), or dark grey (dark-bellied race *bernicla*). Undertail white. Beak blackish, small; legs blackish. Immature similar, but has pale barring across back and lacks white collar marks. In flight, white tail is conspicuous; wingbeats quick. Usually flies in irregular, often-changing, loose flocks, not orderly V-skeins like other geese. *Voice:* soft, low 'rruuk'. *Habitat:* gregarious; breeds on Arctic tundra. In winter, the most maritime goose, favouring estuaries, sheltered bays and nearby marshes and fields. Widespread; locally numerous.

Red-breasted Goose *Branta ruficollis* 55cm Smallest and most compact black goose, with unmistakable plumage. Adult back dark brown; throat and head thick, patterned in blocks of reddish-chestnut outlined in white; crown and nape blackish. Breast black, with white stripe along flanks conspicuous, especially at a distance. Undertail white. Beak black, stubby; legs and feet black. Immature browner, paler and duller. Flight swift and agile, almost duck-like; usually in irregular flocks, not V-skeins. *Voice:* high-pitched, abrupt, disyllabic yap. *Habitat:* grassy steppes and coastal marshes. Rare vagrant over most of Europe, often associating with White-fronts.

anada Goose

Barnacle Goose

rent Goose

Red-breasted Goose

Ruddy Shelduck *Tadorna ferruginea* 60cm Large, goose-like duck with unmistakable orange plumage. Adult male back, neck and underparts uniform orange-chestnut; head buffish. Narrow black collar band. Female has almost white head and lacks collar. Beak black, small; legs black. In flight, shows black tail and striking white forewing and underwing patches contrasting with blackish flight feathers. Immature similar to female, but drabber. *Voice:* nasal disyllabic honk. *Habitat:* more terrestrial than Shelduck. Breeds in holes, often far from water. Winters on grassy areas. Rare vagrant, but beware escapes from wildfowl collections. 🦆🦆🦆

Shelduck *Tadorna tadorna* 60cm Large goose-like duck with striking, pied plumage. Adult predominantly white; head bottle green. Broad chestnut band round base of neck; two long black stripes on back; central black stripe on belly. Beak scarlet; knob at base larger in male. Female may have whitish patch at base of beak. Legs pink. Immature markings grey instead of green or black; lacks chestnut collar. *Voice:* barking 'ak-ak-ak' and deep, nasal 'ark'. *Habitat:* estuaries and sheltered sandy or muddy coasts; occasionally on fresh waters. May breed far from water. Widespread; often numerous. 🦆🦆🦆🦆

Wigeon *Anas penelope* 45cm Medium-sized surface-feeding duck. Adult male back grey; flanks grey and finely marked; undertail black. Breast pink; head chestnut with gold crown stripe. In flight, shows conspicuous white oval patch in wing. Female and immature similar cinnamon brown flecked with darker markings, greyish wing patch in flight. *Voice:* male characteristic plaintive whistle; female low-pitched purr. *Habitat:* breeds on moorland and tundra close to water. Winters on lakes, estuaries, sheltered seas and nearby marshes and grassland. Widespread; often common. 🦆🦆🦆🦆

Gadwall *Anas strepera* 50cm Medium-large surface-feeding duck. Adult male greyish-brown; fine markings visible at close range. Undertail characteristically black. Female and immature similar; speckled brown. In flight both sexes show distinctive black and white patch on trailing edge of wing. *Voice:* rarely vocal, but female produces descending series of 'kaak' quacks. *Habitat:* breeds on freshwater marshes and beside other large fresh waters. Winters in similar areas; occasionally on sheltered coastal waters. Widespread; rarely numerous. 🦆🦆🦆

Teal *Anas crecca* 35cm One of the smallest surface-feeding ducks. Adult male predominantly greyish; conspicuous white stripe on flanks; undertail golden. Breast buff, with fine grey barring. Head chestnut, with dark green patch around eye. Female and immature speckled grey-brown. Fast, erratic flight. *Voice:* male has distinctive low 'krit' and bell-like whistle; female harsh 'quack'. *Habitat:* breeds on boggy or marshy land with reed-fringed pools. Winters in similar habitats, often well inland, and on estuaries and sheltered coastal waters. Common; often numerous. 🦆🦆🦆🦆

Ruddy Shelduck ♂

Shelduck

Wigeon ♂ and ♀

Gadwall ♂

Teal ♂

ESCAPES (see page 25-6)

Mandarin *Aix galericulata* 42cm Small, dumpy, woodland duck. Adult male crown striking grey, broad eye-stripe white and long cheek feathers chestnut. Characteristic orange 'sails' on back. Breast black; flanks buff, finely marked. Female largely grey, with white, spectacle-like mark around eye. *Voice:* rarely vocal. *Habitat:* breeds in holes in trees close to rivers and lakes. Winters on lakes. Escapes now feral in some areas. 🌊🌸

Egyptian Goose *Alopochen aegyptiacus* 70cm In many ways, more like a large Shelduck than a goose. Adult head greyish-brown, with areas of rich chestnut and dark patch around eye; back rich brown, shading to chestnut near rump. Underparts buff, finely barred with black. Beak and relatively long legs pink. Immature drabber. In flight, shows characteristic bold white patches on fore-wing. *Voice:* male rasping sigh; female trumpeting series of honks. *Habitat:* stream- and lakesides in Africa. 🌊

Ruddy Duck *Oxyura jamaicensis* 40cm Squat, stiff-tailed duck. Male upperparts, breast and flanks deep red, shading to white on belly. Head carried low; crown and nape black, bold white face. Beak and feet blue-grey. Female and immature crown blackish, pale buff cheeks; body richly mottled browns, darker above than below. *Voice:* rarely heard, nasal 'raaah'. *Habitat:* freshwater marshes and lakes in North and South America. 🌊

Ring-necked Parakeet *Psittacula krameri* 40cm Large long-tailed parakeet. Adult male largely bright emerald green above and below; with dark brown wingtips and bluish tinge to long, slim, central tail feathers. Collar red, black and pink, narrow; throat black; beak scarlet. Female and immature similar, but duller and lacking collar. *Voice:* vociferous; harsh shrieks. *Habitat:* open woodland, farmland and scrub in Asia and Africa. 🚜🌳

Golden Pheasant *Chrysolophus pictus* 90cm Brilliant pheasant. Adult male throat, breast and belly scarlet; wings brown, patches of dark blue and crimson. Crown golden, drooping gold crest; nape iridescent gold, barred boldly with black. Long rump feathers golden. Tail black, with dark gold mottling, long. Female and immature smaller; buff, richly mottled with browns; tail shorter. Legs relatively long. *Voice:* various crowing calls. *Habitat:* heavily vegetated uplands in China. 🌸🌲🌿

Lady Amherst's Pheasant *Chrysolophus amherstiae* 95cm Brilliant pheasant. Adult male unmistakable: crown blue with scarlet crest. Nape iridescent silver, boldly barred black. Back and wings iridescent greenish-blue, with black barring. Rump gold and scarlet. Throat iridescent blue, shading to green on breast. Belly silvery white. Tail silver with broad black bars, long; shorter outer feathers scarlet. Female and immature richly marked buff; smaller, with shorter tail. *Voice:* far-carrying, crowing calls. *Habitat:* highland forests in Tibet and Burma. 🌸🌲🌿

Mandarin ♂ and ♀

Egyptian Goose

Ruddy Duck ♂

Ring-necked Parakeet

Golden Pheasant ♂

Lady Amherst's Pheasant ♂

Mallard *Anas platyrhynchos* 58cm One of the larger surface-feeding ducks, and the best-known and most widespread duck in Europe. Adult male grey-brown; tail white, with black above and below. Curled black feathers on rump. Head bottle green, separated from chestnut breast by narrow white neck-ring. Beak yellowish-green; legs orange. Female and immature speckled brown, buff and black; beak brownish-orange. In flight, all show broad purple speculum patch between white bars on inner section of wing. *Voice:* male quiet whistle; female harsh quacks. *Habitat:* year-round almost any waters, from small ponds to open seas. Common; almost ubiquitous.

Pintail *Anas acuta* 70cm Large surface-feeding duck, of slim build with relatively long neck. Adult male belly white; flanks finely marked grey; back grey-brown. Head and neck rich brown, with distinctive white mark on side of neck. Beak and legs grey. Tail characteristically black, long and pointed. Female and immature pale grey-brown, marked with darker brown; tail short and pointed. Flight silhouette characteristically slender and elongated. Wings narrow, with inconspicuous brown speculum on trailing edge. *Voice:* rarely vocal; male low whistle; female low, quiet quack and churring growl. *Habitat:* breeds on moors and freshwater marshes close to water. Winters on sheltered coastal waters; sometimes inland.

Garganey *Anas querquedula* 40cm Smallish surface-feeding duck. Adult male belly white, shading to grey on flanks. Back brown; conspicuous long grey and white feathers droop over flanks. Head, neck and breast rich brown; striking white stripe above and behind eye. Female and immature sandy brown, with darker markings. In flight, both sexes show characteristic pale blue-grey patches on forewing. Flight almost as fast and agile as Teal. *Voice:* male distinctive crackling rattle; female short, harsh quack. *Habitat:* freshwater marshes, reed-fringed lakes and ditches. Widespread; rarely numerous.

Shoveler *Anas clypeata* 50cm Medium-sized surface-feeding duck. Adult male brown above; white below, with striking chestnut patches on flanks. Breast white; neck short and head dark bottle green, heavily built. Beak characteristically dark grey, massive and spoon-shaped. Female and immature speckled brown; similarly massive beak brownish-orange. All swim low in the water, head tilted down. In flight, rapid wingbeats and head-up, tail-down attitude are characteristic, as are conspicuous pale grey forewing patches. *Voice:* male low-pitched, double quack 'tuk-tuk'; female quiet quack. *Habitat:* breeds on marshland with reed-fringed pools or lakes. Winters in similar areas; also on reservoirs and sheltered coastal waters. Common.

Mallard ♀ and ♂

Pintail ♂

Garganey ♂

Shoveler ♂

Red-crested Pochard *Netta rufina* 55cm Large diving duck, but which dives relatively infrequently and behaves more as a surface-feeder. Adult male back brown; neck, breast and belly black; conspicuous white flank patches. Head rich chestnut, with paler, golden, erectile crest. Beak bright scarlet. Female and immature dull brown, paler on belly. Crown dark brown, contrasting with characteristic pale grey cheeks. In flight, both sexes show striking broad white band running full length of wing. *Voice:* grating 'kurrr'. *Habitat:* large, reed-fringed areas of fresh or brackish water. Uncommon. 🦆🦆

Pochard *Aythya ferina* 45cm Medium-sized diving duck. Adult male back grey; mostly white below, with breast and undertail black. Head dark chestnut. Female and immature dull rufous brown; paler on cheeks, throat and belly. Both sexes have characteristic, steeply rising forehead. Both have greyish wings with indistinct, paler grey wingbar. Dives frequently. *Voice:* rarely vocal: male hoarse whistle; female harsh growl. *Habitat:* breeds beside large, reed-fringed fresh waters. Winters on large fresh waters, including reservoirs; occasionally along sheltered coasts. Widespread; common. 🦆🦆🦆

Ferruginous Duck *Aythya nyroca* 40cm Small, dark diving duck. Adult male back dark brown; flanks chestnut shading to white on belly and beneath tail. Head and neck rich chestnut. Eye white. Female head and neck chestnut, but otherwise duller and browner. Immature resembles female, but lacks chestnut head. Eye brown. Dives frequently. In flight, bold white wingbars and white undertail conspicuous. *Voice:* rarely vocal; male rasping call; female harsh growl. *Habitat:* breeds near reed-fringed lakes. Winters on large fresh waters. Locally common. 🦆🦆🦆

Scaup *Aythya marila* 45cm Medium-sized diving duck. Adult male back grey, finely marked; flanks and belly white. Head glossy black with greenish sheen; neck, breast black. Rump, undertail black. Female, immature dark brown above; paler on flanks. Adult female has conspicuous, large, white patch at base of beak. Both sexes' eyes golden yellow and beaks grey, black-tipped. Dives frequently. In flight, shows bold white wingbar, and characteristic pale grey back in male. *Voice:* rarely vocal: male crooning whistle; female harsh, double quack. *Habitat:* breeds on marshland near water. Normally winters on coastal seas. Locally common. 🦆🦆🦆🦆

Tufted Duck *Aythya fuligula* 43cm Small, compact diving duck. Adult male black above; purplish sheen to head and drooping crest during breeding season. Breast black; flanks and belly strikingly white. Undertail black. Female and immature dark brown above; paler brown below, shading to pale grey-buff on belly. Wingbeats rapid, with narrow white wingbar running full length of wing. *Voice:* rarely vocal: male soft whistle; female low-pitched growl. *Habitat:* breeds beside reed-fringed ponds, ditches and lakes. Winters on similar and larger waters. Common; often numerous. 🦆🦆🦆

Red-crested Pochard ♂

Pochard ♂

Ferruginous Duck ♂

Scaup ♂

Tufted Duck ♂

Tufted Duck ♀

Eider *Somateria mollissima* 60cm Large, ponderous sea duck. Adult male back white; flanks, belly, rump and tail black. Breast white, tinged pink in breeding season. Head and neck white with black patch across forehead and through eye; cheeks greenish in breeding season. Young males near-black, becoming gradually whiter through series of pied plumages. Female dark brown, uniquely closely-barred with fine black markings. Both sexes' beak characteristically heavy and wedge-shaped, with feathers from cheeks extending down sides. Dives frequently. Flight slow, heavy, low over sea. Female shows faint, narrow, white wingbar; male striking white back and forewings, contrasting with black flight feathers. *Voice:* male loud, moaning, crooning calls; female grating 'coorrr'. *Habitat:* breeds along sea coasts and on islands; occasionally beside fresh waters inland. Winters on shallow coastal seas. Widespread; locally common. ◢◣

King Eider *Somateria spectabilis* 58cm Large, colourful sea duck. Adult male body largely black, with white spot on flank near tail, and white bar visible along folded wing. Breast white, flushed pink in breeding season. Head white; in breeding season unmistakable, with grey crown and nape, yellow eye-stripe and greenish cheeks. Beak orange, with steeply rising orange frontal shield on forehead. Female and immature rufous brown; beak grey and stubby, forehead steep. In flight, male shows striking white forewings, contrasting with black body. Dives frequently. *Voice:* male crooning calls; female grating growl. *Habitat:* breeds on tundra. Winters on northern coastal seas. Rare. ◢◣◣

Steller's Eider *Polysticta stelleri* 45cm Medium-sized sea duck. Adult male largely black above; head white with small greenish crest and black eye-patch in breeding season. Neck black, with white neck-band running into white flanks. Breast and belly rich chestnut, with characteristic black spot on each side of breast. In flight, wings strikingly black and white. Female and immature mottled dark brown. Both sexes have much smaller heads and lighter beaks than Eider. *Voice:* male quiet, crooning calls; female low, Wigeon-like growl. *Habitat:* breeds on tundra. Winters along rocky sea coasts; occasionally on larger lakes. Rare. ◢◣

ider ♂

Eider ♀

King Eider ♂

Steller's Eider ♂

Harlequin *Histrionicus histrionicus* 40cm Small, aptly named sea duck. Adult male unmistakable, with head and body predominantly dark grey-blue; flanks chestnut, marked with striking white streaks and curves. Female and immature brown; paler below; with white cheek patches and spots on head; breast whitish. Beak yellowish-grey, small. In flight, male shows white markings on back and wings; female uniformly brown. Swims in close-packed flocks, tails cocked and heads jerking in unison. Dives frequently. *Voice:* rarely vocal; male quiet whistle; female croak. *Habitat:* breeds beside fast-flowing streams. Winters on rough coasts. Locally common in Iceland; rare elsewhere. ◄▨

Long-tailed Duck *Clangula hyemalis* 50cm Small, long-tailed sea duck. Summer adult male largely dark brown; cheeks and flanks white; tail black, very long and slender. Winter male largely white, with brown face patches; breast and back blackish. Summer female brown above; white below; with white face patches. Tail short, pointed. Winter female and immature have more extensive white on head and neck. Swims buoyantly and dives frequently. In flight, small size and pied appearance are characteristic. *Voice:* vocal; with varied, high-pitched, goose-like honks. *Habitat:* breeds on tundra. Winters along sea coasts. Locally common. ◄▨▨

Common Scoter *Melanitta nigra* 50cm Medium-sized, heavily built sea duck. Adult male unique among ducks with plumage uniformly velvet black. Beak heavy, black and yellow, with black knob in breeding season. Female and immature dull brown; paler below; buffish face patches contrast with brown crown. Dives frequently. Flies characteristically in long straggling lines low over sea, showing uniformly dark wings. *Voice:* male various crooning calls; female harsh growls. *Habitat:* breeds beside moorland lakes and on tundra beside rivers. Winters at sea. Regular; locally common. ◄▨

Surf Scoter *Melanitta perspicillata* 50cm Medium-sized, heavily built sea duck. Adult male almost entirely black, save for white patches on forehead and nape (sometimes inconspicuous). Beak yellow, white and red, massive. Legs red. Female and immature brown; paler below; with buffish face patches; distinguished from Velvet by lack of white in wing. *Voice:* rarely vocal. *Habitat:* breeds beside Arctic coasts and on tundra. Winters at sea. Rare. ◄▨

Velvet Scoter *Melanitta fusca* 55cm Large, heavily built sea duck. Adult male uniform black, but with small white eye-spot (visible only at close range) and white patch (only sometimes visible) in closed wing. Beak yellow with black margins. Female and immature dull brown above; paler below; with buffish, smudgy face patches. Swims buoyantly; dives frequently. In flight, both sexes show characteristic, bold white trailing edge to inner section of wing. *Voice:* rarely vocal; occasional whistles or growls. *Habitat:* breeds beside rivers and lakes, on tundra and in boreal forest fringes. Winters at sea. ◄▨

Harlequin ♂

Long-tailed Duck ♂ (winter)

Common Scoter ♂ (summer)

Surf Scoter ♂ (summer)

Velvet Scoter ♂ (summer)

Barrow's Goldeneye *Bucephala islandica* 52cm
Medium-sized sea duck. Adult male predominantly black above; white below. Back black, with row of small, white, lozenge-shaped patches along closed wing. Head crested, angular in appearance, with purplish sheen and white, kidney-shaped patch on cheek. Eye golden yellow. Female and immature brown above; paler below; head chestnut, dark, angular. Both sexes' beaks greyish, stubby. Swims buoyantly; dives frequently, often in unison. *Voice:* rarely vocal; harsh nasal calls. *Habitat:* breeds (Iceland only) in holes beside lakes and rivers. Winters occasionally on open fresh water; more often on inshore seas. Rare outside Iceland.

Goldeneye *Bucephala clangula* 48cm Medium-sized sea duck. Adult male predominantly black above; white below. Back black, with row of large white patches on closed wing often merging into a bar. Head black with greenish iridescence, crested and angular; small, circular white patch below eye. Female and immature brown above; slightly paler on flanks; belly whitish. Head chestnut, angular. Swims buoyantly, usually in small groups. Dives frequently, often in unison. In flight, wing feathers make characteristic rattling whistle, and white wing patches are conspicuous in both sexes. *Voice:* rarely vocal; male occasionally produces disyllabic, nasal call; female harsh growl. *Habitat:* breeds in old burrows or hollow trees near to water. Winters coastally, or on large fresh waters inland. Regular; rarely numerous.

Smew *Mergus albellus* 40cm Smallest and most compact of the sawbill ducks. Adult male unmistakable: predominantly white with fine black linear markings and grey vermiculated flanks. White crest on crown erected when excited. Female and immature grey-brown, darker above than below; crown dark reddish-brown, contrasting with white face patches. In both sexes, beak grey and slim, with serrated edge visible at close range. In flight, both sexes show conspicuous white patches on inner sections of wing. *Voice:* usually silent. *Habitat:* breeds in hollow trees or ground cavities close to fresh waters and on tundra. Winters on large inland fresh waters, including urban reservoirs; less often on sheltered coastal seas. Widespread but local; rarely numerous.

Barrow's Goldeneye ♂

Goldeneye ♂

Smew ♂

Smew ♀

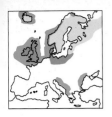

Red-breasted Merganser *Mergus serrator* 55cm
Medium-sized sawbill duck. Adult male black above;
flanks grey, finely marked; belly white. Breast chestnut
with dark brown speckling. Head and bristling, ragged
crest bottle green; throat white; nape black. Beak orange-
red, long and narrow, with serrated edge visible only at
close range. Female and immature grey above; paler
buffish-grey below, shading to white on belly. Breast and
throat white; head and nape chestnut brown, with ragged,
spiky crest. Both sexes show characteristic, elongated,
streamlined appearance both on water and in flight, when
black and white wing patches are conspicuous. Swims
low in water; dives frequently. *Voice:* usually silent.
Habitat: breeds in holes beside rivers and streams; also
along sheltered sea coasts. Winters mostly along
sheltered coasts; also on large fresh waters inland.
Widespread and regular; rarely numerous. ⬤⬤⬤

White-headed Duck *Oxyura leucocephala* 45cm Bulky
medium-sized stiff-tailed duck – Europe's only native
stifftail. Adult male largely chestnut brown above; paler
brown below, with crescentic darker markings. Thick
neck and heavy head dark brown, with characteristic
large white cheek patches. Beak bright blue-grey, large.
Female and immature brown, with dark crown and bar
below eye creating distinctive pattern against buff
cheeks. Tail long, held either flat on water, or upright and
Wren-like in display, when male's white undertail is
conspicuous. Flight whirring, low over water, on uniformly
dark wings. *Voice:* normally silent; male sometimes uses
rattling call. *Habitat:* brackish and freshwater lagoons and
lakes, and adjoining swamps. Local; rare. ⬤

Goosander *Mergus merganser* 63cm Largest of the
sawbill ducks. Adult male back black, with broad white
margin showing on closed wing. Breast, flanks and belly
white, sometimes flushed pink early in breeding season,
but appearing very white at a distance. Head bottle
green, angular in silhouette because of drooping crest.
Female and immature back grey; flanks pale grey,
shading to white on belly. Breast and throat patch white;
head and neck chestnut, with neat, drooping crest.
Swims low in water; dives frequently. Streamlined,
elongate appearance characteristic on water and in flight,
when white wing patches are conspicuous. *Voice:* usually
silent. *Habitat:* breeds in hollow trees, or holes in banks
close to lakes and rivers. Winters on large fresh waters
inland; occasionally along sheltered coasts. Widespread
and regular; rarely numerous. ⬤⬤⬤

ed-breasted Merganser ♂

White-headed Duck ♂

oosander ♂

Goosander ♀

Honey Buzzard *Pernis apivorus* 52cm Buzzard-like raptor, but with long, straight-sided tail. Adult and immature normally dark brown above; underparts white or buffish, streaked with brown; plumages may vary considerably from overall darkish brown to pale buff. Head grey, appearing disproportionately small. Tail long, normally with two dark bars near the base, and single broad bar near the tip. In flight, wings relatively broad, 'fingered' at the tips; underside pale with conspicuous dark patch at 'wrist', and usually also with strikingly dark barring. *Voice:* rapid 'kee-kee-kee', and other squeaky calls. *Habitat:* extensive open forest. Widespread; uncommon, except at favoured migration sites. ♥⚘

Red Kite *Milvus milvus* 62cm Large kite with long, deeply forked tail. Adult back rich rufous brown; head paler, often golden or almost white, with fine dark streaks. Breast and belly rufous, with dark brown streaks. Tail rich chestnut above; buffish-brown below with faint barring. Soars frequently, showing long, narrow-fingered wings, dark with large whitish patches at base of flight feathers. In flight, wings held in characteristic 'M'. Immature resembles adult, but duller; head brownish. *Voice:* buzzard-like mewing. *Habitat:* open woodland and forest, often in hilly country. Widespread; rarely numerous. 🪰♥🌲⚘

Black Kite *Milvus migrans* 53cm Large, predominantly dark kite. Adult and immature various shades of dark brown; immature generally paler on breast than adult. Upright, perching posture. In flight, wings appear long and relatively narrow, with fingered tips; usually show pale, mid-wing patch on underside. Tail long; in flight, often fanned, showing very shallow fork, and twisted characteristically. Flight extremely agile. Social, often soaring or gathering at carrion in flocks. *Voice:* Herring Gull-like mewing. *Habitat:* forests; also urban areas, especially refuse tips. Widespread; more numerous in warmer areas. 🪰🏔️〰️♥⚘

Honey Buzzard

Red Kite

Black Kite

Black Kite

Lammergeyer *Gypaetus barbatus* 110cm Huge, narrow-winged vulture. Adult dark grey-brown above; head and throat paler buffish. Black mark runs from eye to tuft of feathers ('beard') at each side of base of relatively slim beak. Underparts buff, on breast tinged rich cinnamon. Immature duller brown overall; head brownish, lacking beard. In flight, very long, relatively slim wings held only slightly angled, showing little fingering at tips. Together with long, diamond-shaped tail, they produce diagnostic silhouette. *Voice:* shrill, wavering cry. *Habitat:* remote mountainous areas. Rare. ▲

Black Vulture *Aegypius monachus* 105cm Huge, very dark vulture. Adult and immature back and breast dark brown, almost black; head very dark grey, neck grey and ruff blackish – all distinguishing features from Griffon. Beak yellow with black tip, hooked, massive. Wings black, long and broad, heavily fingered. In flight, longer tail, rounded almost to wedge-shaped, helps to separate Black from Griffon. Usually solitary, but may join other vultures at carrion. *Voice:* occasional hisses or grunts. *Habitat:* remote mountain areas and upland plains. Rare. ▲

Egyptian Vulture *Neophron percnopterus* 62cm Smallest European vulture. Adult unmistakable: largely dirty white above and below, often tinged yellow around the head, which has loose crest, and with much black in the wings. Naked face yellowish-pink; beak hooked, but relatively small and slim. Immature initially dark brown, gradually acquiring more white with each moult as it ages. In flight, medium-length narrow, almost pointed wings are held straight at right angles to the body, and with wedge-shaped tail produce diagnostic silhouette. Rarely flocks but often joins other vultures at carrion. *Voice:* normally silent. *Habitat:* mountain areas, upland farms; regular visitor to large urban refuse tips. Widespread in warmer areas, rarely numerous. ▲

Griffon Vulture *Gyps fulvus* 105cm Huge, typical vulture of Europe. Adult sandy brown above and below; breast slightly paler and sometimes streaked. Head and neck pale grey, covered in short down; whitish ruff around shoulders. Beak greyish, massive, hooked. Legs grey; talons weak. Immature browner, with bold feather fringes giving scaly appearance to back; ruff at base of neck brown. In flight, very dark, broad, heavily fingered wings (contrasting in adult with white ruff); tail dark, short, almost square. This and minimal protrusion of head combine to produce characteristic silhouette. Soars for extended periods. Flocks at carrion. *Voice:* occasional grunts and hisses. *Habitat:* remote hilly or mountain country. Uncommon in warmer areas; rarely numerous except at carrion. ▲

Lammergeyer

Black Vulture

Egyptian Vulture (adult)

Egyptian Vulture (immature)

Griffon Vulture

Griffon Vulture

Marsh Harrier *Circus aeruginosus* 53cm Large, broad-winged harrier. Adult male largely brown above; chestnut below. Wings strikingly patterned; patches of brown and grey contrast with black flight feathers. Tail pale grey, long. Adult female largely rich dark brown, with much creamy yellow on head. Immature predominantly brown with darker streaks, lacking yellow patches. Marsh Harriers never show white on rump. Characteristic flight low and steady, with frequent extended glides on wings held stiffly in a shallow 'V'. *Voice:* rarely heard, disyllabic, high-pitched 'kee-ya'. *Habitat:* characteristically marshland with extensive reedbeds. Widespread; locally common.

Hen Harrier *Circus cyaneus* 48cm Medium-sized harrier. Adult male head, back and tail pale grey, with white rump patch. Wings grey; flight feathers blackish. Female and immature rich brown above and below, with darker streaks. Tail brown, with narrow dark bars, long; large white rump patch. Female and immature difficult to distinguish from slightly smaller, slimmer Montagu's. Flight and hunting technique similar to Marsh, but wings appreciably narrower. Sometimes collects in communal winter roosts. *Voice:* chattering 'kee-kee-kee', not often heard. *Habitat:* open country, ranging from moorland and young forestry plantations to farmland and coastal or inland marshes, especially in winter. Widespread; rarely numerous.

Pallid Harrier *Circus macrourus* 45cm Small, pale harrier. Adult male back and tail pale blue-grey, rump greyish; head almost white. Throat and breast white, in contrast to grey of male Hen and Montagu's. Rest of underparts pure white. Wings pale grey, with contrasting greyish flight feathers appreciably paler than other harriers. No black bar on secondaries. Female and immature almost impossible to distinguish with certainty from Montagu's. *Voice:* shrill 'keck-keck-keck'. *Habitat:* open land, including moorland, steppes, plains and hillsides. Rare.

Montagu's Harrier *Circus pygargus* 40cm Small, slim harrier. Adult male pale grey above, lacking white rump patch above grey tail. Underparts greyish white, streaked chestnut on flanks. Wings grey above, with dark blackish flight feathers and dark bar near trailing edge, lacking in male Hen. Female generally brown above; paler below, with darker streaks. Immature similar, but underparts richer rufous brown. Female and immature have comparatively small white rump patch above long, narrow, black-barred brown tail. Wings narrow, pointed; this and more buoyant flight than other harriers are helpful identification characteristics. *Voice:* shrill 'keck-keck-keck'. *Habitat:* open land, ranging from inland and coastal marshes to farmland, moors and sand-dunes. Widespread; only locally numerous.

Marsh Harrier ♀

Hen Harrier ♀

Pallid Harrier ♂

Montagu's Harrier ♂

Goshawk *Accipiter gentilis* 55cm Large, almost buzzard-sized hawk. Adult largely slate grey above, with brownish or greenish tinge. Crown and cheeks dark, separated by striking white eye-stripe extending onto nape. Tail grey-brown with darker bars, relatively long. Underparts white, finely barred with brown. Undertail white, with fluffy feathers expanded in display flights. Immature brown above; buff below with darker streaks; eye-stripe buff. Typical hawk silhouette of long tail and shortish, broad, fingered wings, giving fast manoeuvrable flight in woodland. Female appreciably larger than male. *Voice:* chattering 'gig' or 'keck'. *Habitat:* extensive areas of deciduous or coniferous woodland and forest. Widespread; nowhere numerous. ♠♣♣

Sparrowhawk *Accipiter nisus* 35cm Small, dashing hawk. Male dark grey above; crown grey; occasional small white nape patch. No eye-stripe. Tail grey with several darker bars, long. Underparts distinctive: throat white; breast and belly white but closely barred with chestnut, appearing reddish at distance. Female much larger, grey brown above with white eye-stripe separating dark crown and cheeks. Underparts white, barred with brown. Immature plumage broadly similar to female, but with brown streaks rather than barring on the breast. Short, rounded wings and long tail confer good acceleration and manoeuvrability. *Voice:* rapid 'keck-keck-keck' and similar calls. *Habitat:* forest and woodland of all types. Widespread; often common. ➹♠♣♣

Buzzard *Buteo buteo* 53cm Medium-large, broad-winged raptor. Adult and immature very variable in plumage but normally darkish brown above; whitish below, with heavy darker streaking. Occasional individuals may be pale buff above or dark brown below. In flight, usually dark 'wrist' patch contrasts with generally pale underwing. Soaring habits and flight silhouette are characteristic; wings long, broad, heavily fingered; tail dark, short, fanned. Often perches on exposed poles or trees in upright posture. *Voice:* far-carrying, cat-like mewing. *Habitat:* open country, including farmland and moorland, with tracts of woodland. Widespread; locally common.
⛰➹♠♣♣➴≋

Goshawk (immature)

Goshawk ♀ (adult)

Sparrowhawk ♀

Buzzard

Buzzard

Rough-legged Buzzard *Buteo lagopus* 58cm Large buzzard. Adult and immature pale brown above, with darker streaks; adult may have almost white head with fine dark streaking. Throat white; breast and belly usually pale, but with very variable brown streaks or barring. Tail characteristic, strikingly white with broad black terminal band, best seen in flight. Flight silhouette similar to Buzzard, but soars only occasionally. Frequently hovers clumsily, on slowly beating wings. *Voice:* buzzard-like mewing. *Habitat:* breeds on tundra and barren northern hillsides. Winters on open farmland, coastal and inland marshes. Widespread; irregular in appearance and numbers. ▲ ≋ ♣ ♣ ≈ ⊠

Lesser Spotted Eagle *Aquila pomarina* 65cm Small typical eagle. Adult and immature dark brown above and below, difficult to separate easily from Spotted. Wings long, fingered at the tips, relatively slender; tail rounded, relatively long compared with Spotted. Immature lacks whitish rump patch and heavily white-spotted back of Spotted; only one or two rows of large white spots visible in closed wing. *Voice:* barking 'yak-yak-yak'. *Habitat:* remote montane woodland. Rare, except at established migration points, such as the Bosphorus. ≋ ● ♣ ♣

Spotted Eagle *Aquila clanga* 70cm Larger typical eagle. Adult dark brown above and below, often with whitish rump patch, which is diagnostic if present. Immature heavily pale-spotted on breast and back, especially visible on closed wing. Wings broad, heavily fingered; often flies with outer sections of wings curved downward. Tail disproportionately short, rounded. *Voice:* high-pitched, puppy-like yapping. *Habitat:* forests, especially close to rivers and lakes. Scarce; numerous only at regular migration concentration zones, such as the Bosphorus. ≋ ● ♣ ♣

Steppe Eagle *Aquila rapax* 70cm Large typical eagle. Adult uniformly darkish brown above and below; easily confused with the two Spotted Eagles. Some adults have distinctive tawny patch on nape; none show white rump patch of Spotted. Immature often rather more coffee-coloured. Flight sluggish, on wings held flat; rarely soars. *Voice:* deep, barking 'kow'. *Habitat:* open plains, steppes and mountainsides, normally nesting on the ground. Scarce. Closely-related **Tawny Eagle** *Aquila nipalensis* may stray to Mediterranean basin. ▲ ⊠

Rough-legged Buzzard

Lesser Spotted Eagle

Spotted Eagle (immature)

Steppe Eagle (adult)

Steppe Eagle (immature)

White-tailed Eagle *Haliaeetus albicilla* 88cm Huge 'sea eagle'.
Adult dark brown above and below; tail white, short, wedge-shaped, diagnostic. Beak yellow, massive, hooked. Immature back, shoulders and breast usually paler brown; tail brown, much shorter than that of immature Golden. Beak brown. In flight, all ages show massive, broad, parallel-sided wings, heavily fingered at the tips. Characteristic flight silhouette with broad, straight wings, coupled with relatively short, wedge-shaped tail and relatively long neck and head. Wingbeats slow; often soars. *Voice:* bark-like 'kraa' and harsh 'kri-kri'. *Habitat:* forests, cliffs or crags near to lakes or sea. Widespread; nowhere numerous. ▲ ⬳ ♣

Imperial Eagle *Aquila heliaca* 80cm Huge typical eagle.
Heavy-looking, ponderous, dark brown above and below. Adult head and nape buffish; often pale golden or almost white in older birds. Variable amounts of white can sometimes be seen on shoulders and back: these are diagnostic if present. Spanish race also has striking white leading edge to wing. Immature is often more rufous, with darker streaking. Wings broad, heavily fingered, held horizontal in flight. *Voice:* deep, barking 'owk-owk'. *Habitat:* an open-land eagle; hunts over fields, plains and marshes; nests in isolated trees. Rare. ▲ ➡ ⩳ ♠ ⚎

Golden Eagle *Aquila chrysaetos* 83cm Huge and majestic typical eagle.
Adult uniformly rich dark brown, with golden tinge to head and nape. Beak massive and hooked. Immature has characteristic white patches in wings and white tail with broad black terminal band. White areas get smaller with age, causing possible confusion with other eagles. Impressively long, broad, heavily fingered wings, held slightly above the horizontal when soaring, but with tips often curled downwards. Tail comparatively long and broad. *Voice:* rarely heard, barking 'kaah'. *Habitat:* remote mountain and forest areas, down to sea level in places. Widespread; never numerous. ▲ ♣ ◤

Booted Eagle *Hieraaetus pennatus* 48cm Buzzard-sized eagle, occurring in two colour forms.
Dark-phase adult rich uniform chestnut brown above and below; tail grey. Pale-phase adult brown above; buff below with dark brown streaks; tail pale grey. Immature resembles duller version of adult of appropriate phase. Flight rapid, almost nimble among trees; wings relatively slender, and long in the tail. Seen from below, black-outlined white under-wings are characteristic of pale phase in flight. *Voice:* high-pitched, descending 'keeee'. *Habitat:* wooded hills and valleys, often with clearings. Uncommon. ▲ ♣ ♠

White-tailed Eagle

Imperial Eagle

Golden Eagle

Booted Eagle (immature)

Short-toed Eagle *Circaetus gallicus* 65cm Small, pale, buzzard-like eagle. Adult and immature brown above, whitish below; head and breast have varying degrees of darker streaking and barring. Brown of upperparts may vary considerably, but underparts characteristically appear near-white, except for dark wingtips visible in flight. Head loose-feathered and appears bulky, almost owl-like. Tail long with faint darker bars; often held fanned, especially when bird hovers clumsily with legs dangling – a characteristic habit. *Voice:* harsh 'jeee' and barking 'ock-ock'. *Habitat:* well-wooded hillsides and gorges rich in snakes and lizards, favourite foods. Widespread; nowhere numerous in warmer areas.
▲ 🏔 🌳 🌲 🌿 🏞

Bonelli's Eagle *Hieraaetus fasciatus* 70cm Medium-large, long-tailed eagle. Adult brownish above, largely white below with darker streaks on breast and belly. In flight, pale greyish tail with broad dark brown terminal band and pale forewings contrasting with generally darker feathers elsewhere on underside of wing are characteristic. Immature brown above, rufous below, with lightly barred tail. From below, flight silhouette is distinctly long-tailed and slender-winged, reminiscent of large Hen Harrier. *Voice:* rapid 'key-key-key'. *Habitat:* rocky hills and valleys. Scarce. ▲

Osprey *Pandion haliaetus* 58cm Medium-sized fish-hunting raptor. Adult and immature brown above; head white, with large brown patch through eye. Crown loosely crested. Underparts largely white, with band of brown streaks across breast. Wings dark above; generally pale below, with dark wingtips and dark 'wrist' patch. In flight, wings characteristically held in 'M', and arched. Beak grey, relatively small and hooked. Legs and large feet, with powerful long talons, grey. Plunge-dives for fish. *Voice:* rarely heard, brief whistle. *Habitat:* lakes and streams; saline lagoons and reservoirs. Widespread; rarely numerous. 🦐 🌊

Lesser Kestrel *Falco naumanni* 28cm Small falcon. Adult male back bright chestnut, diagnostically without spots (*see* Kestrel); head grey; tail grey with black terminal band. Underparts pinkish-buff, with dark brown streaks. Female and immature brown above, paler buffish below, heavily barred and streaked. In flight, from below appears much paler than Kestrel; hovers only occasionally. Gregarious; feeds, flies and roosts in small flocks. *Voice:* very vocal; chattering 'chee' and 'chet' calls, plaintive whistles. *Habitat:* open farmland, rocky hillsides and towns with old buildings. Widespread; sometimes common. 🏍 🐛 🏞

Short-toed Eagle

Bonelli's Eagle

Osprey

Lesser Kestrel ♂

Kestrel *Falco tinnunculus* 35cm Medium-sized falcon. Adult male back chestnut brown with heavy dark brown spots; head grey; tail grey, with black terminal bar. Underparts buff, with darker spots. Female and immature brown above, buffish below, with heavy brown spots and streaks. Long pointed wings sometimes appear rounded. Hovers frequently and expertly. *Voice:* shrill, repetitive 'ki-ki-ki'. *Habitat:* widely varied, from towns and cities, farmland and marshes to moors, mountains and sea coasts. Common.

Red-footed Falcon *Falco vespertinus* 27cm Small, slim-winged falcon. Adult male dark grey above and below; flanks, thighs and undertail coverts chestnut. Legs and feet dark red. Female and immature grey-brown above; head pale buff and crown chestnut. Underparts pale buffish, with darker streaks, sparser in female. Wings dark, long and pointed. Agile in flight in pursuit of insects; also hovers regularly. Often occurs in small flocks. *Voice:* high-pitched 'ki-ki-ki'. *Habitat:* lightly-treed grassland and farmland; woodland edges and marshland with occasional trees. Only locally common.

Merlin *Falco columbarius* 30cm Small low-flying falcon. Adult male slate grey above, rich chestnut-buff below, with dark brown streaks. Female and immature dark brown above, buff below, streaked dark brown. Fast-flying and agile falcon, hunting small birds in low-level chases across open country. *Voice:* chattering 'ki-ki-ki'. *Habitat:* breeds on moors and grassy hillsides. Winters over farmland and inland and coastal marshes. Widespread; uncommon.

Hobby *Falco subbuteo* 28cm Small long-winged falcon. Adult dark slate grey above, conspicuously white on face and sides of neck (almost appearing as collar in distant view), with marked black moustachial streaks. Underparts pale buff with heavy brownish streaking, shading to rich chestnut on lower flanks, thighs and undertail coverts. Immature dull grey-brown above; buff below, with dark streaking, but lacking chestnut. Extremely fast in flight, resembling a giant Swift in silhouette. *Voice:* repeated 'kew' and chattering 'ki-ki-ki'. *Habitat:* heaths and open woodland; occasionally farmland and marshes. Widespread; locally common.

Kestrel ♂

Kestrel ♀

Red-footed Falcon (immature)

Merlin ♀

Hobby

Eleonora's Falcon *Falco eleonorae* 35cm Medium-sized long-winged falcon, occurring in two colour forms. Dark-phase adult slate grey above; dark grey below with rufous tinge. Legs and talons yellow (*see* Red-footed). Pale-phase adult brown above, with black cap and black moustachial stripes contrasting with white cheeks. Immature drabber, browner version of corresponding adult. Flight fast, Hobby-like, in pursuit of birds and insects. *Voice:* harsh 'kek-kek-kek'. *Habitat:* confined to sea cliffs on Mediterranean islands. Local and scarce.

Gyr Falcon *Falco rusticolus* 58cm Largest, most robust falcon, occurring in two colour forms. Rare pale-phase adult almost white above and below, with sparse darker flecks. Commoner dark-phase adult grey-brown above, white below, heavily marked with dark brown streaks. Intermediate forms occasionally occur. Immature resembles drab version of appropriate adult plumage. Purposeful, powerful flight, with relatively broad wings and long tail. *Voice:* rarely heard; chattering. *Habitat:* rocky outcrops and tundra; sea cliffs on northern coasts. Rare.

Peregrine *Falco peregrinus* 45cm Large, powerful falcon. Adult crown, back and tail steel grey; dark moustachial streaks contrast with white cheeks. Underparts white, with delicate, brownish-grey barring. Immature much browner; breast buffish, heavily streaked with dark brown. Females substantially larger than males. Flight fast and strong; periods of wingbeats interspersed with glides. Often hunts by 'stooping' – high-speed power-dive of great force onto prey. *Voice:* chattering 'kek-kek-kek' is commonest. *Habitat:* rocky, mountainous areas and cliffs year-round; also moors and marshes in winter. Widespread; nowhere numerous.

Eleonora's Falcon

Gyr Falcon

Peregrine (adult)

Peregrine (immature)

Willow Grouse *Lagopus lagopus* 40cm Medium-sized, skulking game bird. Summer adult male mottled rich chestnut brown above and below; almost black tail feathers and striking white wings conspicuous in flight. Beak short, stubby; red fleshy wattles visible over eyes at close range. Summer female and immature drabber, greyer; lacking wattles, but with white wings. Both sexes all-white in winter; only black tail feathers contrast. No black face patch as in Ptarmigan. Remains in concealment until danger threatens closely; then whirrs off on fast-beating, downcurved, short wings. *Voice:* powerful 'go-back-urrr'. *Habitat:* heather moorland, willow scrub, tundra edges. Widespread; locally common.

Red Grouse *Lagopus lagopus scoticus* 40cm Medium-sized, skulking game bird. Scottish sub-species of Willow, confined to Britain and Ireland. Summer adult male richer reddish-chestnut than Willow, but female similar. In both sexes wings dark brown, not white. Both retain chestnut or brown plumage entire through winter. Behaviour, voice and habitat as Willow.

Ptarmigan *Lagopus mutus* 35cm Medium-sized, largely terrestrial game bird. Summer adult male head, neck and back mottled greyish-brown; tail black. Breast and belly white; wings white, conspicuous in flight. Red fleshy wattles visible over eyes at close range. Summer adult female largely mottled chestnut brown, with white wings. Immature similar. In winter, both sexes all-white except for black tail, and small black eye-patch in male. Runs rather than flies. *Voice:* various croaks; male brief, crowing 'song'. *Habitat:* high altitudes or high latitudes year-round. Widespread, but sporadic; rarely numerous.

Black Grouse *Tetrao tetrix* 50cm Large game bird. Male unmistakable: plumage iridescent jet black; bright red wattles over eyes; tail black and white, lyre-shaped. In flight, white 'shoulder' and wingbar conspicuous in blackish rounded wings. Female and immature mottled grey-brown, with relatively long, slightly forked tail. Displays communally at lekking grounds. Fast, high flight when disturbed. *Voice:* in display, astonishing variety of cackling, bubbling and crooning calls. *Habitat:* heaths, moors and open woodland. Widespread; only locally common.

Hazelhen *Bonasa bonasia* 35cm Small, woodland game bird. Adult male grey-brown above, barred with dark brown. Head brown, with slight crest. Underparts primarily white; sides of breast and flanks rich rufous brown with darker markings. Throat distinctly black, with broad white moustachial streak extending onto shoulders. Female and immature similar but rather duller; throat white, not black. In flight, shows characteristic broad black band near tip of grey tail. Often perches in trees. *Voice:* high-pitched, trilling whistle. *Habitat:* hilly woodlands, particularly of aspen and birch. Widespread; rarely numerous.

Willow Grouse (winter)

Red Grouse ♂ (summer)

Ptarmigan ♂ (winter)

Ptarmigan ♀ (summer),

Black Grouse ♂

Hazelhen ♂

Capercaillie *Tetrao urogallus* 85cm Huge, turkey-like game bird. Adult male unmistakable: largely iridescent black above and below, but back brownish. Head feathers form shaggy crest. Displays with long tail fanned. Female and immature smaller (still large for game birds), richly marked chestnut brown. *Voice:* both sexes have disyllabic 'kok-kok'; male song accelerating series of 'hiccups', ending in 'pop' as of cork withdrawn from bottle. *Habitat:* coniferous woodland. Widespread. ▲♣♣

Chukar *Alectoris chukar* 33cm Medium-sized game bird. Adult grey-brown above; buffish below, boldly barred black and brown on flanks. Striking head pattern of large white bib extending well down breast (*see* Red-legged Partridge), surrounded by black border. Beak and legs bright red. Immature sandy brown, lacking head pattern. Flight low and direct, on whirring wings. *Voice:* 'chuck-arr'. *Habitat:* open rocky hillsides and scrub. Locally common. ▲♣🌿

Red-legged Partridge *Alectoris rufa* 35cm Medium-sized game bird. Adult grey-brown above; buffish below, boldly barred with black, white and chestnut on flanks. Striking head pattern of white chin and upper throat, surrounded by black border and black streaking extending onto breast. Immature sandy brown, lacking distinctive head pattern. Flight low and direct on whirring wings. *Voice:* 'chuck, chuck-arr'. *Habitat:* dry, farmland heath and scrub. Locally common. ♣🌿

Grey Partridge *Perdix perdix* 30cm Medium-sized game bird. Adult back, face and upper throat buff-streaked brownish; nape and breast dove grey, paling towards belly. Bold chestnut barring on flanks. Dark brown, inverted-horseshoe patch on belly larger in male than female. Immature streaked sandy brown. Flight low, direct and fast, on whirring wings. *Voice:* 'chirrick, chirrick'. *Habitat:* arable fields, grassland, heaths and scrub. Widespread; locally common. ♣🌿

Quail *Coturnix coturnix* 18cm Small, secretive game bird. Adult plumage flecked and streaked mixture of sandy browns, browns and pale buff, with broad buff stripes on crown. Male has small black bib. Immature resembles female. Flies only as last resort; then for the shortest possible distance. *Voice:* more often heard than seen: characteristic 'wet-my-lips' call. *Habitat:* dry grassland, heaths and cereal fields. Widespread; rarely numerous. ♣🌿

Pheasant *Phasianus colchicus* 85cm Large, long-tailed game bird. Adult male unmistakable: body iridescent bronze, beautifully marked; head glossy bottle green, with scarlet face patches; tail very long. Female and immature sandy buff with darker streaks; tail shorter. Flight rapid; long glides after bursts of flapping. Take-off explosive. *Voice:* male has ringing 'cork-cork', followed by loud wing-claps. *Habitat:* farmland, heaths, scrub, open woodland. Widespread; numbers influenced by release of captive-reared birds. ♣♦♣♣

Capercaillie ♂

Chukar

Red-legged Partridge

Grey Partridge

Quail

Pheasant ♂

Water Rail *Rallus aquaticus* 28cm Medium-sized, skulking crake. Adult predominantly leaden grey on face and underparts, with flanks boldly barred black and white and striking white undertail coverts. Upperparts rich buffish-brown, speckled and streaked with dark brown. Beak reddish, long, slender and slightly downcurved. Legs and toes yellowish and long. Immature darker, more speckled above and barred below. Flies rarely, fluttering low with legs trailing. *Voice:* various noisy pig-like grunts and squeals. *Habitat:* dense reedbeds and heavily vegetated swamps. Widespread; rarely numerous; difficult to see. 🌾

Spotted Crake *Porzana porzana* 23cm Small, skulking crake. Adult streaked brownish over much of upperparts, greyish below; characteristic white spots on breast and wings. Pale bars on flanks visible at close range. Undertail distinctly buff. Beak yellow with black tip, short; legs and toes greenish. Immature resembles duller, paler version of adult. Flies rarely. *Voice:* repetitive, high-pitched 'whit' call at dusk, produced with metronomic regularity. *Habitat:* densely vegetated swamps and lakesides. Widespread; difficult to see. 🌾

Baillon's Crake *Porzana pusilla* 17cm Small, extremely secretive crake. Adult predominantly olive-brown above, with inconspicuous pale spots; mostly grey below, with distinctive bold black and white barring on the flanks (*see* Little). Beak greenish-yellow with dark tip, short; legs yellowish-pink. Immature brown above and buff below; striking, bold, dark brown barring on flanks. Flies rarely. *Voice:* shrill trilling. *Habitat:* densely vegetated swamps and lakesides; reedbeds. Locally fairly common; difficult to see. 🌾

Little Crake *Porzana parva* 17cm Small, extremely secretive crake. Adult male predominantly speckled brown above; greyish below, barred with pale grey on flanks. Beak yellow with dark tip and red spot at base, short. Legs green (contrast Baillon's). Female and immature brown above; rich buff below, with faint flank barring. Rarely flies. *Voice:* harsh, high-pitched trilling. *Habitat:* densely vegetated, swampy areas and reedbeds. Widespread; difficult to see. 🌾

Corncrake *Crex crex* 23cm Noisy but skulking medium-sized crake. Adult predominantly richly mottled buffish-brown above, with strikingly chestnut wings. Throat grey; rest of underparts buff, barred with brown on flanks. Chestnut patches in wings characteristic in flight, which is feeble, with brownish legs trailing. Beak yellow with dark tip, short. Immature resembles paler, washed-out version of adult. *Voice:* absolutely diagnostic dry 'crex, crex', repeated endlessly day and night. *Habitat:* hay meadows, unkempt grassland. Widespread; locally common, but diminishing. 🐦🌾

Water Rail

Spotted Crake ♀

Baillon's Crake

Little Crake ♂

Corncrake

Moorhen *Gallinula chloropus* 33cm Medium-sized crake. Adult velvety brownish-black, with characteristic white streak along flanks. Undertail coverts white, conspicuous when tail jerked while swimming. Forehead scarlet, fleshy; beak red with yellow tip. Legs and long toes green. Immature drab grey-brown, darker above than below. Swims well; upends, but does not dive. Flies feebly and low over water, legs trailing. *Voice:* several ringing calls, including 'whittuck'. *Habitat:* fresh waters, from smallest pool to largest lake. Common.

Coot *Fulica atra* 38cm Medium-large crake. Adult uniformly dull, velvety black. Short beak and fleshy forehead patch diagnostically white. Legs and feet grey, with distinctive lobed webbing to toes. Immature dark grey-brown above, paler below. Flies low over water, revealing conspicuous white trailing edges to wings. Swims buoyantly; dives frequently. *Voice:* single or repeated strident 'kowk'. *Habitat:* larger expanses of fresh or brackish water, including reservoirs in winter; occasionally on sheltered estuaries. Common.

Common Crane *Grus grus* 110cm Huge, stork-like crane. Adult predominantly greyish above and below. Long neck black in front, white behind; small red crown patch. Bushy plumes above tail give bottom-heavy appearance, especially in spring. Beak grey, long, dagger-shaped. Legs grey, long. Immature grey-brown; paler below. Flies on broad, fingered wings, often in V-formation, neck and legs outstretched (*see* Grey Heron). *Voice:* trumpeting calls in flight; wild whooping during display. *Habitat:* extensive bog and tundra areas. Regular on old-established migration routes and breeding grounds.

Little Bustard *Tetrax tetrax* 43cm Wary, medium-sized, stout, long-necked, long-legged game bird. Summer adult male mottled sandy buff above; white below. Head, neck and collar show striking black and white patterns. Female, immature and winter male mottled buff above; paler, almost white, below. In flight, powerful wings show distinctive black and white pattern. *Voice:* rarely vocal; hissing 'dahg'. *Habitat:* plains, open grassland and large fields. Locally fairly common; rarely easy to see.

Great Bustard *Otis tarda* 100cm Huge bustard, one of the heaviest flying birds. Adult male richly mottled golden brown above; white below. Long neck and head grey, with white moustachial tufts. Beak yellow, short and stout. Legs yellowish, long and strong. Female and immature drabber, less finely marked and lacking moustachial tufts. Flies with neck and legs outstretched, broad wings strikingly patterned in black and white. Wary. *Voice:* seldom-heard grunts. *Habitat:* open plains, large grassy and arable fields. Rare and local.

Moorhen

Coot

Common Crane (summer)

Little Bustard ♂ (summer)

Great Bustard ♂ (summer)

Oystercatcher *Haematopus ostralegus* 43cm

Conspicuously pied, medium-sized wader. Adult back, head and neck black; white below. Tail white, with black terminal band. In flight, usually in noisy flocks, black wings show conspicuous white wingbars. Beak orange, long and fairly stout. Legs and feet pink, thick and fleshy. Winter adult and immature show some black on beak, and white collar mark on neck. *Voice:* noisily vociferous; various 'kleep' calls and pipings. *Habitat:* breeds on coastal marshes, grassy islands, sand-dunes etc, and on inland damp grassland. Winters on rocky, sandy or muddy coasts and estuaries. Widespread, often common, usually in flocks in winter. ◄ ▧ ▧

Black-winged Stilt *Himantopus himantopus* 38cm

Unmistakable medium-sized wader, with extremely long legs. Adult back and wings black; head, neck and underparts white, with varying amounts of grey or black on nape. Beak black, long and very slender. Legs rich pink, almost ridiculously long, enabling it to wade and feed in deeper water than other waders. Immature browner above; legs greyish-pink. Flight apparently feeble for wader, showing dark undersides to wings but no wingbars, with legs trailing conspicuously well beyond tail. *Voice:* noisily vociferous; yelping 'kyip' call. *Habitat:* saltpans, coastal lagoons and marshes. Locally common. ◄ ▧

Avocet *Recurvirostra avosetta* 43cm

Medium-sized wader, with unmistakable pied plumage and upturned beak. Adult predominantly white above and below, with black crown and nape, black bars on back and wings, and black wingtips. Beak black and long, extremely slender towards the tip, which is markedly upturned. Feeds by sweeping beak from side to side in shallow water. Legs grey, relatively long. Immature similarly patterned, but browner. *Voice:* vocal; 'kloo-oot' call, varying from flute-like to strident if alarmed. *Habitat:* saline or brackish lagoons and pools. May overwinter on sheltered estuaries. Locally common. Breeds colonially; often winters in flocks. ◄ ▧

Stone Curlew *Burhinus oedicnemus* 40cm

Medium-sized, thick-set and slow-moving wader. Adult and immature head, neck, back and breast buff, finely marked with brown, paling to white on belly. Dark stripe through strikingly large, glaring golden eye, with whitish-buff stripes above and below. Beak yellow with black tip, short, plover-like. Legs yellow, relatively long, with conspicuously large, knobbly joints. In flight, which is swift and direct, double white wingbars and white wing patches are conspicuous. Secretive, often solitary, and largely nocturnal. *Voice:* weird wailing calls and shrieks. *Habitat:* breeds on dry heaths and arable fields. Scarce. ◄ ▧

Oystercatcher

Black-winged Stilt (winter)

Avocet

Stone Curlew

Pratincole *Glareola pratincola* 25cm Comparatively small shorebird, almost more like a tern than a wader. In silhouette, on the ground and in flight, resembles large Swallow. Adult largely sandy brown above, paling to white on belly. Characteristic buff throat patch edged in black. Beak dark, tiny. Legs black, short. Immature speckled brown above; lacking throat patch below. Flight Swallow-like, showing black wingtips, diagnostic chestnut undersides to wings (*see* Black-winged), white rump and black, deeply forked tail. *Voice:* tern-like 'keeyik' and chattering calls. *Habitat:* breeds colonially on coastal mudflats, saltpans and grassland. Only locally common.

Black-winged Pratincole *Glareola nordmanni* 25cm Comparatively small shorebird, more like a tern than a wader. Adult and immature normally indistinguishable from Pratincole, unless reasonably close-range view can be obtained of underwing in flight. Pratincole has chestnut underwings (caution: in poor light, may appear blackish at a distance), whereas Black-winged has diagnostic black underwings. Voice and habitat as Pratincole. Scarce or vagrant.

Little Ringed Plover *Charadrius dubius* 15cm Small, fast-moving wader. Adult pale sandy brown above; white below. Bold black and white head pattern, with white band between black forehead and sandy crown. Black collar band; yellow eye-ring. Beak yellowish, stubby. Legs pinkish. Immature lacks black and white pattern, and has brownish, incomplete collar. In flight, shows characteristically plain, pale brown wings, with little trace of wingbars. Usually single or in pairs. *Voice:* plaintive, piping 'tee-you', trilling song. *Habitat:* sandy coasts, saltpans and lagoons; inland on quarries, sandpits etc. Widespread.

Ringed Plover *Charadrius hiaticula* 20cm Small, fast-running plover. Adult sandy brown above; white below. Black and white facial pattern, lacking upper white forehead stripe and yellow eye-ring of Little Ringed. Black collar. Beak yellowish with black tip, stubby; legs yellow. White wingbar conspicuous in flight. Immature marking brownish, not black. Rarely in large flocks. *Voice:* fluting 'too-lee'; trilling song. *Habitat:* sandy coasts and saltpans; occasionally inland on river banks and excavations. Widespread; relatively common.

Kentish Plover *Charadrius alexandrinus* 15cm Small, fast-moving plover. Adult pale, sandy brown above; white below. Crown chestnut in summer, richer in male. Black and white forehead pattern; black mark through eye. Dark brown or blackish patches on shoulders; lacks complete collar. Immature paler and drabber, lacking chestnut crown and black markings. In flight, white wingbar visible in brown wings. *Voice:* fluting 'poo-eet'; soft, repeated 'wit'; long, trilling song. *Habitat:* sandy beaches, saltpans, muddy lagoons. Locally common.

Pratincole

Black-winged Pratincole (immature)

Little Ringed Plover

Ringed Plover

Kentish Plover (adult)

Kentish Plover (immature)

Dotterel *Charadrius morinellus* 22cm Medium-small, upland plover. Summer adult mottled grey-brown above, with black crown and distinctive bold white eye-stripe. Throat white; breast and nape grey, in continuous collar. Belly chestnut, darker on flanks, separated from breast by clear but narrow white band. Undertail white. Beak dark, stubby; legs yellow, relatively long. Female brighter than male. Winter adult and immature buff above, paler below, with faint eye-stripe and breast band. No wingbar visible in flight. Tame. *Voice:* piping trill. *Habitat:* breeds on tundra, mountain tops at lower altitudes. Lowland heaths, fields and marshes on migration. Scarce.

Golden Plover *Pluvialis apricaria* 28cm Medium-sized plover. Summer adult striking, with richly flecked, golden crown, nape and back separated from glossy black face, throat and belly by broad white margin. Beak stubby; legs grey, long. Winter adult and immature flecked dull golden buff above; buff below, shading to white on belly, with no black. No wingbar visible in flight. Often gregarious. *Voice:* fluting whistle 'tloo-ee'. *Habitat:* breeds on tundra and moorland, winters on coastal marshes and inland on damp fields and grassland. Locally common; sometimes in large flocks.

Grey Plover *Pluvialis squatarola* 28cm Medium-sized, often solitary plover. Summer adult strikingly handsome: upperparts richly black-flecked silver grey, separated from black face, throat, breast and belly by broad white margin. Winter adult and immature flecked grey-buff above; white below. In flight, shows faint wingbar and characteristic bold black patches in 'armpits' beneath wings. Beak black, stubby; legs black, long. *Voice:* plaintive, fluting 'tee-too-ee'. *Habitat:* breeds on northern tundra. Winters on sheltered coastal bays and estuaries. Widespread; rarely numerous.

Lapwing *Vanellus vanellus* 30cm Medium-large plover. Adult unmistakable; black above with purplish-green iridescent sheen. Cheeks greyish but throat, breast and crown black. Conspicuous, long, slender, upturned crest. Flanks and belly white; undertail coverts rich chestnut. Tail white, with terminal black bar. Immature browner, with buff fringes to feathers, giving scaly appearance to back. Beak black, stubby; legs brown, long. Flight characteristic; floppy, on black and white, rounded wings. Gregarious. *Voice:* characteristic 'pee-wit'. *Habitat:* breeds on fields, moorland, marshes. Winters on arable land, grassland, estuaries. Common.

Knot *Calidris canutus* 25cm Medium-small wader. Summer adult brown above, with golden, scaly markings; distinctly rusty below. Winter adult and immature non-descript; flecked grey-brown above, whitish below. Beak dark, straight, medium length; legs dark, medium length. Faint, white wingbar visible in flight. Gregarious, gathering in close-packed flocks, thousands-strong. *Voice:* occasional grunts. *Habitat:* breeds on Arctic tundra. Winters on sand and mudflats of sheltered coastal bays and estuaries. Widespread; locally numerous.

Dotterel ♂

Golden Plover (summer)

Grey Plover (winter)

Lapwing

Knot (winter)

TRANSATLANTIC WANDERERS (see page 26)

Black Duck *Anas rubripes* 40cm Mallard-like, surface-feeding duck. Adult back, wings and belly predominantly dark purplish-brown. Head pale brown. In flight, shows white undersides to wings, contrasting with dark belly. Upper wings show trace of white trailing edge. *Voice:* similar to Mallard. *Habitat:* shallow, coastal and freshwater marshes in North America; occasionally wanders east. 🦆🌾

American Golden Plover *Pluvialis dominica* 22cm Closely similar to Golden. Summer adult gold above, flecked black and white. Face, throat black, broadly edged white; belly black; flanks, undertail black, not white as in Golden. No wingbar. *Voice:* whistling 'oodle-oo'. *Habitat:* breeds on tundra. Winters on marshes in North America, migrating south to South America or south-west into Asia. Occasionally wanders east. 🚜🌾🌊

Lesser Yellowlegs *Tringa flavipes* 24cm Medium-sized, slim wader. Summer adult back grey-brown, flecked white. Head, neck, breast white, finely streaked grey; belly white. Winter adult, immature greyer, drabber, paler. Legs yellow, comparatively long. In flight, white rump contrasts with dark back and black-barred white tail. *Voice:* soft 'tew-tew'. *Habitat:* breeds on tundra, open woodland in northern North America. Winters in Central and South America. Occasionally strays east. 🌾🌊

White-rumped Sandpiper *Calidris fuscicollis* 17cm Small, Dunlin-like wader. Summer adult speckled brown, with bronze feather edges on back, nape and crown. Clear, white eye-stripe. Underparts white, streaked brown on throat, breast and flanks. In winter, duller; greyish band on upper breast. In flight, appears long-winged; whitish wingbar and white rump patch above blackish tail. *Voice:* distinctive, high-pitched squeak in flight. *Habitat:* North American tundra-breeding. Winters southern South America. Occasionally strays east. 🌾🌊

Pectoral Sandpiper *Calidris melanotos* 22cm Relatively large, long-necked, long-legged wader. Summer adult richly marked browns, blacks and buffs above. Face, neck and throat buff; brown streaks form band between breast and white belly. In winter, duller; throat, breast greyish; clear pectoral band. In flight, faint wingbar and white rump split by black central feathers. Tail grey. *Voice:* fluting 'chuurk'. *Habitat:* breeds on North American, Asiatic tundra. Winters South America, Australasia. American birds wander east. 🌾🌊

Ring-billed Gull *Larus delawarensis* 47cm Medium-sized gull. Adult resembles Herring Gull, but much smaller; legs yellowish, beak yellow with black vertical band near tip. Immature much paler than immature Herring; all ages more buoyant in flight, showing darker underwings. *Voice:* shrill 'kyow'; angry 'ka-ka-ka'. *Habitat:* breeds on central North American freshwater lakes. Winters coastally. Occasionally wanders east. 🌊🌾

114

Black Duck

American Golden Plover

Lesser Yellowlegs

White-rumped Sandpiper

Pectoral Sandpiper

Ring-billed Gull

Sanderling *Calidris alba* 20cm Small, fast-running wader. Summer adult rufous cinnamon above, with scaly, buff markings; white below. Winter adult and immature distinctly pale silver grey above; pure white below. Grey-black smudge mark through eye. Beak dark, short; legs dark. Runs at speed on sand, typically following waves in and out. In flight, white wingbar conspicuous on dark, blackish wings. Often occurs in small flocks. *Voice:* short 'quick'. *Habitat:* breeds on Arctic tundra. On passage and in winter, on sandy bays and beaches. Locally common.

Little Stint *Calidris minuta* 13cm Tiny, short-beaked wader. Summer adult chequered buff and rich browns above, with characteristic, double, pale buff V-marking on back. Underparts white. Winter adult and immature brownish-grey above, less clearly marked but with 'V' normally still visible; whitish below. Beak dark, short and finely pointed. Legs blackish (*see* Temminck's). In flight, shows pale wingbar and characteristic tail pattern of dark central feathers flanked by grey outer feathers. *Voice:* terse 'chit'. *Habitat:* breeds on tundra. On migration, muddy saline lagoons and creeks; inland freshwater marshy areas. Widespread; rarely numerous.

Temminck's Stint *Calidris temminckii* 13cm Tiny, drab wader. Summer adult mottled buffs and browns above; paler, almost whitish, below, with indistinct broad spotted band across breast. Winter adult and immature drab grey, shading to white below. Beak dark, short and finely pointed. Legs yellowish (*see* Little) but colour may be concealed by mud. In flight, shows pale wingbar and characteristic tail pattern with blackish central feathers flanked by white outer ones. Often solitary. *Voice:* short, characteristic, rattling trill 'tirrrrr'. *Habitat:* breeds on damp moorland and tundra. At other times, fresh or saline muddy pools and swamps.

Curlew Sandpiper *Calidris ferruginea* 20cm Smallish wader with downcurved beak. Summer adult strikingly chestnut brown above and below, with duller, darker brown wings. Winter adult and immature characteristically pale, mottled grey-brown above; whitish-buff below. Head and neck shaded brown; clear white eye-stripe. Neck often appears relatively long; stance upright. Beak dark, relatively long and noticeably downcurved. Legs dark grey, relatively long. In flight, shows clear wingbar, and conspicuous characteristic white rump and black tail pattern. Often in flocks. *Voice:* distinctive, soft, trilling 'chirrup'. *Habitat:* breeds on tundra close to water. At other times, sheltered bays and estuaries, saline lagoons, freshwater marshes and swamps. Regular, but in varying numbers from year to year.

Sanderling (winter)

Little Stint (winter)

Temminck's Stint (winter)

Curlew Sandpiper (winter)

Curlew Sandpiper (summer)

Purple Sandpiper *Calidris maritima* 20cm Small, dark wader, characteristic of rocky shores. Summer adult back rich brown, with buff, scaly markings. Underparts almost entirely white, browner on flanks. Winter adult and immature distinctive purplish-leaden grey on upperparts and breast; paler grey below. Throat white. Pale yellowish eye-ring. Beak yellow with black tip, distinctive, medium length and slightly downcurved. Legs yellow, relatively short. In flight, shows indistinct wingbar but some white on inner flight feathers; tail pattern shows small white patches on each side of rump, and dark tail. *Voice:* disyllabic 'wit-wit'. *Habitat:* breeds on moorland and tundra. At other times, characteristic wader of seaweed-clad rocky shores. Locally common. 🏔🦆🦆

Broad-billed Sandpiper *Limicola falcinellus* 15cm Small, secretive wader. Summer adult rich brown above, heavily streaked and mottled with chestnut and buff. Winter adult and immature duller and less richly marked, but retaining buff stripes on back. In flight, shows uniformly dark brown wings; no wingbar. Tail has dark central stripe, and brown-barred white outer feathers. Beak dark, relatively long; 5mm breadth only visible from some angles and at close range. Legs greenish. *Voice:* deep trill. *Habitat:* breeds on tundra and moorland with occasional scrubby trees. Winters on inland waters and coastal lagoons. Scarce. 🦆🌊🦆

Dunlin *Calidris alpina* 18cm Small, widespread, long-billed wader. Summer adult rich bronze with darker rufous brown speckling above; breast pale, dark-streaked; characteristic black belly patch. Winter adult and immature dull, speckled grey-brown or buffish-brown above, paling to near-white on underparts. Beak dark, relatively long and slightly downcurved. Legs dark, relatively short. In flight, shows clear, pale wingbar and white patches on each side of dark rump and tail. Gregarious, often in huge flocks. *Voice:* call nasal 'treeer'; song purring trill, delivered in flight. *Habitat:* breeds on damp grassland, moorland and tundra. At other times, sheltered coastal bays, estuaries and lagoons; inland on marshes and swamps. Common. 🦆🏔🦆🌊🦆

Ruff *Philomachus pugnax* 30cm Medium-sized wader, male appreciably larger than female. Adult male in breeding season unmistakable, with copious ruff of feathers round neck usually chestnut, black, white, or combination of these. Back mottled rich brown; rest of underparts white. Smaller female mottled rich buffs and browns above; pale buff below. Winter male and immature similar to female. Beak yellowish with dark tip, medium-long. Legs variable in colour, but usually yellow or orange, relatively long. In flight, appears long-winged and leisurely, showing pale wingbar. Tail pattern characteristic, with dark central bar separating large, white, oval patches on each side of rump. Gregarious. Forms communal displays or leks in spring. *Voice:* rarely vocal. *Habitat:* breeds on tundra, freshwater marshes, wet fields and swamps. At other times, coastal lagoons and inland muddy pools. 🦆🦆🌊🦆

Purple Sandpiper (summer)

Broad-billed Sandpiper (winter)

Dunlin (winter)

Dunlin (summer)

Ruff ♂ (winter)

Ruff ♂ (summer)

Jack Snipe *Lymnocryptes minimus* 20cm Small, long-billed, secretive wader. Adult and immature have characteristic Snipe-like plumage of rich brown, mottled and streaked with black, buff and grey. Beak yellowish, only medium-long. Legs greenish-grey, comparatively short. In display flight, fanned tail makes noise like muffled drums. Shy, well-camouflaged and difficult to flush. Flies only short distances before pitching down, without calling. In flight, wingbars and long, buff back markings are conspicuous, contrasting with uniformly brown, wedge-shaped tail. *Voice:* normally silent. *Habitat:* breeds beside freshwater swamps, lakes etc. Winters on fresh and salt marshland, with plentiful muddy creeks and pools. Regular; rarely numerous.

Common Snipe *Gallinago gallinago* 28cm Small but very long-beaked wader. Adult and immature rich brown, plentifully barred and streaked with chestnut, buff and black, with three, bold, yellowish-buff, longitudinal stripes on crown. Beak brownish, straight and very long. Legs greenish, comparatively short. Characteristically swift, zig-zag flight when flushed, usually rising and travelling some distance. Wingbars and striped back conspicuous. Tail rounded; shows dark band. Display flight soaring and diving, when fanned tail produces throbbing, bleating noise. *Voice:* almost always calls on taking flight, and frequently in flight; harsh 'scarp'. In breeding season, clock-like 'tick-er, tick-er'. *Habitat:* breeds on freshwater marshes, swamps, wet meadows, moorland. Winters in similar habitats, salt marshes and saline lagoons.

Woodcock *Scolopax rusticola* 35cm Medium-large, heavily built, woodland wader. Adult and immature superficially Snipe-like, but much more heavily built, and with bolder barring and finer mottling on rich brown plumage. Breast grey-buff and barred, not streaked. Head angular with large bulging eyes; crosswise yellowish bands across rich brown crown. Beak yellowish-brown, long, stout. Legs pinkish, short, giving squat stance, and stout. Rarely flies until danger is close at hand. During winter and spring displays establishes regular 'roding' flight paths through woodland glades. *Voice:* during display, frog-like 'orrrt-orrrt', with repeated, high-pitched, sneezing 'swick' calls; otherwise silent. *Habitat:* aberrant wader, usually preferring damp woodland year-round; rarely seen on fresh or coastal marshes. Widespread; difficult to see.

Jack Snipe

Common Snipe

Woodcock

Woodcock

Black-tailed Godwit *Limosa limosa* 40cm Large long-beaked wader. Summer adult striking, with back mottled brown and chestnut; head and neck cinnamon brown; underparts whitish, with chestnut barring on flanks. Winter adult and immature are grey or grey-brown above, paling to near-white below. In flight, always shows striking, broad, white bar in blackish wings, and characteristic black-tipped white tail. Beak pinkish-red, blackish towards the tip, very long and straight. Legs black, long. Gregarious. *Voice:* noisy 'wicka-wicka-wicka', particularly in breeding season. *Habitat:* breeds on damp meadows and marshes. Winters on estuaries, sheltered sandy or muddy bays; occasionally on freshwater marshes. Locally common.

Bar-tailed Godwit *Limosa lapponica* 40cm Large long-beaked wader. Summer adult back richly marked brown; head, neck and breast rufous cinnamon brown; belly chestnut. Winter adult and immature mottled grey to grey-brown above, shading to white below. In flight, shows no wingbars; tail pattern is of dense, narrow, dark brown barring across white tail (*see* Black-tailed). Beak reddish but darker towards the tip, very long, characteristically slightly but noticeably upturned. Legs black and long. Gregarious, sometimes in large flocks. *Voice:* rarely vocal, except in breeding season: usually harsh 'kirrick'. *Habitat:* breeds on Arctic tundra. Winters on muddy or sandy estuaries; sheltered coastal bays. Common; locally numerous.

Whimbrel *Numenius phaeopus* 40cm Large Curlew-like wader. Adult and immature greyish-brown above, with copious white and darker brown flecking. Underparts pale buff with darker brown streaking, shading to white on belly. Crown dark brown, with three characteristic yellow-buff longitudinal stripes. Beak grey-brown, long (but not as dramatically as Curlew) and downcurved. Legs blue-grey, comparatively long. In flight, shows no striking wing markings, only small whitish rump patch and buff tail with darker bars (*see* Curlew). Rarely gregarious. *Voice:* short, high-pitched, piping whistle, usually repeated several times in quick succession. *Habitat:* breeds on moorland and tundra, on migration (occasionally overwinters) usually on coastal marshes. Widespread; rarely numerous.

Curlew *Numenius arquata* 58cm Very large unmistakable wader. Adult and immature sandy buff above, with whitish and brown flecks and streaks. Underparts pale buffish-fawn with darker brown streaks, shading to white on belly. Characteristic beak brownish-black, exceptionally long and markedly downcurved. Legs blue-grey, relatively long. In flight, shows clear white rump extending well up back, and dark-barred buff tail; no distinctive wingbars. Often gregarious in winter. *Voice:* characteristic 'coor-lee' calls at all times, augmented in breeding season by song-flight with remarkable bubbling trills. *Habitat:* breeds on moorland, marshes and wet meadows. Winters on sandy or muddy coasts and estuaries. Widespread; often common.

Black-tailed Godwit (winter)

Bar-tailed Godwit (winter)

Whimbrel

Curlew

Spotted Redshank *Tringa erythropus* 30cm Medium-sized wader. Summer adult unmistakable, sooty black speckled with white markings. Winter adult and immature strikingly pale grey above; white below. Beak dark red at base, long, slender. Legs deep blood red, relatively long. Characteristically feeds by wading (occasionally swimming) in deeper water than Redshank. In flight, shows no wingbars but conspicuous white rump. *Voice:* explosive and distinctive 'chew-it'. *Habitat:* breeds on Arctic tundra and marshland with scattered bushes. On migration and in winter on fresh and salt marshes, estuaries and sheltered bays. Regular; rarely numerous.

Redshank *Tringa totanus* 28cm Medium-sized wader. Summer adult rich brown above, with pale flecks and fine dark brown streaks; buff below, with brown streaking, shading to white on belly. Winter adult and immature duller greyer-brown above; grey-buff below, shading to white on belly and flanks. Beak reddish, slim, medium-long. Legs bright red. Bold white wingbar distinctive in flight, barred with dark brown. Wary and noisy. *Voice:* several piping calls, usually variants of 'tu-lee-lee'. *Habitat:* breeds on fresh and salt marshes, wet meadows and moorland. Winters on salt and fresh marshes, estuaries and sandy bays.

Marsh Sandpiper *Tringa stagnatilis* 23cm Small, strikingly slim, Greenshank-like wader. Summer adult back grey-brown; black centres and pale margins to feathers give strikingly spotted appearance. Head and neck buff, forehead white; underparts largely white, with brown streaks on sides of breast. Winter adult and immature paler and greyer. Beak relatively long, very slender and straight (*see* Greenshank). Legs greenish, relatively long, and much slimmer than those of Greenshank. In flight, dark wings show no wingbars, but white rump is striking. Tail white with fine dark barring. Feet project well beyond tail. *Voice:* high-pitched twittering 'tee-oo', and variants. *Habitat:* breeds on tundra and freshwater marshes. On migration and in winter usually on freshwater marshes; occasionally on saline lagoons. Scarce.

Greenshank *Tringa nebularia* 30cm Medium-sized wader. Summer adult grey-brown above, richly flecked with black and silver; strikingly white below. Winter adult and immature paler and drabber grey. Beak greenish, medium-long, relatively stout and characteristically slightly but detectably upturned (*see* Marsh Sandpiper). Legs green, long, relatively stout. In flight, shows all-dark wings with no wingbars, and striking white rump extending well up back. Tail white, with dark brown barring. Rarely gregarious. *Voice:* characteristic, far-carrying, tri-syllabic 'tu-tu-tu'. *Habitat:* breeds on damp moorland, marshes and tundra. On migration and in winter on coastal lagoons and sheltered sandy or muddy estuaries and bays; occasionally on fresh marshes. Widespread; rarely numerous.

Spotted Redshank (winter)

Spotted Redshank (summer)

Redshank

Marsh Sandpiper (winter)

Greenshank (winter)

Green Sandpiper *Tringa ochropus* 23cm Small, dark wader. Adult and immature crown, nape and back dark greenish-grey, faintly speckled with whitish buff, more marked in adult in summer. Underparts white, with dark streaks on breast. Beak dark, medium length. Legs·dark green, relatively long. Flight jerky and Snipe-like, all-dark wings contrasting characteristically with white rump. Tail white, with black barring. Underwings blackish, not white as in Wood Sandpiper. Often bobs. Usually solitary. *Voice:* fluty, trilling song; when flushed, whistling 'tee-loo-eet'. *Habitat:* breeds close to water in swampy forested areas; may use old nests in trees. On migration and in winter, coastal and inland pools, creeks and marshes. Regular; never numerous. 🪶🌊🌲🔲

Wood Sandpiper *Tringa glareola* 20cm Small, fairly dark, slimly built wader. Summer adult brownish above, copiously flecked with white; white below with light flecking and streaking on neck and sides of breast. Clear, pale, buff-white eye-stripe below dark cap. Winter adult and immature duller, grey-brown. Beak dark, medium-short and straight. Legs characteristically yellow, relatively long (*see* Green). In flight, shows whitish underwings, white rump and white tail with faint dark barring; no wingbars. Solitary, or in small flocks. *Voice:* distinctive 'chiff-if-if' call; musical, yodelling song-flight. *Habitat:* breeds on swampy moorland and tundra, sometimes with scattered trees. On migration and in winter, inland and coastal marshes and pools. Widespread and regular; rarely numerous. 🪶🌊🔲

Terek Sandpiper *Xenus cinereus* 24cm Medium-small, comparatively squat wader, with upturned beak. Summer adult crown, nape and back pale brownish-grey; dark centres to feathers form·irregular but conspicuous V-marking across closed wings and onto back. Underparts whitish, with faint dark streaks on sides of neck and breast. Winter adult and immature paler grey, with less distinct markings. Beak dark, relatively long and characteristically noticeably upturned. Legs distinctive orange-yellow. In flight, white rump and white trailing edge to dark wings are conspicuous. *Voice:* fluting 'du-du-du-du'. *Habitat:* breeds on tundra and wetlands along boreal forest margins. Winters on coasts and saline lagoons. Rare. 🪶🌊🔲

Common Sandpiper *Actitis hypoleucos* 20cm Small wader with distinctive flight. Summer adult sandy brown above, flecked with·white; white below, with brown streaking on throat and on sides of breast forming half-collar. Winter adult and immature duller, less spotted. Beak dark, short and straight. Legs greenish. Flight low over water and fast, with characteristic, rapid, shallow wingbeats and downcurved wings. In flight, shows white wingbar, brown rump, brown tail with brown-barred white outer feathers.·Bobs incessantly. *Voice:* distinctive, trilling 'twee-wee-wee...' call; song high-pitched 'tittyweety-tittyweety'. *Habitat:* breeds beside lakes, rivers and streams. On migration and in winter on fresh and salt marshes; sheltered coasts. Widespread. 🪶🌊🔲

Green Sandpiper

Wood Sandpiper

Terek Sandpiper

Common Sandpiper

Turnstone *Arenaria interpres* 23cm Small, dumpy harlequin-like wader. Summer adult back rich pale chestnut; head, neck and underparts white, all boldly patterned with black. Winter adult and immature retain pied parts of plumage, but chestnut is replaced with grey. Feeds among seaweeds on rocky shores; well camouflaged. In flight, white wingbars and pied plumage are unmistakable. Beak dark, short, flattened from top to bottom; used to overturn weed and stones. Legs yellowish. *Voice:* staccato, chattering 'tuk-uk-tuk' call. *Habitat:* breeds on tundra and rocky Arctic coasts. Winters on rocky coasts; rare inland. Widespread; often common.

Red-necked Phalarope *Phalaropus lobatus* 17cm Small, slim aquatic wader. Summer adult mottled brown and buff above; head dark brown. Throat and chin white; reddish stripe on side of slim neck. Underparts white. Female brighter than male. Winter adult and immature pale grey-brown above, with white head and neck and dark smudge surrounding eye; white below. Beak dark, short, very finely pointed. In flight, shows double white wingbar and black tail with grey outer feathers (*see* winter Sanderling). Characteristically, swims buoyantly much of the time, often spinning to disturb food. *Voice:* sharp 'prip'. *Habitat:* breeds beside moorland or tundra pools. Many winter at sea, but may occur on inshore waters; occasionally inland. Rare.

Grey Phalarope *Phalaropus fulicarius* 17cm Small, dumpy aquatic wader. Summer adult unmistakable, with throat, breast and flanks chestnut, paling to white on belly. Back brown with buff markings; head and nape grey, with large white cheek patch. Female brighter than male. Winter adult and immature pale grey above; white below. Beak short, noticeably stouter than Red-necked. In flight, shows single, bold wingbar, dark rump and tail with grey outer feathers (*see* winter Sanderling). Characteristically, spends much time swimming buoyantly, spinning to disturb food. *Voice:* sharp 'whit' or 'prip'. *Habitat:* breeds in Iceland, beside lakes on tundra. Most winter well out at sea, but some pass inshore on migration; occasionally inland. Rare.

Turnstone (winter)

Red-necked Phalarope ♀ (summer)

Grey Phalarope (winter)

Grey Phalarope ♀ (summer)

Arctic Skua *Stercorarius parasiticus* 45cm Medium-sized skua, occurring in two colour forms. Dark-phase adult uniformly chocolate brown. Pale-phase adult sandy brown above, with blackish cap; neck, breast and belly buffish-white. Adult tail has slim central feathers noticeably elongated. Immature rich brown, heavily speckled and barred; lacks long central tail feathers. Beak and legs greyish-brown, gull-like. In flight, all stages show striking white patches in long slender wings. Slim silhouette and agile flight help separate from Pomarine. Pursues other birds to steal food. *Voice:* yelping 'tuk-tuk'; harsh 'eee-air'. *Habitat:* breeds colonially on moorland, remote islands and tundra. On migration, inshore waters. Regular; rarely numerous, except on breeding grounds.

Pomarine Skua *Stercorarius pomarinus* 50cm Medium-sized skua, occurring in two colour forms. Dark-phase adult uniformly dark brown with darker markings, except for striking white patches in wing, visible in flight. Pale-phase adult sandy brown above, with dark crown, pale buff neck and throat, and broad brown breast band. Belly whitish. White patches in dark brown wings striking in flight. Adult tail has central feathers elongated, conspicuously broad and twisted. Immature uniformly rich honey brown, with darker barring and speckling. Shows white in wings, but lacks elongated tail feathers. In flight, heavier build and steady flight distinguish Pomarine from Arctic. *Voice:* harsh 'which-yoo'. *Habitat:* breeds colonially on tundra. On migration, coastal seas. Scarce, except on breeding grounds.

Long-tailed Skua *Stercorarius longicaudus* 53cm Smallish, slim skua, with very long tail; distinctively the smallest, slimmest and most tern-like of the skua family in flight. Adult brown above, with dark crown. Neck and rest of underparts buffish-white. Central tail feathers slim and elongated; may reach 18cm beyond rest of tail. Immature grey-brown, finely barred and streaked with pale grey; lacks long central tail feathers. Adult and immature show striking white flash in wing. Pursues other birds to steal food. *Voice:* rarely vocal; occasional high-pitched 'kreee' in breeding season. *Habitat:* breeds on tundra. On migration, may pass through inshore waters. Rare, except on breeding grounds.

Great Skua *Stercorarius skua* 60cm Size and shape of Great Black-backed Gull. Adult and immature bulky and heavy, but powerful in flight. Adult plumage dark brown, with paler and darker flecking; cheeks slightly paler and crown slightly darker than elsewhere. Adult has central tail feathers slightly but not noticeably elongated. In flight, striking bold white flashes in dark wings immediately separate Great Skua from immature large gulls. Pursues other birds up to Gannet-size to pirate food. *Voice:* barking 'tuk' or 'uk-uk-uk'; rasping 'skeeer'. *Habitat:* breeds on moorland, tundra and remote islands. On migration, may pass through coastal waters. Regular, but scarce on migration; only locally numerous in colonies.

Arctic Skua (pale)

Arctic Skua (dark)

Pomarine Skua

Long-tailed Skua

Great Skua

Little Gull *Larus minutus* 27cm One of the smallest and most tern-like of gulls. Summer adult largely white, with jet-black hood. Wings grey above, lacking black markings, but characteristically sooty grey below. Beak dark red, small, legs red. Winter adult lacks black head. Immature has white underwing, slightly forked black-tipped tail, and black M-marking across upperside of wings, distinctive in flight. Swims buoyantly. Flight distinctive, tern-like, often dipping down to pick food from water surface. Gregarious. *Voice:* high-pitched 'kek-kek-kek'; repeated, drawn out 'kay-eee'. *Habitat:* breeds on freshwater marshes. Most winter at sea; some occasionally occur inland, especially on migration. Regular; locally fairly common.

Mediterranean Gull *Larus melanocephalus* 38cm Medium-sized gull. Summer adult largely white, with coal-black hood. Wings pale grey, distinctively with white tips and no black markings. Beak orange-red with black band near tip, relatively large. Legs reddish-brown. Winter adult lacks dark head, but has grey smudge through eye. Immature has brown diagonal mark on inner part of wing, and distinctive largely black outer part of wing and flight feathers. In flight, broad black terminal band visible on white tail. Occasionally gregarious. *Voice:* various yelping 'keeer' and harsh 'kwaar' cries. *Habitat:* breeds on lakes and marshes, fresh and saline. Winters along coasts and in estuaries. Rare inland. Scarce except near colonies.

Sabine's Gull *Larus sabini* 32cm Smallish, maritime gull. Summer adult unmistakable, with largely white plumage and grey hood with black border. Beak black with yellow tip, short. In flight, grey inner portion of wing and black outer flight feathers enclose triangular white patch, creating striking pattern. Tail white, quite deeply forked. Immature has similarly striking wing pattern in flight, but forked tail has black tip. Flight dipping and tern-like; often feeds on wing. *Voice:* rasping, tern-like 'keeer'. *Habitat:* breeds on swampy tundra. Winters out at sea in northern oceans. Scarce.

Black-headed Gull *Larus ridibundus* 35cm Medium-sized gull. Summer adult largely white, with chocolate hood. Wings pale silver grey, with black-tipped white flight feathers and white leading edge characteristic in flight. Beak and legs blood red. Winter adult lacks brown hood; nape and smudge through eye greyish; beak and legs brownish. Immature has brownish bars on inner portion of wing; black terminal band on white tail visible in flight. Gregarious. *Voice:* various yelping 'keeer' and drawn-out 'kwaar' calls. *Habitat:* breeds colonially on dunes, islands, fresh and salt marshes. In winter, almost ubiquitous coastally and inland, including urban areas but excluding mountainous regions. Common; often abundant.

Little Gull (adult)

Little Gull (immature)

Mediterranean Gull (immature)

Sabine's Gull

Black-headed Gull (winter)

Black-headed Gull (summer)

Slender-billed Gull *Larus genei* 42cm Medium-sized gull. Adult similar to Black-headed, but lacking brown hood in summer and grey head markings in winter. Small white head with high sloping forehead, long slim neck and long red bill normally held downpointed are all diagnostic features. Immature similar to young Black-headed, but separable by unusual head and beak profile; also less brown on wings. *Voice:* similar 'keeer' and drawn-out 'kwaar' calls to Black-headed. *Habitat:* breeds colonially on coastal marshes. Winters on coastal waters. Only locally common near colonies.

Audouin's Gull *Larus audouinii* 47cm Medium-sized gull of very restricted distribution. Adult largely white; upper surface of wings pale grey, shading gradually to black tips to flight feathers; small white marking visible in flight. Legs black. Immature grey-brown above; whitish below. Beak pattern diagnostic: adult beak mostly red, with black band before yellow tip; immature beak yellow with black band near tip. Rarely gregarious. *Voice:* nasal 'gee-ow'. *Habitat:* breeds on remote rocky islets in Mediterranean. Winters nearby. Rare.

Common Gull *Larus canus* 40cm Medium-sized gull. Adult predominantly white, occasionally with grey flecks around head and nape. Wings grey above; black and white tips to flight feathers. Beak, legs characteristic greenish-yellow. Immature pale brown above, whitish below; crown, nape streaked grey-brown. Gregarious. *Voice:* high-pitched 'kee-you' and high 'gah-gah-gah' calls. *Habitat:* breeds on remote hillsides, islands, moorland and tundra. Widespread on migration and in winter, on farmland, urban parks, refuse tips, reservoirs and coasts. Often common.

Lesser Black-backed Gull *Larus fuscus* 53cm Medium-large gull. Adult predominantly white; back and wings slate grey. Wingtips black, with small white markings. Beak yellow, with red spot near tip; legs characteristically yellow. Immature mottled brown and white above, whitish below; often impossible to distinguish from young Herring Gull. Gregarious. *Voice:* powerful 'kay-ow'; various laughing 'yah' calls and mewings. *Habitat:* breeds on clifftops, islands, sand-dunes and moorland. Migrates southwards in winter to coastal and inland habitats, including urban parks, reservoirs and refuse tips. Widespread; often common.

Herring Gull *Larus argentatus* 55cm Medium-sized gull. Adult predominantly white; back and wings pale silver grey. Wingtips black, with bold white markings. Beak yellow, with red spot near tip. Legs pink; yellow in southern and south-western races. Immature mottled brown and white above, largely white below; beak and legs brownish (*see* Lesser Black-backed). Gregarious. *Voice:* noisily vocal; various mewing cries, harsh 'kay-ow', 'yah-yah-yah' laughing calls. *Habitat:* breeds on remote islands, moors, sand-dunes, cliffs and buildings. Winters on coasts, farmland, town parks, reservoirs and refuse tips. Common; often very numerous.

Slender-billed Gull (winter)

Audouin's Gull

Common Gull

Lesser Black-backed Gull

Herring Gull (adult)

Herring Gull (immature)

Iceland Gull *Larus glaucoides* 55cm Medium-sized, very pale gull. Adult predominantly white above and below; wings very pale grey, completely lacking black at tips of flight feathers. Beak yellowish with red spot near tip, relatively small and light. Legs pink. Immature pale coffee brown above and below, becoming almost pure white, even on wings, in second year. At rest, wingtips protrude beyond tip of tail, and small head and beak profile also aid separation from Glaucous, as does yellow eye-ring visible in adult at close range. *Voice:* very similar to Herring. *Habitat:* breeds on Arctic cliffs, islands and tundra. Winters in northern seas. Rare.

Glaucous Gull *Larus hyperboreus* 67cm Large, very pale gull. Adult predominantly white above and below; wings pale grey, entirely lacking black tips. Beak yellow with red spot near tip, large and strong (*see* Iceland). Eye-ring orange, visible at close range. Legs pink. Immature mottled, pale coffee brown, becoming almost pure white, including wings, in second year. At rest, folded wings barely reach tip of tail. Great Black-backed Gull-like profile and size aid separation from Iceland. *Voice:* similar to Herring, perhaps higher-pitched. *Habitat:* breeds colonially on cliffs and islands in Arctic. Winters coastally; occasionally inland. Scarce.

Great Black-backed Gull *Larus marinus* 68cm Largest European gull. Adult largely white, with black back and jet black wings, in flight showing conspicuous white trailing edge and white spots near tips of flight feathers. Beak yellow with red spot near tip, large and strong. Legs pale pink. Immature speckled brown and white; tail white with broad black terminal bar. Takes four years to reach adult plumage. Flight powerful, heavy. *Voice:* gruff 'kow-kow-kow'. *Habitat:* breeds on coastal islands and cliffs. Most maritime of large gulls, often wintering at sea; also commonly in coastal waters and inland, especially near refuse tips. Widespread.

Kittiwake *Rissa tridactyla* 40cm Medium-sized, slim-winged gull. Adult largely white, wings pale grey. Tips of flight feathers black, with no white patches. Beak lemon yellow with vermilion gape visible at close range, small. Legs distinctively black. Immature similar, but with blackish collar, black M-markings across wings and black-tipped, shallowly forked tail visible in flight. Wings characteristically long and slender; flight buoyant and tern-like. Gregarious. *Voice:* very vocal at colony; distinctive 'kitti-waaake' calls. *Habitat:* breeds colonially on sea cliffs; occasionally buildings. In winter, most well out to sea; some remain in inshore waters. Widespread; locally numerous.

Iceland Gull

Glaucous Gull

Great Black-backed Gull

Kittiwake

Gull-billed Tern *Gelochelidon nilotica* 38cm Medium-sized sea tern. Adult in summer predominantly white; crown black; back, rump and wings pale grey. Tail greyish-white, shallowly forked. Beak all-black, stout, relatively short (*see* Sandwich). Winter adult lacks dark cap. Immature back and crown brown-speckled grey, with brownish-grey streaks. *Voice:* rasping 'tzar-tzar-tzar' and deep 'kay-wreck'. *Habitat:* breeds colonially on sandy beaches and islands, normally close to sea. Hunts over sea, lagoons and saltpans, characteristically also over nearby fields. Uncommon.

Caspian Tern *Sterna caspia* 53cm Giant among terns. Summer adult white with black bristling cap, grey back and wings with dark grey tips. Tail white, shallowly forked. Beak strikingly coral red, large. Winter adult and immature have grey-flecked crowns and brownish-orange beaks. Enormous size and heavy gull-like flight are distinctive. *Voice:* deep, harsh, crow-like 'kraaa-uh' and 'kaaah'. *Habitat:* breeds in small colonies on beaches, usually close to salt water. On migration, over lagoons, coastal waters and occasionally inland. Scarce.

Sandwich Tern *Sterna sandvicensis* 40cm Medium-sized tern. Summer adult predominantly white, with grey wings and shaggy-crested black crown (*see* Gull-billed). Tail white, appreciably forked. Beak black with character-istic yellow tip, long; legs black. Winter adult has white forehead and grey-flecked crown. Immature similar to winter adult, but with grey-brown, scaly markings on back. Gregarious. *Voice:* characteristic, harsh, heavily disyllabic 'kay-wreck' and hurried 'kirrick'. *Habitat:* breeds in dense but notoriously mobile colonies on sandy beaches and islands; feeds at sea. Migrates through coastal waters. Reasonably common.

Roseate Tern *Sterna dougallii* 38cm Medium-sized, slim sea tern. Summer adult white, with pink on breast in spring. Wings grey; forked tail white, with extremely long streamers. Crown black. Beak characteristically black with blood red patch at base. Winter adult has white forehead. Immature greyer above, with grey-brown scaly markings and appreciably shorter tail streamers. Gregarious in breeding season. *Voice:* distinctive soft 'chee-vee' or chow-ick'. *Habitat:* breeds colonially, often with other terns, on sandy or pebbly beaches, or short grass in islands. Feeds offshore. Rare.

Common Tern *Sterna hirundo* 35cm Medium-sized sea tern. Summer adult predominantly white, with black cap and grey wings with appreciably darker tips (*see* Arctic). Tail white, deeply forked. Beak red with black tip; legs red. Winter adult has white forehead. Immature darker, with sandy grey markings on back and wings. Gregarious. *Voice:* harsh 'kee-aarh' with emphasis on second syllable; hurried 'kirri-kirri-kirri'. *Habitat:* breeds colonially on coastal beaches, islands, and inland on sand or gravel beside fresh water. Feeds over coastal lagoons, inshore waters and various inland fresh waters, especially on migration. Common.

Gull-billed Tern (winter)

Caspian Tern (summer)

Sandwich Tern

Roseate Tern (summer)

Common Tern (summer)

Arctic Tern *Sterna paradisaea* 37cm Medium-sized sea tern. Summer adult white, with black cap. Wings grey, distinctively pale and translucent near tips. Tail white, with long streamers. Beak entirely red (*see* Common). Legs red, very short. Winter adult has white forehead, dark beak and legs. Immature similar, but with sandy brown back and wing markings. *Voice:* short, sharp 'keee-ah', with emphasis on first syllable. *Habitat:* breeds colonially on beaches, islands and grassy areas near sea. Feeds at sea. On migration, only occasionally seen inland. Widespread; locally common. 🐟🐦

Little Tern *Sterna albifrons* 22cm Small, stubby sea tern. Adult white, with grey wings showing blackish tips. Crown black, forehead white; more extensive in winter. Beak characteristically yellow with black tip. Immature similar, but lacking bold head pattern, grey-brown marks on back and wings. Flight distinctively flickering. Gregarious. *Voice:* high-pitched 'kree-ik' and hurried 'kirri-kirri-kirrick'. *Habitat:* breeds on coastal beaches; occasionally inland. Feeds in shallow inshore seas and lagoons. Regular; nowhere numerous. 🐟🐦〰

Whiskered Tern *Chlidonias hybridus* 25cm Small, plump marsh tern. Summer adult grey above; black cap contrasts with distinctive white cheeks. Underparts ash grey, paler on belly. Tail pale grey, shallowly forked. Beak red, comparatively small; legs red. Winter adult pale grey above, white below, with dark grey crown and smudge around eye. Immature similar, but with white forehead and brownish markings on back and nape. *Voice:* rarely vocal; croaks and rasping calls. *Habitat:* breeds colonially on freshwater swamps and marshes. On migration, usually over freshwater areas; occasionally sheltered salt waters. Only locally common. 🐟🐦〰

Black Tern *Chlidonias niger* 25cm Small, dark marsh tern. Summer adult largely dark sooty grey above and below; head, breast and belly jet black. Tail dark grey, shallowly forked. Beak and legs black. Winter adult grey above, white below, with dark crown, white forehead and black 'half-collar' marks on shoulders. Immature similar to winter adult, but browner. Characteristic flight, dipping down to water surface to feed. Gregarious. *Voice:* rarely vocal; occasional 'krit' or kreek'. *Habitat:* breeds colonially on swamps and marshes. On migration, coastal and frequently inland. Regular; locally common. 🐟🐦〰

White-winged Black Tern *Chlidonias leucopterus* 25cm Small marsh tern. Summer adult unmistakable; greyish-white above, with head, breast and belly jet black. Tail pale grey, shallowly forked. Upperside of wings almost white; underside black, except for pale flight feathers. Beak and legs dark red. Winter adult largely greyish-white; crown and back blackish; wings dark grey. Lacks collar marks (*see* Black). Immature similar, but brownish-grey. Flight as Black. Gregarious. *Voice:* rarely vocal; occasional 'kit' or 'kreek'. *Habitat:* breeds colonially on freshwater lakes and marshes. On migration, both coastal and inland waters. Only locally common. 🐟🐦〰

Arctic Tern (summer)

Little Tern (summer)

Whiskered Tern (summer)

Black Tern (summer)

White-winged Black Tern (winter)

Guillemot *Uria aalge* 40cm Medium-sized auk. Summer adult chocolate brown above (northern birds almost black); white below. Some ('bridled' form, commoner in north) have white eye-ring and stripe behind eye. Beak long, dagger-shaped; legs grey. Winter adult and immature similar, but grey, not brown. Whirring flight low over sea, showing white trailing edge to wing. Long and low-bodied while swimming; stance upright on cliffs. Dives frequently. Gregarious. *Voice:* vocal during breeding season; various 'cooing' and 'mooing' calls. *Habitat:* breeds colonially on sea cliff ledges. Winters in coastal seas. Locally common. ✿

Razorbill *Alca torda* 40cm Medium-sized auk. Summer adult jet black above; strikingly white below. Beak black with white vertical line near tip, large and deep. White line on face from eye to base of beak. Bold, white wingbar, conspicuous in flight, as is white trailing edge to wing. Winter adult and immature similar, but greyer. *Voice:* gruff growl, usually only on breeding grounds. *Habitat:* breeds on rock-strewn sea cliffs. Winters in coastal seas. Locally fairly common. ✿

Black Guillemot *Cepphus grylle* 33cm Medium-sized auk. Summer adult unmistakable; largely velvet black, except for striking white wing patch. Beak black with vermilion lining; legs striking vermilion. Winter adult and immature almost photographic negative of this; flecked grey above, white below, but with blackish wings retaining white patch. Often solitary. *Voice:* strange, bell-like twittering. *Habitat:* rocky shores and adjacent seas year-round. Local; rarely numerous. ✿

Puffin *Fratercula arctica* 30cm Medium-sized auk. Summer adult unmistakable; black above, white below, with large white face patch and huge parrot-like beak coloured grey-blue, yellow and red. Legs and feet bright orange-red. Winter adult and immature drabber, with smoky grey face patch and much smaller, dark beak. Flight whirring, low over sea; characteristically lacks white wingbar. Gregarious. *Voice:* low growls in breeding season. *Habitat:* breeds on coastal cliffs, screes and clifftop grassland, often in large colonies. Most winter out at sea; some remain inshore. Locally common. ✿

Little Auk *Alle alle* 20cm Small, dumpy auk. Summer adult velvet black above, with black head and neck. Wings black, with fine white streaks. Beak black, small and stubby; legs black. Winter adult and immature greyish-black above; sides of face, throat, breast and belly white. Gregarious in summer. *Voice:* vocal only near colonies: shrill, chattering calls. *Habitat:* breeds in immense colonies on Arctic cliffs. Most winter far out to sea; only occasionally close to land. Scarce away from breeding grounds. ✿

Guillemot (summer)

Razorbill (summer)

Black Guillemot (summer)

Puffin (summer)

Little Auk (summer)

Rock Dove *Columba livia* 33cm Medium-sized pigeon. Adult and immature uniformly soft dove grey above and below, adult with metallic sheen on many of feathers of nape of neck, absent in immature. In flight, shows diagnostic white rump patch, and two black bars in rounded wings. Beak dark, short; legs reddish. Flight swift and direct. Gregarious. *Voice:* purring and cooing, often prolonged. *Habitat:* remote rocky coasts and caves; mountainous areas. Local. Ancestor to widespread feral pigeons of town centres.

Stock Dove *Columba oenas* 33cm Medium-sized farmland and woodland pigeon. Adult and immature uniformly dull leaden grey above and below. Adults have greenish metallic sheen on nape and pinkish flush to breast. In flight, shows distinctive black border to wing, with two indistinct, irregular black wingbars. Rump grey. Flight swift and direct. Beak dark, short; legs reddish. Gregarious. *Voice:* booming 'coo-ooh', particularly in spring. *Habitat:* nests in holes on farmland and woodland; occasionally on coasts. Widespread; locally common.

Woodpigeon *Columba palumbus* 40cm Large, cumbersome pigeon. Adult and immature delicate grey-brown above; paler dove grey below. Adult has metallic sheen on nape and conspicuous white collar patches, lacking in immature. Beak dark pink, short; legs pinkish. In flight, white crescentic wingbars are striking and diagnostic. Flight fast but clumsy. Gregarious. *Voice:* distinctive 'coo-*coo*-coo, coo-coo'. *Habitat:* breeds in woodland and scrub; feeds in woodland, on all types of farmland and in urban areas. Widespread; often common.

Turtle Dove *Streptopelia turtur* 28cm Medium-small pigeon. Adult rich bronze, mottled with brown and black on back and wings; head and neck grey. Underparts pinkish-buff, shading to white on belly. Adult has chequered black and white collar patches. Immature duller and browner, lacking collars. Wings dark-tipped; tail blackish, with diagnostic narrow white border visible in flight (*see* Collared). Flight swift and direct. Gregarious. *Voice:* distinctive and prolonged purring. *Habitat:* woodland, farmland with hedges, scrub. Widespread; fairly common.

Collared Dove *Streptopelia decaocto* 28cm Medium-small, sandy-coloured pigeon. Adult and immature back and wings sandy brown; head, neck, breast and belly appreciably paler pinkish-buff. In flight, wings show dark tips and conspicuous blue-grey forewing patches. Tail brown with broad white terminal band striking in flight. Black and white, continuous, crescentic collar band distinctive in adult, lacking in immature. Gregarious. *Voice:* in flight, dry 'aaah'; strident 'coo-*coo*-coo'. *Habitat:* farmland, parks, urban areas. Widespread; common.

Stock Dove

Stock Dove

Woodpigeon

Turtle Dove

Collared Dove

Black-bellied Sandgrouse *Pterocles orientalis* 35cm
Medium-sized, short-legged, pigeon-like game bird. Adult
male sandy buff above, with darker markings; head
buffish-grey, throat chestnut. Underparts largely grey-buff,
but with characteristic narrow black breast band and
striking black belly. Beak stubby; legs very short. Female
and immature sandy brown with heavy mottling; speckled
band across breast; belly blackish. In flight, swift and
direct, often in flocks, showing dark wingtips and black
belly. *Voice:* 'churr-urr-urr'. *Habitat:* arid grassland,
marshes and steppes. Extremely localized.

Pin-tailed Sandgrouse *Pterocles alchata* 33cm Pale,
medium-sized, pigeon-like game bird. Adult male mottled
bronze, browns and buffs above, with contrasting pale
brown head, dark chin and greenish-buff neck. Breast
band pale chestnut, edged black above and below.
Underparts white (*see* Black-bellied). Female and
immature paler, and lacking dark throat. Swift and direct in
flight, often in flocks. Uniformly brownish wings and long,
slender, pointed tail characteristic in flight. *Voice:*
hiccoughing 'catarr, catarr' in flight. *Habitat:* arid
grasslands. Extremely localized.

Cuckoo *Cuculus canorus* 33cm Slim and long-tailed, like a
medium-sized falcon. Adult and immature dove grey
above; head and neck grey. Long tail blackish, with white
bars on underside visible at close range. Underparts
white, finely barred grey. Rare rufous form (female and
immature only) has rich brown upperparts. Beak black
with yellow at base, short; legs yellow, short. *Voice:*
characteristic 'cuck-oo' and variants; female bubbling trill;
male rasping chuckle. *Habitat:* woodland, farmland, heath,
scrub, moorland and marshes. Widespread; often
numerous.

Great Spotted Cuckoo *Clamator glandarius* 40cm
Large, boldly marked cuckoo. Adult largely brown above,
boldly marked with white. Head darker brown, with greyish
crest often conspicuous. Long tail brown on upper
surface, conspicuously barred with white on underside.
Throat white; rest of underparts pale creamy white.
Immature similar, but with russet-shaded underparts and
chestnut wings conspicuous in flight. Lacks crest. Eye red;
beak dark, yellow at base. Legs grey, short. *Voice:* harsh,
rasping shriek. *Habitat:* dry woodland, farmland and olive
groves (often parasitizes Magpies and Azure-winged
Magpies). Regular; rarely numerous.

Black-bellied Sandgrouse ♂

Pin-tailed Sandgrouse ♂

Cuckoo

Great Spotted Cuckoo

Barn Owl *Tyto alba* 35cm Well-known, pale medium-sized owl. Adult and immature pale sandy brown above, delicately flecked with brown, grey and white. Underparts white in birds from north-western Europe, including Britain and Ireland; rich buff, even almost chestnut, in birds from western and southern Europe. Facial disc white, characteristically heart-shaped. Eyes dark brown, large. Stance upright; legs long and 'knock-kneed'. Wings relatively long, appearing very pale in flight. Usually nocturnal; in winter, may hunt in daylight. *Voice:* various snoring noises when roosting; occasional strident shriek at other times. *Habitat:* open woodland, farmland, heaths, villages. Widespread; nowhere numerous.

Scops Owl *Otus scops* 20cm Small, secretive owl. Adult and immature uniformly brown, occurring in two colour phases; one reddish-tinged, the other greyish. Plumage finely marked with grey, white and buff. Head shape distinctive, with short, upright 'ear' tufts. Oblong facial disc pale grey. Eyes bright yellow, with dark pupil. Always roosts well-concealed in daylight; hunts at night. *Voice:* penetrating, repetitive and monotonous 'peeuu'. *Habitat:* open woodland, town parks and gardens, olive groves. Widespread.

Eagle Owl *Bubo bubo* 68cm Huge, the bulkiest European owl. Adult and immature rich chestnut brown, darker above than below, and copiously marked with fine darker streaks and bars. Throat pale buff. Facial disc poorly defined, brownish; eyes strikingly orange, with dark pupils. 'Ear' tufts long and conspicuous. Wings dark brown, long and broad in flight, giving Eagle Owl a massive appearance. Largely nocturnal. *Voice:* reverberating 'boo-hoo'. *Habitat:* extensive forests and woodland. Scarce.

Snowy Owl *Nyctea scandiaca* 60cm Huge, unmistakable and spectacular owl. Adult male almost entirely white, with delicate sparse brown flecking. Larger female white; barred and streaked, often copiously, with dark brown on back, and to lesser extent on breast and belly. Facial disc poorly defined; eyes golden, with dark pupil. Stance upright; often perches in open. Wings long and broad, largely white, making bird very conspicuous in flight. Often hunts in daylight. *Voice:* rarely vocal. *Habitat:* breeds on tundra. Winters on open lands. Numbers very variable, dependent on lemming populations. Irregular and scarce.

Barn Owl (pale-breasted)

Barn Owl (dark-breasted)

Scops Owl

Eagle Owl

Snowy Owl ♂

Hawk Owl *Surnia ulula* 38cm Medium-sized, daylight-hunting owl. Adult and immature brownish above, with copious paler spots and streaks. Underparts largely whitish, with grey-brown barring. Oblong facial disc white, with distinctive bold black margin; eyes golden, with black pupil. Long tail conspicuous in flight and when perched, giving silhouette like large-headed hawk. Often perches conspicuously on tree-tops, cocking tail like clumsy, gigantic Wren. Wings comparatively short and rounded; flight hawk-like. *Voice:* rapid series of abrupt whistles. *Habitat:* northern birch and conifer forests. Locally fairly common. ●🌲🌲◣

Pygmy Owl *Glaucidium passerinum* 17cm Very small but aggressive owl. Adult and immature brownish above, with white spots and streaks. Underparts whitish, with dense dark brown streaking. Stance upright, showing relatively small, rounded head. Facial disc pale, with series of concentric fine dark rings around yellow eyes. Whitish 'eyebrows' visible at close range. Often hunts in daylight, choosing conspicuous perches and jerking tail up and down. Wings relatively short and rounded; flight deeply undulating. *Voice:* ascending series of whistles. *Habitat:* conifer forests. Locally fairly common. ●🌲🌲

Little Owl *Athene noctua* 23cm Small, bold owl, often seen in daylight. Adult and immature grey-brown above, with bold white spots and streaks. Underparts whitish or greyish-buff, heavily streaked with dark brown. Head comparatively large, flat-crowned. Oblong facial disc greyish with paler margin; eyes bright yellow, with dark pupils. Stance squat but upright; often perches on posts; bobs occasionally if approached. Flight undulating on short, conspicuously rounded wings. Hunts during evening and at night. *Voice:* various puppy-like yelps; penetrating 'poo-oop'. *Habitat:* woodland, farmland, heaths, surburban areas; occasionally coasts. Widespread; locally fairly common. 🚜🌊●🌲🌲🏜

Tawny Owl *Strix aluco* 38cm Medium-sized, round-headed owl. Adult and immature brown above, quite frequently rich chestnut, occasionally almost grey; with fine black streaks and bold buff blotches. Underparts buffish-brown, finely marked with darker brown. Head large, conspicuously rounded. Roughly circular facial disc grey-buff with narrow black border. Eyes large, all-dark. Nocturnal hunter, markedly round-winged in flight. Secretive during day, when whereabouts are often revealed by flocks of agitated small birds. *Voice:* well-know, tremulous 'hoo-hoo-hoooo' and sharp 'kew-wit'. *Habitat:* woodland, farmland, urban areas. Widespread: the commonest owl. 🚜🏙●🌲🌲

Hawk Owl

Pygmy Owl

Little Owl

Tawny Owl

Ural Owl *Strix uralensis* 60cm Huge northern owl. Adult and immature resemble giant Tawny, but with uniformly pale grey-brown plumage, marked with darker streaks. Head rounded; roughly circular facial disc buff, with faint darker markings. Eyes all-dark, comparatively small. Stance upright; often hunts in daylight, flying on broad, medium-length wings. *Voice:* low-pitched 'how-how-how'. *Habitat:* coniferous and mixed forests; occasionally mountain areas. Rare. ♠♣

Great Grey Owl *Strix nebulosa* 68cm Huge, round-headed owl. Adult and immature grey-brown above, finely marked with brown, buff and black. Underparts grey-buff, with bold dark streaking. Head comparatively large, almost spherical; almost circular facial disc marked with concentric grey rings, and with white crescent on each side of beak. Eyes yellow with dark pupil, comparatively small. *Voice:* low-pitched, booming 'hoo'. *Habitat:* northern coniferous forests. Uncommon. ♣♣

Long-eared Owl *Asio otus* 35cm Slim, long-winged, medium-sized owl. Adult and immature rich brown above, finely marked with black, brown and buff, producing immaculate camouflage against tree trunk. Underparts rich buff, with bold dark brown streaks. Head rounded; conspicuous 'ear' tufts. Roughly circular facial disc orange-brown with black border. Eyes strikingly golden or flame-coloured, with black pupils. Stance upright; often slim. In flight, shows relatively long wings with dark patch at 'wrist'. In winter, may roost communally. *Voice:* relatively silent; in breeding season, series of deep 'poop' calls. *Habitat:* woodland, more often coniferous than deciduous. Widespread; never numerous. ♠♣♣♣

Short-eared Owl *Asio flammeus* 38cm Medium-sized open-country owl. Adult and immature sandy brown above, with brown and buff markings; paler below, heavily marked with dark brown streaks. Head rounded; inconspicuous 'ear' tufts. Roughly circular facial disc, pale buff with dark border and dark brown patches surrounding yellow eyes. Stance horizontal and harrier-like. Characteristically hunts in daylight, flying low over open ground; bouncing flight alternates with glides. Shows pale undersides to wings, with conspicuous dark 'wrist' patches. *Voice:* rarely vocal. *Habitat:* open country; usually tundra, moorland or marshes. Widespread; erratic in distribution and numbers. ♠♣♣♣

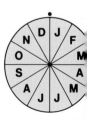

Tengmalm's Owl *Aegolius funereus* 25cm Smallish, northern owl. Adult rich brown above, with bold grey-buff spots; greyish-white below, with dark brown streaking. Head rounded; facial disc roughly rectangular, whitish with distinctive raised dark 'eyebrows'; eyes yellow, with dark pupils. Stance squat and upright. Largely nocturnal. *Voice:* repetitive, short whistle. *Habitat:* forest and woodland, favouring conifers. Numbers and distribution variable, depending on availablity of prey; sometimes locally fairly common. ▲♣♣

Ural Owl

Great Grey Owl

Long-eared Owl

Short-eared Owl

Tengmalm's Owl

Nightjar *Caprimulgus europaeus* 28cm Medium-sized, hawk-like, but difficult to see. Adult and immature rich reddish-brown above and below; distinctively and beautifully mottled with browns, greys and buffs, producing excellent camouflage against a branch, or dead leaves on the woodland floor. Small white patches on sides of neck. Male has white patches near wingtips, and at tip of each side of tail. Beak tiny, eyes large. Often seen at dusk, hunting for insects in strangely silent flight, when hawk-like silhouette is characteristic. *Voice:* characteristic, long drawn-out churring, augmented by wing-claps in display. *Habitat:* heaths, open woodland and scrub. Widespread; only locally common. **Red-necked Nightjar** *C. ruficollis* is very similar, but has sides of face, chin and throat rufous, with pinkish-buff crescentic band round throat. *Voice:* characteristic series of 'ker-chek' calls. *Habitat:* restricted to dry scrub in southern Spain and Portugal. ♦♠♠➤➤

Swift *Apus apus* 18cm Small, with characteristic sickle-shaped wings. Adult sooty black above and below, except greyish-white throat visible at close range. Immature dull grey, with pale grey scaly markings. Beak and legs tiny; eyes large and dark. Wings distinctively long and narrow, sickle-shaped; flight fast and character-istically flickering. Tail short, shallowly forked. Often gregarious. Highly mobile bird, spending much of its life on the wing. *Voice:* shrill, very high-pitched scream. *Habitat:* breeds colonially in urban areas; feeds over almost any habitat. Widespread; locally common. **Pallid Swift** *A. pallidus*, relatively common around Mediterr-anean cliffs, mountains and towns, is very similar, but browner and with large pale throat patch. Flight slower and silhouette stockier, with larger head, than Swift. ▲♠♨➤➤

Alpine Swift *Apus melba* 20cm Appreciably larger than Swift, with pied plumage. Adult sandy brown above; predominantly white below, but with broad brown breast band. Immature similar, but with pale, scaly markings on back. Wings characteristically long, powerfully sickle-shaped; flight stronger and faster even than Swift. Tail dark, shallowly forked. Gregarious. *Voice:* surprisingly loud, musical trill. *Habitat:* mountain areas; also coastal cliffs and towns. Breeds colonially. Locally common. ▲♠➤➤

Nightjar

Nightjar

Swift

Alpine Swift

Kingfisher *Alcedo atthis* 17cm Small but unmistakable. Adult electric blue-green above; dark blue crown, with paler blue flecks. Cheeks chestnut and white. Underparts bright chestnut. Immature slightly duller, with heavily flecked crown. Beak all-black or showing some red at base, long, dagger-shaped. Legs and feet bright scarlet and tiny. Dumpy silhouette with oversized beak and head, and arrow-like flight on whirring wings low over water, are characteristic. *Voice:* shrill, ringing 'cheet'. *Habitat:* lakes, rivers and streams; occasionally coasts in winter. Widespread.

Bee-eater *Merops apiaster* 28cm Medium-sized, swallow-like and unmistakable. No other European bird possesses such dazzling array of plumage colours. Adult and immature green, chestnut, gold and white above; yellow, black and turquoise blue below. Tail long, with extended central tail feathers in adult. Beak dark, long and downcurved. Legs short. Flight swooping and agile. Gregarious. *Voice:* in flight, characteristic, bell-like 'prewit'. *Habitat:* open, dry country: breeds in holes in sandy banks; often feeds over lakes and marshes. Only locally common.

Roller *Coracias garrulus* 30cm Medium-large and unmistakable, especially in flight. Adult back chestnut; head, neck and underparts blue. Wings dark brown, with electric blue patches strikingly obvious in flight. Tail dark blue above, bright blue below. Immature resembles much greyer, drabber version of adult. Characteristic tumbling display flight. Often perches conspicuously on posts or overhead wires. *Voice:* harsh 'kraak'. *Habitat:* open bushy or scrub country; farmland. Fairly widespread; rarely numerous.

Hoopoe *Upupa epops* 28cm Medium-sized, with unmis-takable fawn and pied plumage. Adult and immature head, neck and breast unusual and characteristic pinkish sandy fawn; belly white. Long, black-tipped, pale ginger crest on head, erected into fan when excited or alarmed. Back and wings boldly barred black and white; tail black, with white bar. Beak dark, long, slender and downcurved. Legs short. Flight characteristically flopping. *Voice:* characteristic, far-carrying, repetitive 'poo-poo-poo'. *Habitat:* open country with trees and scrub, orchards, olive groves. Widespread; rarely numerous.

Kingfisher

Bee-eater

Roller

Hoopoe

ORIENTAL ACCIDENTALS (see page 26)

Sharp-tailed Sandpiper *Calidris acuminata* 18cm
Relatively large, slightly angular wader. Summer adult
rich brown above. Crown dark; pale stripe over eye. Neck
grey-brown, streaked; shading to buff on breast, with
bold V-shaped markings. Winter adult duller, greyer;
breast greyish, faintly streaked. Immature as summer
adult; lacks V-shaped markings. *Voice:* twittering 'teet-
trrt'. *Habitat:* breeds on Siberian tundra; migrates to
coastal marshes in Australasia.

Spur-winged Plover *Hoplopterus spinosus* 27cm
Strikingly plumaged, Lapwing-sized plover. Adult back
and wings brownish; crown and nape jet black,
contrasting white cheeks and sides to throat. Centre of
throat, breast, flanks jet black; undertail white. Immature
duller. In flight, brown, white and black upper wing
patterning characteristic. *Voice:* metallic 'tick'; repetitive
'did-ee-do-it'. *Habitat:* northern African marshes.

White-breasted Kingfisher *Halcyon smyrnensis* 28cm
Large, strikingly coloured kingfisher. Adult mantle, rump
and tail iridescent blue; darker blue wings show brown
shoulders when perched and in flight. Head bright
chocolate; throat, front of neck and much of breast white;
flanks and belly chocolate. Beak scarlet, relatively
massive, dagger-shaped. *Voice:* far-carrying, distinctive
laugh. *Habitat:* fresh and coastal waters throughout Asia;
now breeds in far south-eastern Europe.

Citrine Wagtail *Motacilla citreola* 18cm Wagtail with
diagnostic yellow head. Summer adult male back
greenish-grey; wings blackish, broad white feather
margins; tail black, white outer feathers, long. Nape
black; rest of head and underparts rich sulphur yellow.
Female and winter male similar to Yellow, but have
double white wingbar and yellow forehead. *Voice:*
'sweep'. *Habitat:* grassland, tundra and marsh in Russia
and Asia.

Blyth's Reed Warbler *Acrocephalus dumetorum* 13cm
Small, unstreaked warbler. Adult similar to Marsh; pale
olive green above, whitish stripe over eye; whitish below,
flanks shaded buff. Greyish legs darker than Marsh,
wings relatively shorter. *Voice:* 'check' and chack' calls;
song melodious, with mimicry. Tempo measured; regular
pauses, unlike Marsh's babble. *Habitat:* scrub, dense
undergrowth in far north-eastern Europe.

Pallas's Warbler *Phylloscopus proregulus* 10cm Tiny,
pale-rumped leaf warbler. Adult predominantly greenish-
olive above; dark mark through eye; characteristically
three yellowish stripes along crown, and yellowish rump
patch. Dark brownish wings show two yellowish-white
bars. Underparts white; legs brown. Immature similar, but
yellower. Active, Goldcrest-like warbler, often feeding in
canopy. *Voice:* high-pitched, distinctive 'tweet'. *Habitat:*
coniferous or mixed woodland in eastern Asia. Amazingly,
in some years, dozens reach western Europe.

Sharp-tailed Sandpiper (winter)

Spur-winged Plover

White-breasted Kingfisher

Citrine Wagtail

Blyth's Reed Warbler

Pallas's Warbler

Wryneck *Jynx torquilla* 18cm Small, drab and elongated, and though related to woodpeckers untypical of them in its camouflaged plumage and in its soft tail feathers. Adult and immature brown above, finely mottled and streaked with black and fawn, with characteristic, buff V-marking. Underparts pale buff, with brownish barring. Tail long, brown with dark barring; not stiff, as in other woodpeckers. Beak black, short, strong. Often feeds on ground. *Voice:* persistent laughing 'kee-kee-kee'. *Habitat:* open land with old trees. Widespread; inconspicuous. ᴪ♦♣❈▩

Black Woodpecker *Dryocopus martius* 45cm Largest, most striking European woodpecker. Adult and immature unmistakable; glossy, all-black plumage relieved only by bright, golden eye and crimson crown, more extensive in male than female. Tail appears relatively long in flight, which is deeply undulating. Beak grey with black tip. *Voice:* harsh 'klee-oh'; also drums often and loudly. *Habitat:* large tracts of old forest with mature trees, both deciduous and coniferous. Locally fairly common. ♦♣❈

Green Woodpecker *Picus viridis* 30cm Medium-sized woodpecker. Adult strikingly green and gold above; greenish-grey below, with darker barring on flanks. Crown and nape red in both sexes; striking moustachial streaks black in female, red and black in male. Beak grey with black tip, relatively long; Immature paler, with reddish crown; heavily buff-spotted on upperparts, and barred on breast and flanks. Often feeds on ground. Flight deeply undulating; gold rump conspicuous. *Voice:* characteristic ringing laugh, 'yah-yah-yah'; drums relatively rarely. *Habitat:* open, dry grassland, heath, scrub and deciduous woodland. Widespread. ᴪ♦♣❈▩

Grey-headed Woodpecker *Picus canus* 25cm Medium-sized woodpecker. Adult predominantly green above, with yellowish rump and browner wings and tail. Underparts uniformly pale grey. Head grey; scarlet forehead patch only in male. Moustachial streak black in both sexes. Immature resembles female, but drabber; scaly markings on breast. Flight deeply undulating. *Voice:* gradually diminishing laugh; drums frequently (*see* Green). *Habitat:* open, deciduous or mixed forest. Widespread; never numerous. ▲ᴪ♦❈▩

Wryneck

Black Woodpecker

Green Woodpecker

Grey-headed Woodpecker

Great Spotted Woodpecker *Dendrocopos major* 23cm
Smallish pied woodpecker. Adult barred boldly in black
and white on upperparts. Forehead white, crown and
neck black (with scarlet nape patch only in male); white
cheeks and patches on sides of neck. Underparts
whitish, with extensive area of red beneath tail. Immature
greyer; crown and tail scarlet. Flight undulating, showing
bold barring across back and striking white wing
patches. Beak black, short, stout. *Voice:* explosive 'kek'
or 'chack'; drums often. *Habitat:* all types of woodland,
urban parks, gardens, farmland with large trees.
Widespread; often common. 🚜🏭🌷🌲🌿

Syrian Woodpecker *Dendrocopos syriacus* 23cm
Smallish pied woodpecker. Adult and immature closely
resemble appropriate ages and sexes of Great Spotted.
Distinguishing features are that white cheeks and sides of
nape merge, giving paler-headed appearance, and are
separated from white throat by narrow black moustachial
streak. Feathers beneath tail pinkish, not bright red.
Voice: harsh 'chack'; drums frequently. *Habitat:* open
woodland and parkland. Locally fairly common.
🚜🏭🌷🌲🌿

Middle Spotted Woodpecker *Dendrocopos medius*
20cm Smallish pied woodpecker. Adult and immature
generally similar to Syrian, but Middle Spotted has
completely red crown and much shorter black moustachial streaks in all plumages. Underparts pale buff, tinged
pink and streaked with brown on flanks; undertail pinkish.
Voice: distinctive, guttural 'gate-gate-gate' calls; drums
relatively rarely. *Habitat:* favours high limbs in mature
deciduous woodland and forest. Locally fairly common.
🚜🏭🌷🌲🌿

Lesser Spotted Woodpecker *Dendrocopos minor* 15cm
Sparrow-sized, smallest European Spotted Woodpecker.
Adult and immature predominantly black above, with
ladder-like white barring across back. Lacks white wing
patches. Head pattern distinctive: nape black, forehead
white; male crown red, immature reddish, female white.
Underparts, including undertail, whitish, sparsely
streaked. *Voice:* distinctive, repetitive, shrill 'kee-kee-kee';
drumming frequent and high-pitched. *Habitat:* deciduous
woodland, parks, orchards, olive groves. Widespread.
🚜🏭🌷🌲🌿

Three-toed Woodpecker *Picoides tridactylus* 23cm
Smallish, northern pied woodpecker. Adult and immature
predominantly blackish above; back white between dark
wings, particularly conspicuous in flight as wing barring is
not as striking as in other Spotted Woodpeckers, and as
white wing patches are absent. Head dark, with narrow
white streaks down nape and sides of throat. Male crown
characteristically yellow; female and immature speckled
black and white. Underparts greyish, barred densely
brown on flanks. Flight typically fast and direct. *Voice:*
harsh 'chack'; rarely drums. *Habitat:* birch and conifer
woodland. Unusual. 🏔🌷🌲🌿

Great Spotted Woodpecker ♀

Syrian Woodpecker ♂

Middle Spotted Woodpecker ♂

Lesser Spotted Woodpecker ♂

Three-toed Woodpecker ♀

Calandra Lark *Melanocorypha calandra* 20cm One of the largest larks. Adult and immature predominantly sandy brown above, richly marked with grey-buff and darker brown; whitish below, with conspicuous broad blackish band across upper breast, indistinct in immature. Beak brownish, relatively long and heavy. In flight, wings characteristically look almost black, with striking white trailing edge. Tail dark brown, with white outer feathers. *Voice:* song musical, extended, with much mimicry; call wheezy 'chirrup'. *Habitat:* arid farmland and stony rough ground. Locally common.

Short-toed Lark *Calandrella brachydactyla* 13cm Tiny, pale lark. Adult and immature pale sandy brown above, mottled with rufous brown. Underparts predominantly whitish, except for often inconspicuous dark grey smudge on each side of base of neck. Beak pale buff, short and stubby; legs pinkish. In flight, dark, almost black tail with white outer feathers conspicuous. *Voice:* call sparrow-like 'chirrup'; song higher-pitched and simpler than Skylark, produced in characteristically erratic, bouncing song-flight. *Habitat:* arid, open landscapes. Locally common.

Lesser Short-toed Lark *Calandrella rufescens* 13cm Tiny, dark lark. Adult and immature similar in build to Short-toed, but plumage is appreciably darker grey-brown above, with paler feather edges. Underparts whitish; throat, breast and flanks heavily streaked with brown. Beak pale, stubby; legs pinkish. In flight, dark tail with white outer feathers conspicuous. *Voice:* call abrupt 'prritt'; song rich and varied, produced in circling song-flight (*see* Short-toed). *Habitat:* arid open ground, especially dry mudflats and saltpans. Only locally common.

Crested Lark *Galerida cristata* 17cm Typical lark with striking crest. Adult and immature rich fawn above, tinged chestnut and with brown streaking; pale buffish-white below, throat and breast finely streaked with dark brown. Long, brown, dark-streaked crest on crown often held erect. Beak brownish, relatively long; legs pale brown. In flight, brown tail with striking sandy chestnut outer feathers. *Voice:* call characteristic 'doo-dee-doo'; song similar to Skylark, but usually produced from ground. *Habitat:* open land, farms, roadside verges, often near towns. Common; strangely, extremely rare in Britain and Ireland.

Calandra Lark

Short-toed Lark

Lesser Short-toed Lark

Crested Lark

Skylark *Alauda arvensis* 18cm The typical lark. Adult and immature buffish-brown above; back and wings richer chestnut brown, all feathers with dark centres and pale fringes. Head pale buff, with dark brown streaks; short crest raised when excited. Pale buff eye-stripe extending as pale margin to cheek patch. Underparts pale buff, heavily streaked brown on breast. Wings dark brown, flight feathers blackish. Tail blackish, with white trailing edge visible in flight. Beak pale brown, stout; legs pinkish-brown. *Voice:* call liquid 'chirrup'; song characteristic, produced in song-flight hovering or circling high above ground, musical, varied and extended, containing much mimicry of other birds. *Habitat:* open farmland, marshes, moors, heaths and mountains. Often abundant.
▲ ➤ ▓ ☷ ◣ ▦

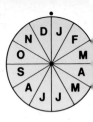

Woodlark *Lullula arborea* 15cm Small short-tailed lark. Adult and immature rich brown above, with chestnut and buff markings. Crown chestnut with fine black streaks; conspicuous pale buff eye-stripe over characteristic chestnut cheek patch. Underparts pale buff, streaked brown on breast. Tail short, chestnut brown with buff outer feathers. *Voice:* call 'tee-loo-ee'; song produced in spiralling song-flight, similar to Skylark, but rich in 'loo-loo-loo' phrases. *Habitat:* open woodland and heaths, occasionally in mountain regions. Widespread; locally common. ➤ ♦ ♠ ♣ ▦

Shore Lark *Eremophila alpestris* 18cm Scarce lark with striking head pattern. Adult predominantly pale sandy brown above, very lightly marked with darker browns. Summer head pattern characteristic; face and throat yellow; black stripe on forehead and sides of crown, ending in short, pointed crests. Black patch running from beak to below and behind eye; black 'bib' on upper breast. Beak and legs black. Winter adult and immature head and breast have poorly-defined blackish speckled pattern. In flight, shows uniformly brown wings; tail pale brown with white outer feathers. *Voice:* pipit-like 'see-ee'; song produced in flight high-pitched, repetitive, rather feeble and simple version of Skylark's. *Habitat:* breeds on Arctic tundra. Winters on coastal marshes and farmland. Scarce. ▲ ➤ ▓ ◣

Skylark

Skylark

Woodlark

Shore Lark

Sand Martin *Riparia riparia* 12cm Tiny hirundine. Adult and immature sandy brown above, immature with pale feather fringes giving scaly appearance; whitish below, with characteristic brown band across breast. Tail brown, short, shallowly forked. Beak and legs black, tiny; eyes relatively large. Spends much time on wing. Gregarious. *Voice:* soft, rattling trill; sharp 'chirrup' alarm call. *Habitat:* breeds colonially in sandy banks, often feeds by hawking over nearby fresh waters. Widespread; locally numerous.

Crag Martin *Ptyonoprogne rupestris* 15cm Small, dark hirundine. Adult and immature grey-brown above, shading to dull greyish-white below; immature often has scaly appearance. Broader in wing and heavier-built than Sand. Tail blackish, hardly forked at all; white spots near tip visible at close range. Gregarious. *Voice:* rarely vocal. *Habitat:* rocky sea cliffs, mountain gorges and occasionally towns and cities. Locally fairly common.

Swallow *Hirundo rustica* 20cm The typical small hirundine. Adult and immature dark glossy blue-black over much of upperparts; dark chestnut face patch and white spots on tail conspicuous in flight. Underparts predominantly white. In flight, shows slender, curved wings, slim silhouette and long, deeply forked tail with narrow streamers; tail longer in adult than immature, and longer in male than female. Flight swift, swooping; feeds on wing. *Voice:* prolonged, musical twittering; call sharp 'chirrup'. *Habitat:* breeds in buildings on farmland and in urban areas; feeds over most habitats. Common.

Red-rumped Swallow *Hirundo daurica* 18cm Small hirundine. Adult and immature have characteristic pattern on upperparts; crown, back, wings and tail dark blackish-blue, interrupted by chestnut-buff nape and diagnostic, large, pale chestnut rump patch. Tail long, deeply forked. Underparts whitish, tinged buff. More like House Martin than Swallow in silhouette; distinguished by long forked tail. *Voice:* scolding chatter of alarm; song melodious twittering. *Habitat:* open, rocky and dry country, often nesting under bridges and culverts. Local.

House Martin *Delichon urbica* 12cm Tiny pied hirundine. Adult glossy blue-black above, with rather duller, blackish flight feathers and diagnostic bold white rump patch. Tail blue-black, shallowly forked. Underparts white. Legs and toes feathered and white, visible when collecting mud for nest. Immature greyer; lacking iridescent sheen. Gregarious. *Voice:* unmusical, rattling twitter. *Habitat:* nests colonially on buildings, often in towns, occasionally on cliffs; feeds over open land and fresh waters. Widespread; often numerous.

Sand Martin

Crag Martin

Swallow

Red-rumped Swallow

House Martin

Richard's Pipit *Anthus novaeseelandiae* 18cm Large, dark, long-legged pipit. Adult and immature brown above, broadly streaked with black. Head darker brown, with pale stripe over eye and distinct, dark cheek patch. Underparts predominantly buffish-white; throat and breast boldly streaked with black. Tail dark, with whitish outer feathers, relatively long. Legs pale brown, long. *Voice:* characteristic harsh 'rrripp'. *Habitat:* marshy grassland and steppes; rice paddies. On passage, often in wet habitats. Scarce. 🦆🌿🦆

Tawny Pipit *Anthus campestris* 17cm Relatively large, pale pipit. Adult pale, greyish sandy brown above, with faint dark markings; whitish below; in spring, breast flushed with pink. Conspicuous pale eye-stripe. Immature browner and more heavily marked above, with dark streaking on breast and flanks. Legs pinkish. Large for pipit, long-legged and wagtail-like. *Voice:* characteristic 'tseep' call. Song (often on ground) repetitive 'seely-seely-seely'. *Habitat:* arid areas, including saltpans, grassland and marshes. Widespread; locally fairly common. 🦆🌿🌾

Tree Pipit *Anthus trivialis* 15cm Predominantly woodland pipit. Adult and immature rich yellow-brown above, with plentiful, fine, darker brown streaks. Breast buff, shading to white on belly. Conspicuous dark brown streaks on breast and flanks. Rather stockier in build than Meadow; legs pinkish. *Voice:* call distinctive 'tee-zee'; song, usually produced in parachuting display flight, characteristic, descending trill, ending in series of 'see-aah' notes. *Habitat:* woodland clearings and heathland with trees. Widespread; locally common. 🌲🌳🌿🌾

Meadow Pipit *Anthus pratensis* 15cm Small, nondescript pipit. Adult and immature brownish above (shade varying from yellowish through olive to greenish), with abundant darker streaks. Underparts pale grey-buff, shading to white on belly, with dark streaks on breast and flanks. Legs dark brown. *Voice:* call thin 'seep'; song (often produced in parachuting song-flight) weak, descending trill (*see* Tree). *Habitat:* open moorland, heath, farmland and marshes. Widespread; often common. 🦆🌿🌾🦆🌾

Red-throated Pipit *Anthus cervinus* 15cm Small, dark pipit. Adult in spring and early summer distinctive because of plain pinkish face, throat and upper breast. Rest of upperparts buffish-brown, with heavy darker streaks, including on the rump – a distinguishing feature at close range from Meadow. Winter adult and immature off-white below, with dark streaks on breast and flanks. *Voice:* call harsh, distinctive 'zeeh'. Song similar to Meadow. *Habitat:* breeds on tundra and northern scrub, open habitats on passage. Only locally common. 🦆🌿🌾

Richard's Pipit

Tawny Pipit

Tree Pipit

Meadow Pipit

Red-throated Pipit (summer)

Rock Pipit *Anthus petrosus* 17cm Largish, dark pipit. Adult and immature largely brownish-grey above, with plentiful darker streaks; pale grey-buff below, with heavy dark brown markings. Legs grey, relatively long. Tail dark, with characteristic smoky grey outer tail feathers, long. *Voice:* call strident 'zeep'; song strong, descending trill, often produced in parachuting display flight. *Habitat:* rocky coastlines. Widespread; not numerous.

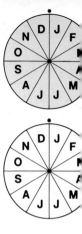

Water Pipit *Anthus spinoletta* 17cm Largish pipit. Summer adult grey-buff above, with faint, fine, dark brown markings; pale buff below, shading to white on belly, often without any darker streaking; characteristic pink flush to breast, most marked in spring. Dark tail has white outer feathers at all times (*see* Rock). Winter adult and immature darker and greyer; breast grey-buff with bold darker streaks. *Voice:* strident 'zeep' and descending, trilling song, often given in parachuting display flight. *Habitat:* breeds on open rocky areas in mountains. Winters in lowlands, often on coasts or inland marshes. Scarce.

Grey Wagtail *Motacilla cinerea* 18cm Longest-tailed of the European wagtails. Summer adult male dove grey above, with bold white eye-stripe separating grey crown from darker cheeks; lemon yellow below, particularly rich beneath tail. Summer male also has white moustachial streaks and black bib, absent in winter. Female and immature duller; breast whitish, and yellow confined to undertail. Tail black with white outer feathers, long. *Voice:* call high-pitched 'chee-seek'; song resembles Blue Tit, 'tsee-tsee-tsee', followed by trill. *Habitat:* fast-moving watersides – streams, rapids, sluices etc. Widespread.

White Wagtail *Motacilla alba alba* 18cm The typical pied-plumage wagtail of continental Europe. Summer adult male back silvery grey, with white forehead and black nape. Cheeks white; throat and breast black; rest of underparts white. Summer female similar, but duller. Winter adult and immature have grey back, smoky nape, white face and throat, grey moustachial stripes (*see* Pied) and indistinct blackish collar. *Voice:* call soft, disyllabic 'swee-eep'; twittering song. *Habitat:* open grassland and watersides in farmland and urban areas. Common.

Pied Wagtail *Motacilla alba yarrellii* 18cm The typical pied wagtail of Britain and Ireland. Summer adult male jet black above; head and breast black, interrupted by white cheeks and forehead. Underparts white, grey on flanks. Summer female similarly patterned, but dark grey on back and wings. Winter adult has dark grey back, and white face and throat surrounded by black markings. Immature even drabber and less well marked. Ever-active. *Voice:* explosive, disyllabic 'chis-ick' call; twittering song. *Habitat:* open land, grass or farmland, urban areas, often near water. Common.

Rock Pipit

Water Pipit

Grey Wagtail ♀

White Wagtail ♂ (summer)

Pied Wagtail ♂ (summer)

THE 'YELLOW' WAGTAILS (see page 26)

Yellow Wagtail *Motacilla flava flavissima* 17cm
Comparatively short-tailed, yellowish wagtail. Summer adult male largely olive green above, with some yellow on nape and bold yellow eye-stripe separating greenish crown from darker cheek patch; rich canary yellow below. Tail black, white edges. Summer female brownish above, with buff shading running onto sides of breast and flanks; much paler yellow below. Winter adult duller, resembling immature; grey-brown above, with whitish eye-stripe over dark cheek patch; pale buff below, often only trace of yellow under tail. Often gregarious. *Voice:* call rich 'tseep'; song musical twittering. *Habitat:* damp meadows, farmland and marsh areas. Locally common.

Blue-headed Wagtail *Motacilla flava flava* 17cm The 'yellow' wagtail of much of central Europe. Only adult male in summer can easily and safely be distinguished from other races; female and immature resemble Yellow. Back greenish-olive as in Yellow; underparts rich yellow. Head pattern distinctive: crown rich blue-grey, separated by long white eye-stripe running from beak to nape (*see* Spanish) over pale-flecked blue-grey cheek patch with whitish lower margin. Voice, habits and habitat as Yellow. Widespread, locally common.

Spanish Wagtail *Motacilla flava iberiae* 17cm The 'yellow' wagtail of Spain, Portugal and parts of southernmost France. Female and immature extremely difficult, if not impossible, to separate from other races. Summer adult male has olive green back and distinctive head pattern, with blue-grey crown, black cheek patches and white throat; underparts rich yellow. Eye-stripe white and narrow, running only from behind eye to nape (*see* Blue-headed, Grey-headed). Voice, habits and habitats as Yellow. Locally common.

Black-headed Wagtail *Motacilla flava feldegg* 17cm The 'yellow' wagtail of the Balkans. Female and immature extremely difficult to separate from other races. Summer adult male very striking; back olive green contrasting with jet black crown, nape and cheeks; underparts rich yellow. No eye-stripe. Throat yellow. Voice, habits and habitats as Yellow. Locally common.

Grey-headed Wagtail *Motacilla flava thunbergi* 17cm The 'yellow' wagtail of central and northern Scandinavia. Female and immature extremely difficult to separate from other races. Summer adult male back olive green; crown and nape slate grey, cheek patch jet black, bordered at base by narrow white moustachial stripe; underparts rich yellow. Chin and throat yellow. Italian race, **Ashy-headed** *M. f. cinereo-capilla*, is very similar, but has broad, white moustachial stripe merging into white chin and throat. No eye-stripe. Voice, habits and habitats as Yellow. Locally common.

Yellow Wagtail ♂

Yellow Wagtail ♀

Blue-headed Wagtail ♂

Spanish Wagtail ♂

Black-headed Wagtail ♂

Grey-headed Wagtail ♂

Waxwing *Bombycilla garrulus* 17cm Starling-like. Adult and immature pinkish-brown above; paler sandy brown below. Black bib, black eye-patch and chestnut crest. Wings black; white bars and yellow margins to flight feathers. Adult has small, wax-like, red feather-ends in wings. Tail blackish; yellow band across tip. Flies like Starling; feeds like parrot. *Voice:* distinctive, bell-like trill. *Habitat:* breeds in mixed conifer forest and scrub. Occasionally winters in urban gardens. Common on breeding grounds; irregular elsewhere.

Dipper *Cinclus cinclus* 17cm Dumpy bird, resembling thrush-sized Wren. Adult rich dark brown above, with striking white throat and breast. Belly rich chestnut (Britain and Ireland) or blackish (rest of Europe). Immature scaly grey, darker above than below. Flight fast, whirring and low over water. Characteristically stands, bobbing, on rocks before plunging into river. *Voice:* call loud 'zit'; song fragmented warbling. *Habitat:* fast-flowing, clear rivers in hilly country; occasionally lakes or sheltered coasts. Locally common.

Wren *Troglodytes troglodytes* 10cm One of the smallest European birds. Adult and immature rich chestnut brown, barred with dark brown above; rather paler below with less barring. Tail characteristically narrow, carried cocked upright. Flight low and direct, on short, rounded, whirring wings. *Voice:* call scolding 'churr'; song musical, extended and astonishingly loud. *Habitat:* well-vegetated habitats of all kinds; also cliffs and mountain screes. Widespread; often common.

Dunnock *Prunella modularis* 15cm Small, drab. Adult brown above, with darker markings. Head, nape and breast distinctive leaden grey; belly buff. Immature browner, lacking grey; pale-speckled above. *Voice:* call shrill 'seek'; song brief, suddenly interrupted, melodious warble. *Habitat:* woodland of all types, farmland, scrub, town parks and gardens. Widespread; locally common.

Alpine Accentor *Prunella collaris* 17cm Small, secretive. Adult rich brown above, marked with dark brown and buff. Throat and breast pattern characteristic; chin and throat white, finely barred with grey, shading to grey breast. Flanks buff, with chestnut markings. Immature paler, buff-speckled above, lacking throat and flank pattern. *Voice:* call short trill; song brief warble. *Habitat:* breeds in mountainous areas. Winters at lower altitudes, sometimes on coasts. Local.

Rufous Bush Chat *Cercotrichas galactotes* 15cm Small, skulking bird. Adult and immature distinctive pale rufous brown above, with white eye-stripe separating crown from black areas around eye. South-eastern race grey-brown above. Underparts pale buff. Tail characteristic, rufous with black and white tips to feathers, long, often characteristically fanned. *Voice:* vocal, often in song-flight; distinctive, ascending series of fluting notes. *Habitat:* dry bush heath or scrub areas. Uncommon.

Waxwing

Dipper

Wren

Dunnock

Alpine Accentor

Rufous Bush Chat

Robin *Erithacus rubecula* 13cm Small, well-known bird. Adult predominantly sandy brown above, with orange-red face, throat and breast broadly edged with dark grey. Grey on lower breast extensive, shading to white on belly. Narrow, buff wingbars conspicuous in perched bird, not striking in flight. Tail unmarked sandy brown. Immature darker brown above; pale buff below, copiously speckled and barred. *Voice:* call sharp 'tick'; song high-pitched warble. *Habitat:* woods, parks and urban gardens, usually with plentiful undergrowth. Widespread; common.

Thrush Nightingale *Luscinia luscinia* 17cm Small, comparatively long-tailed thrush. Adult drab, darkish brown above, with characteristic, long, dark rufous tail. Underparts predominantly greyish-buff; often faintly speckled or barred across the breast, visible only at close range. Immature sandy brown above; paler below, copiously speckled, but with striking rufous tail. Immature rarely distinguishable from Nightingale. Long, strong legs suit largely terrestrial habits. *Voice:* call sweet 'hoo-eet'; song loud and melodious, almost as varied as Nightingale. *Habitat:* the 'northern Nightingale', favouring dense undergrowth and swampy thickets. Locally common.

Nightingale *Luscinia megarhynchos* 17cm Small, drab thrush, but an incomparable songster. Adult olive brown above, with striking, long, round-ended, rufous tail. Underparts pale buff, almost white on belly and appreciably paler than Thrush Nightingale, always unmarked. Immature sandy brown above; paler below, copiously spotted but with long rufous tail. Legs relatively long and strong, suited to terrestrial habits. *Voice:* call soft 'hoo-eet'; song long, loud and melodious, richly varied and containing some mimicry of other birds, often produced night and day. *Habitat:* dense woodland undergrowth and swampy thickets. Widespread; locally common.

Bluethroat *Luscinia svecica* 15cm Small, secretive thrush. Summer adult male brown above, with characteristic chestnut patches on each side of base of tail often striking as it dives for cover. Throat and breast characteristic; bright blue, fringed with black and chestnut, with central spot white (southern race) or red (northern race). Breast colours duller, but still distinctive at other seasons. Female throat white fringed with black. Immature resembles slim, immature Robin, but has characteristic chestnut tail markings. *Voice:* call sharp 'tack'; song extended, high-pitched, melodious warble. *Habitat:* northern swampy scrub or heathland. Locally fairly common.

Robin (adult)

Robin (immature)

Thrush Nightingale

Nightingale

Bluethroat

Black Redstart *Phoenicurus ochruros* 15cm Small, very dark chat. Summer adult male dark ash grey above, sooty black on face and breast, white on belly. Rump and tail (often flicked) conspicuously chestnut red. White wingbar striking, especially in older birds. Winter plumage duller; retains chestnut tail. Female uniformly drab, dark grey-brown, but with characteristic chestnut red tail. Immature dark brown with copious paler spots; tail chestnut. *Voice:* call sharp 'tick'; song rapid, but brief, rattling warble. *Habitat:* mountain screes and towns, including large factory sites. Widespread; locally common.

Redstart *Phoenicurus phoenicurus* 15cm Small, red-tailed chat. Summer adult male unmistakable; strikingly pale blue-grey above, with white forehead and characteristic chestnut tail. Face and throat black; breast bright chestnut; belly white. Winter adult altogether browner and less well-marked. Female brown above; fawn below, with chestnut tail. Immature brown; paler below, copiously buff-flecked like immature Robin, but with chestnut tail, paler and shorter than tail of immature Nightingale. *Voice:* call melodious 'tu-eet'; song brief, melodious warble ending in dry rattle. *Habitat:* woodlands of all descriptions; sometimes scrub. Widespread; locally common.

Whinchat *Saxicola rubetra* 13cm Small, upright chat. Summer adult male speckled brown and fawn above, with bold white eye-stripe separating crown from characteristic dark cheek patch. Tail dark brown, with distinctive white markings at base visible in flight. Underparts pale orange. Wings and tail constantly flicked. Winter adult appreciably duller. Female paler and duller than male. Immature paler and duller, heavily streaked on underparts. Often perches on low bushes or tufts of grass. *Voice:* call harsh 'teck'; song short, high-pitched warble, often produced in song-flight. *Habitat:* open grassland, heath and scrub. Widespread; only locally numerous.

Stonechat *Saxicola torquata* 13cm Small, upright and noisy chat. Summer adult male back dark brown, rump pale and tail black. Head and throat black, with characteristic white patches on side of neck. Breast orange-buff, shading towards white on belly. Winter plumage patterned similarly, but obscured by pale feather fringes. Female similarly patterned, but browner and heavily streaked; lacks white rump. Immature brown above; paler below, copiously buff-speckled. Frequently perches on bushes, with wings and tail flicking. *Voice:* call sharp 'tchack'; song high-pitched, scratchy warble, often produced in song-flight. *Habitat:* heath and scrub, often with gorse, inland or coastal. Widespread; locally common.

Black Redstart ♂

Black Redstart ♀

Redstart ♂

Whinchat ♂

Stonechat ♂

Stonechat ♀

Wheatear *Oenanthe oenanthe* 15cm Small, pale chat. Summer adult male pale grey above, with black eye-patch. Wings blackish; tail black, with characteristic white inverted V-marking on rump and base of tail conspicuous in flight. Underparts apricot-buff. Winter adult browner. Female grey-brown above; buff below, with brown eye-patch. Immature similar, but copiously speckled with buff. Both show distinctive tail and rump pattern. Largely terrestrial; runs in short bursts, then characteristically pauses, tail cocked. Greenland race larger, brighter-coloured and with more upright stance. *Voice:* call harsh 'tack'; song brief, scratchy warble, often produced in song-flight. *Habitat:* open areas of heath, grassland or moorland, often with scanty vegetation. Widespread; locally common. 🏍🐟🌊🏞

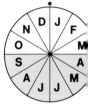

Black-eared Wheatear *Oenanthe hispanica* 15cm Small, terrestrial chat. Adult male pale cinnamon brown above and below, with black wings and characteristic white inverted V-marking on rump and tail prominent in flight. Two forms occur; one with large black patch through eye; other with completely black face and throat. Winter adult appreciably duller. Female and immature similar to Wheatear, but with darker cheeks and wings. *Voice:* call harsh 'tchack'; song high-pitched, scratchy warble. *Habitat:* dry, open, often stony areas with little tall vegetation. Locally common. 🏍🏞

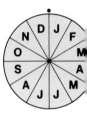

Black Wheatear *Oenanthe leucura* 17cm Relatively large, very dark chat. Adult male unmistakable; entirely jet black, except for characteristic white Wheatear-marking on rump and tail. Female dark sooty brown; immature brown with paler speckling; both show typical rump and tail pattern. Largely terrestrial. *Voice:* call high-pitched 'pee-pee-pee'; song brief, rich warble. *Habitat:* arid, rocky, mountainous areas; rocky coasts and cliffs. Locally fairly common. 🏔🐟

Wheatear ♂

Wheatear ♀

Black-eared Wheatear ♂

Black Wheatear ♂

Rock Thrush *Monticola saxatilis* 20cm Colourful thrush. Summer adult male unmistakable; head, nape, breast and rump blue; back white; wings black; belly and tail chestnut. Female, winter male and immature altogether drabber; brown above, and buff below with copious dark scaly markings; all have characteristic chestnut tail. Largely terrestrial. *Voice:* call brief 'tack'; song varied, fluting warble. *Habitat:* high altitude, mountainous areas. Widespread; rarely numerous.

Blue Rock Thrush *Monticola solitarius* 20cm Dark thrush. Summer adult male unmistakable; head and body characteristic slate blue; wings and tail blackish. Winter male appreciably darker slate blue. Female and immature duller; brown above; fawn below with copious speckling. Largely terrestrial and often very shy. *Voice:* call harsh 'tchick'; song loud and musical, often delivered from prominent perch. *Habitat:* rocky or mountainous areas, occasionally towns; always at lower altitudes than Rock Thrush. Widespread; rarely numerous.

Ring Ouzel *Turdus torquatus* 25cm The 'mountain Blackbird'. Summer adult male unmistakable; largely sooty black, with bold white crescentic patch on breast. Winter male greyer, with white patch smudged sooty grey. Female largely brown with darker speckling; pale buff, crescentic bib sometimes poorly marked. Immature brown with paler, scaly markings; lacks bib. In flight, wings appear pale grey, a useful distinguishing feature from Blackbird. *Voice:* call characteristic 'chack'; song loud, repetitive, echoing 'chew-chew-chew'. *Habitat:* upland fields, moorland and mountainsides, especially near rocky ravines. Widespread; never numerous.

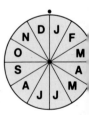

Blackbird *Turdus merula* 25cm Familiar and comparatively long-tailed. Male unmistakable, with entirely glossy, velvet black plumage and contrasting orange beak and eye-ring. Female dark brown above; paler below, with dark-bordered whitish throat; beak dark, with trace of yellow at base. Immature rather more ginger brown than female, heavily buff-spotted. *Voice:* call loud 'chink' or 'chack', often persistent; song fluting, varied, extended and melodious. *Habitat:* farmland, woodland, heaths and urban areas. Widespread; often abundant.

Rock Thrush ♂ (winter)

Blue Rock Thrush ♂ (summer)

Ring Ouzel ♀

Blackbird ♂

Fieldfare *Turdus pilaris* 25cm Comparatively long-tailed thrush. Adult crown, nape and rump dove grey; back, mantle and wings rich golden russet brown, shading to white on belly. Immature browner above; fawn below, heavily speckled. Often gregarious. *Voice:* call very characteristic series of laughing 'chacks'; song scratchy warble. *Habitat:* breeds in northern forests, parks and gardens. Winters on open farmland and open woodland. Widespread; often common. 🏍🏔🌸🌲🏕

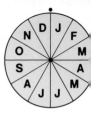

Song Thrush *Turdus philomelos* 23cm Smallish, short-tailed, upright thrush. Adult olive or sandy brown above, tinged yellowish-buff, with pale eye-stripe above darker brown cheek patch. Wings and tail chestnut brown. Underparts greyish-white, tinged cinnamon, heavily streaked with dark brown. Immature similar, but with copious yellow-buff speckling on upperparts. In flight, underwings are pale sandy brown (*see* Redwing, Mistle). *Voice:* call thin 'seep'; song (often from prominent perch) series of musical notes, each repeated two or three times. *Habitat:* woods, parks, gardens and farmland with plentiful trees. Widespread; often common. 🏍🏔🌸🌲🏕

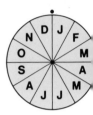

Redwing *Turdus iliacus* 20cm Smallish, dark, short-tailed thrush. Adult dark russet brown above, with conspicuous buffish eye-stripe and moustachial streak on either edge of dark cheek patch. Underparts whitish, streaked dark brown, with conspicuous reddish flanks. Immature similar but duller, with copious sandy speckling on back. In flight, characteristic red underwing prominent. Often gregarious. *Voice:* call extended 'see-eep'; song slow series of fluting notes; *Habitat:* breeds in northern forests, parks and gardens. Winters in woodland and on open farmland; occasionally parks and gardens. Widespread; often numerous. 🏍🏔🌸🌲

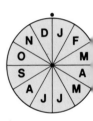

Mistle Thrush *Turdus viscivorus* 27cm Largish, pale and relatively long-tailed thrush. Adult pale grey-brown above; wings dark brown; tail dark with pale grey-buff outer feathers, long. Underparts whitish, heavily spotted with brown. In flight, characteristic white underwing conspicuous. Immature greyer, appears much paler because of copious pale scaly feather margins on upperparts. *Voice:* call angry, extended rattle; song simple and slow but tuneful, often produced early in spring and usually delivered from prominent perch. *Habitat:* woodland, parks, gardens and well-treed farmland; often open grassland in winter. Widespread. 🏍🏔🌸🌲

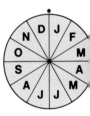

Fieldfare

Song Thrush

Redwing

Mistle Thrush

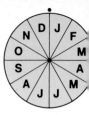

Cetti's Warbler *Cettia cetti* 15cm Small, unstreaked warbler. Adult and immature have entire upperparts rich reddish-brown, shading to buff on sides of breast and flanks, and to white on belly. Tail rich brown, relatively long and conspicuously rounded at tip. Secretive, normally flying only short distances between clumps of vegetation. *Voice:* call sharp 'teck; song explosive burst of metallic 'cher-chink' notes. *Habitat:* damp, heavily vegetated marshes, ditches, swamps and scrub. Non-migratory. Widespread; locally common.

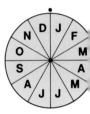

Fan-tailed Warbler *Cisticola juncidis* 10cm Tiny, heavily streaked warbler. Adult and immature grey-buff above, heavily streaked with dark brown; paler greyish-fawn below, lightly streaked. Tail grey-brown, very short, rounded, often flicked Wren-like. Secretive, except in song-flight, flying only short distances on short, rounded, whirring wings. *Voice:* usually in fluttering yo-yo-like song-flight, when plaintive, repetitive 'zee-eek' notes are diagnostic. *Habitat:* open areas with low, dense clumps of vegetation, often marshy, but sometimes quite arid. Non-migratory. Locally fairly common.

Grasshopper Warbler *Locustella naevia* 13cm Tiny, dark-streaked warbler. Adult and immature dark, dull grey-brown above, with dense darker brown streaks. Underparts greyish-buff, often spotted on throat, paling to near-white on belly. Greyish eye-stripe. Tail brown, with wedge-shaped tip. Extremely secretive, normally moving through cover rather than flying in the open. *Voice:* often sings at night; song characteristic, high-pitched, extended trill, often of some minutes' duration, recalling unreeling fishing line. Rarely on prominent perch, often ventriloquial; therefore difficult to locate. *Habitat:* areas of dense, shrubby vegetation, ranging from reedbeds to young plantations. Widespread; rarely numerous.

Savi's Warbler *Locustella luscinioides* 15cm Small, unstreaked warbler. Adult and immature brown above, tinged with rufous, unstreaked. Faint grey-buff eye-stripe. Underparts whitish, shading to buff on flanks. Tail reddish-brown, characteristically long, wedge-shaped at tip. Secretive, but on calm evenings will sing on exposed reed stems. *Voice:* similar to Grasshopper, but lower-pitched and produced in shorter bursts. Ventriloquial. *Habitat:* almost confined to extensive reedbed areas. Widespread; locally quite common.

River Warbler *Locustella fluviatilis* 13cm Tiny warbler with streaked breast. Adult and immature dull olive brown above, lacking streaks (*see* Grasshopper), shading to pale grey-buff on flanks and to white on belly. Throat and breast streaked dark brown, more conspicuously in adult than immature. Tail slightly rufous-tinged, rounded. Secretive; rarely flies in open. *Voice:* harsh alarm call; song similar to Grasshopper but louder and with clearly separated notes. *Habitat:* damp thickets and forest glades with dense undergrowth. Widespread; only locally common.

Cetti's Warbler

Fan-tailed Warbler

Grasshopper Warbler

Savi's Warbler

River Warbler

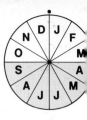

Moustached Warbler *Acrocephalus melanopogon* 13cm Tiny, heavily streaked warbler. Adult and immature back chestnut brown, with bold blackish streaks. Characteristic blackish crown separated from dark cheeks by conspicuous white eye-stripe. Flanks pale ginger-buff; belly white. Tail brown, tinged chestnut, wedge-shaped at tip; frequently and characteristically cocked. Secretive, but often sings from tops of reeds. *Voice:* call harsh 'chuck' and scolding alarm rattle; song rapid and extended warble, based on rich 'lu-lu-lu' notes. *Habitat:* dense, swampy vegetation near water, reedbeds. Non-migratory in some areas. Locally fairly common.

Sedge Warbler *Acrocephalus schoenobaenus* 13cm Tiny, heavily streaked warbler. Adult and immature back olive brown, heavily streaked with blackish-brown. Crown brown, with narrow blackish stripes, separated by clear whitish eye-stripe from grey-brown cheeks. Underparts whitish, tinged buff on flanks. Tail brown, tinged chestnut. Inquisitive, but rarely flies far in the open. *Voice:* explosive 'tuck' of alarm; song (often produced in short, vertical song-flight) rapid, repetitive, metallic jingle, often loud and interspersed with chattering notes. *Habitat:* reedbeds and adjacent shrubby swamps. Widespread; often common.

Reed Warbler *Acrocephalus scirpaceus* 13cm Tiny, unstreaked warbler. Adult and immature rich reddish-brown above, lacking darker streaks. Faint, buffish eye-stripe. Underparts whitish, shading to buff on flanks. Tail reddish-brown, relatively long and tapered towards tip. Legs normally dark brown. *Voice:* alarm call 'churr'; song prolonged and repetitive, with spells of chirruping, more musical and less twangy than Sedge, with some mimicry. *Habitat:* normally reedbeds, sometimes other heavily vegetated freshwater margins. Widespread; often common.

Marsh Warbler *Acrocephalus palustris* 13cm Tiny, unstreaked warbler. Adult and immature greenish or yellowish olive-buff above, with faint buff eye-stripe; whitish below, shaded pale yellowish-buff on breast and flanks. Tail olive brown, tapered towards tip. Legs usually pinkish (*see* Reed). Secretive. *Voice:* loud alarm 'chuck'. Song diagnostic (best way of distinguishing Marsh from Reed) extended, exceptionally musical, varied with wide range of inserted passages of expert mimicry of other birds. *Habitat:* damp, marshy areas and thickets. Widespread; locally fairly common.

Great Reed Warbler *Acrocephalus arundinaceus* 20cm Small, but large for a warbler. Adult and immature dull unstreaked greyish-brown above, with bold buffish eye-stripe; shading to pale greyish-buff below, with throat and belly almost white. Tail grey-brown, relatively long, tapered towards tip. Thrush size, powerful beak and strident song are good diagnostic features. *Voice:* loud, grating and metallic, with repeated phrases, 'gurk-gurk-gurk', 'karra-karra-karra' and others. *Habitat:* extensive reedbed areas. Widespread; rarely numerous.

Moustached Warbler

Sedge Warbler

Reed Warbler

Marsh Warbler

Great Reed Warbler

Olivaceous Warbler *Hippolais pallida* 13cm Tiny warbler. Adult and immature grey-brown above, with darker brown wings and tail. Narrow grey-buff eye-stripe. Underparts white, shading to grey-buff on flanks. Beak comparatively long and broad. Legs dark brown. Resembles brownish version (not yellowish or greenish) of Melodious. Tail flicked frequently. *Voice:* call 'teck'; song rapid, often harsh, jangle of notes with repetitive phrases reminiscent of Sedge. *Habitat:* open woodland, parks and gardens, often near water. Locally fairly common. 🌿

Dusky Warbler *Phylloscopus fuscatus* 12cm Small, brownish leaf warbler. Adult and immature brown above, slightly darker on crown, wings and tail, characteristically lacking any trace of green or yellow. Clear whitish or rusty eye-stripe. No wingbars. Underparts white, shading to buff on flanks, often with rusty tinge. Secretive. *Voice:* call harsh and distinctive 'tchack', frequently produced. *Habitat:* deep scrub, often in or near marshy areas. Vagrant from Asia, usually in passage seasons. 🌿🌲🌿🌿

Icterine Warbler *Hippolais icterina* 13cm Tiny warbler. Adult and immature greyish-green above, with bold and rich yellow eye-stripe; bright lemon yellow below. Wings and tail brownish. Legs blue. At rest, wingtips extend halfway down tail (*see* Melodious). Paler patch in closed wing visible at close range. Raises crown feathers if alarmed or excited, otherwise flat-capped silhouette and large beak are characteristic of the *Hippolais* group of warblers. *Voice:* call hard 'tack'; song (usually on open perch) varied and sustained jingle of notes. *Habitat:* woodland undergrowth, parks, gardens. Widespread; locally common. 🚜🌿🌿

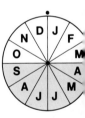

Melodious Warbler *Hippolais polyglotta* 13cm Tiny warbler. Adult and immature greyish-green above, with rich yellow eye-stripe; rich yellow below. Wings and tail brown, with no pale panel in wing. Closed wingtips reach only to base of tail (*see* Icterine). Beak relatively long and broad; legs brownish (*see* Icterine). *Voice:* sparrow-like chattering and soft 'hoo-eet'; song extended, slow initially but then rapid, melodious. *Habitat:* woodland undergrowth, scrub, parks and gardens. Southern European counterpart of Icterine. Widespread; locally common. 🚜🌿🌿🌿

Olivaceous Warbler

Dusky Warbler

cterine Warbler

Melodious Warbler

Spectacled Warbler *Sylvia conspicillata* 13cm Tiny warbler. Adult male mantle and head grey, with inconspicuous white eye-ring. Wings rich chestnut; tail blackish, with white outer feathers. Throat white; breast pale grey shaded with pink, fading to white on belly. Female and immature duller and browner above; Legs pale pinkish. Secretive. *Voice:* call rattling churr; song high-pitched warble with little variety, often from exposed perch. *Habitat:* arid scrub and maquis. Local; sometimes fairly common. 🐦 ⌷

Dartford Warbler *Sylvia undata* 13cm Tiny, dark, long-tailed warbler. Adult dark grey above; tail dark grey, long, often cocked. Underparts characteristically dark red with white flecks, paling to white beneath tail. Red eye-ring and chestnut eye visible at close range. Legs brownish. Immature dull brown above, grey-buff below. Often secretive. *Voice:* call loud 'chuck' or metallic 'tchurr'. Song (often in song-flight) quiet, brief, scratchy warble. *Habitat:* tall, dry heathland, maquis or gorse. Locally common. ⌷

Radde's Warbler *Phylloscopus schwarzi* 14cm Small, brownish leaf warbler. Adult and immature drab brown above, with long pale buff or yellowish eye-stripe accentuated by dark, almost black, border to cheeks. Throat white; band across breast (sometimes indistinct) and flanks cinnamon brown; belly whitish, sometimes with faint yellowish streaks, especially in immature. Beak appreciably stouter than other leaf warblers. *Voice:* call sharp 'tchack'; song soft, hesitant warble. *Habitat:* dense undergrowth. Vagrant from eastern Asia, usually in passage seasons. 🌲 🌿 🌿 ⌷

Subalpine Warbler *Sylvia cantillans* 13cm Tiny, dark warbler. Adult male dark grey above (but not as dark as Dartford); wings dark brown; tail dark brown with broad, white edges. Throat and breast chestnut red, with white moustachial stripe. Belly white. Female and immature much less richly coloured than male. Legs brown. Secretive. *Voice:* call sharp 'tchack'; song brief, musical warble, lacking harsh, metallic notes, often given in song-flight. *Habitat:* arid scrub, heath and maquis; woodland clearings. Locally fairly common. 🐦 🌿 🌲 🌿 ⌷

Spectacled Warbler ♀

Dartford Warbler ♀

Radde's Warbler

Subalpine Warbler ♀

Sardinian Warbler *Sylvia melanocephala* 13cm Tiny warbler. Adult male grey above; head black, distinctive, with bold red eye-ring round dark eye. Tail almost black, white-edged. Underparts white, strikingly so at throat, shading to grey on flanks. Legs brown. Female and immature considerably duller and browner, with cap much the same colour as mantle. Secretive, but active. *Voice:* call scolding chatter; song extended, scratchy warble interspersed with melodious phrases, often produced in bouncing song-flight. *Habitat:* scrub, maquis and bush-covered rocky hillsides. Widespread; often common. 🚜🌳🌲🌿👑

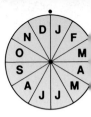

Rüppell's Warbler *Sylvia rueppelli* 14cm Tiny, dark warbler. Adult male darkish-grey above, with characteristic black head and throat separated by conspicuous white moustachial streaks. Underparts white, shading to pale grey on flanks. Tail blackish, with white edges. Female and immature similarly patterned, but appreciably paler and browner. Eyes and legs rich red. *Voice:* call dry, extended rattle; song similar to Whitethroat, but including rattling phrases akin to Lesser Whitethroat. *Habitat:* rocky, scrubby areas and hillsides. Local and uncommon. 🌲🌿👑

Orphean Warbler *Sylvia hortensis* 15cm Small, but comparatively large for a warbler. Adult head dark grey, with blackish cheeks and characteristic staring white eye. Rest of upperparts dark grey-brown; tail edged with white. Underparts white, tinged pinkish-buff on flanks. Beak relatively long and slender; legs grey. Immature paler and greyer. *Voice:* call sharp 'tchack'; song in south-western European race unmusical and repetitive; in south-eastern race strikingly different, being loud, Blackbird-like and melodious. *Habitat:* open woodland, parks, olive groves. Widespread; locally quite common. 🚜🌳🌲🌿

Barred Warbler *Sylvia nisoria* 15cm Small, but large for a warbler. Adult largely dull grey above, with slightly darker shading round distinctive staring white eye. Tail white-edged, relatively long and broad. Underparts whitish, with very variable amounts of crescentic grey-brown barring. Immature duller, usually lacking most of breast barring. Beak relatively long; legs pinkish-brown. *Voice:* call harsh 'tack'; song extended, melodious warbling, mixed with chattering calls, often produced in song-flight. *Habitat:* hedges, scrub, woodland clearings, shrubberies. Widespread; occasionally fairly common. 🚜🌳👑

Sardinian Warbler ♂

Sardinian Warbler ♀

Rüppell's Warbler ♂

Orphean Warbler ♂

Barred Warbler

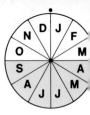

Lesser Whitethroat *Sylvia curruca* 13cm Small, dull warbler. Adult largely grey-brown above, with brown wings and white-edged tail. Crown grey, with distinctive blackish patch through eye. Underparts white, tinged pink on breast and flanks in early summer. Legs bluish. Immature duller, lacking pink flush on underparts. Secretive. *Voice:* call short 'tack'; song brief warble, followed by repetitive rattle on single note. *Habitat:* farmland hedges, woodland clearings, scrubby hillsides. Widespread; rarely numerous. ◢●▩

Whitethroat *Sylvia communis* 14cm Small, active warbler. Adult male grey above, with characteristic pale chestnut wings and white-edged dull brown tail. Throat strikingly white; rest of underparts whitish, tinged pinkish-buff. Female and immature browner and paler, but with chestnut wings still evident. Legs brownish (*see* Lesser). Active, but fairly secretive except in song. *Voice:* call rasping 'tschack'; song rapid, scratchy warble, usually produced in song-flight. *Habitat:* heath, scrubby hillsides, maquis and woodland clearings. Widespread; locally common. ◢●▩

Garden Warbler *Sylvia borin* 15cm Small warbler, lacking distinctive features. Adult and immature characteristically drab greyish-olive above; whitish below, shaded grey or buff, especially on flanks. Faint pale eye-stripe. Legs bluish. Secretive. *Voice:* call sharp 'tack'; song extended, liquid, melodious warbling, usually produced in deep cover. *Habitat:* well-grown thick scrub or dense woodland undergrowth; tall trees seem unnecessary (unlike Blackcap). Widespread; occasionally quite common. ◢●♣♣▩

Blackcap *Sylvia atricapilla* 15cm Small warbler. Adult male greyish-olive above, with characteristic black crown; pale grey below. Female and immature have grey plumage with browner tinge; characteristic caps are brown in female, ginger-chestnut in immature. Legs bluish. *Voice:* call sharp 'tack'; song melodious warble, similar to but briefer than Garden Warbler, usually ending in rising note. *Habitat:* parks, gardens and woodland, with both well-developed undergrowth and tall trees. Widespread; locally quite common. ●♣♣

Lesser Whitethroat ♂

Whitethroat ♂

Garden Warbler

Blackcap ♂

Blackcap ♀

Greenish Warbler *Phylloscopus trochiloides* 11cm Tiny leaf warbler. Adult and immature greyish-green above, with distinct yellow eye-stripe. Wings brownish, with single white wingbar that is sometimes indistinct, except at close range. Underparts whitish, shading to greyish- or yellowish-buff (immature) on flanks. Legs grey-brown. *Voice:* call high-pitched, disyllabic 'chee-wee'; song loud trill, terminating with brief warble. *Habitat:* deciduous woodland, parks, gardens and dense tall scrub. Locally common. ●▲♠

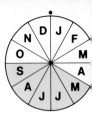

Yellow-browed Warbler *Phylloscopus inornatus* 11cm Tiny leaf warbler. Adult and immature yellowish-green above, with prominent creamy white eye-stripe and pale green rump. Wings brownish, with double whitish wingbars, usually quite distinct; pale edges to secondary feathers are often visible. Underparts whitish, shading to yellow on flanks, especially in immature. Tail dark brown, relatively short. Often hunts flying insects like miniature flycatcher. *Voice:* call high-pitched, shrill 'soo-eet'; song high-speed, twittering 'fitifitifiti' monotone, interspersed with trills. *Habitat:* mixed and coniferous woodland, often with well-developed undergrowth. Rare, but regular, passage migrant, especially in late autumn. ▲♠

Bonelli's Warbler *Phylloscopus bonelli* 10cm Tiny leaf warbler. Adult and immature greenish-olive above, with strikingly yellow rump. Whitish eye-stripe is indistinct. Brownish wings lack wingbars, but yellow feather edges create golden central panel. Underparts characteristic silvery white. Legs brownish. *Voice:* soft, plaintive and markedly disyllabic 'hoo-eet'; song even trill, similar to Wood, but of slower pace and with more clearly separated notes, often produced in two phrases of different pitch. *Habitat:* mixed or coniferous woodland, often in hilly country. Widespread; often locally common. ●▲♠

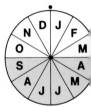

Wood Warbler *Phylloscopus sibilatrix* 13cm Small but one of the larger leaf warblers. Adult and immature yellowish-olive above, with distinct yellowish eye-stripe; face, throat and breast rich yellow. Rest of underparts strikingly white. Wings brown, with yellowish feather fringes, but lacking wingbars. Legs pale pinkish-brown. *Voice:* call liquid 'dee-you'; song characteristic trill, based on accelerating repetition of 'sip' notes, often produced in song-flight. *Habitat:* mature deciduous woodland, often with comparatively little undergrowth. Widespread; locally common. ●▲♠

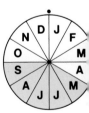

Greenish Warbler

Yellow-browed Warbler

Bonelli's Warbler

Wood Warbler

Chiffchaff *Phylloscopus collybita* 10cm Tiny, drab leaf warbler. Adult and immature drab brownish-olive above; wings brown, lacking wingbars; tail brown. Pale yellow eye-stripe. Underparts whitish, shaded buff on flanks, often yellow-tinged in immature. Legs usually blackish. *Voice:* call plaintive 'hoo-eet'; song striking and diagnostic, monotonous series of 'chiff', 'chaff' notes. *Habitat:* favours mature woodlands, with both tall trees and well-developed undergrowth; rarely in scrub, except on migration. Widespread; often common. 🐦🌱🌲🌳

Willow Warbler *Phylloscopus trochilus* 10cm Tiny leaf warbler. Adult and immature pale olive green above, with clear whitish eye-stripe; whitish below, strongly tinged with yellow in immature, especially on flanks. Legs usually brown (*see* Chiffchaff). *Voice:* call plaintive 'too-eet'; song characteristic, melodious, silvery, descending warble, with final flourish. *Habitat:* woodlands with dense undergrowth, heath, parkland; in the far north, scrub without trees. Widespread; common.
🐦🌱🌲🌳🏞️🏚️

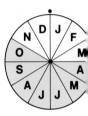

Goldcrest *Regulus regulus* 9cm Tiny, one of the smallest European birds. Adult and immature olive green above; tail brown, short; wings brownish with double white wingbar. Head pattern is characteristic, with crown-stripe yellowish-gold in female, flame-coloured in male, broadly edged in black; diffuse, white eye-ring. Immature lacks this head pattern. Underparts whitish. Beak dark, short and finely pointed; legs dark brown. *Voice:* call very high-pitched 'tsee'; song high-pitched, descending series of 'tsee-tsee' notes, terminating in flourishing trill. *Habitat:* woodland of all sorts; occasionally parks and gardens. Widespread; common. 🐦🌱🌲🌳

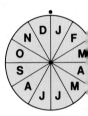

Firecrest *Regulus ignicapillus* 9cm The smallest European bird. Adult and immature olive green above, tinged golden bronze on mantle in adult; tail brown, short; wings brownish, with double white wingbars. Head pattern (lacking in immature) striking and diagnostic, with orange crown-stripe (flame-coloured in male) edged in black, and contrasting with bold white stripe over eye. Underparts whitish. *Voice:* call rasping, high-pitched 'tsee'; song monotonous, accelerating repetition of 'tsee' notes, lacking final flourish of Goldcrest. *Habitat:* woodland of all types. Widespread; locally common. 🐦🌱🌲🌳

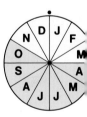

Chiffchaff

Willow Warbler

Goldcrest

Firecrest

Spotted Flycatcher *Muscicapa striata* 15cm Small, elongated flycatcher. Adult and immature drab brown above, with dark brown, closely spaced streaks on crown; buff below, shading to white on belly, with brown streaking on breast. Immatures have pale scaly markings on back when freshly fledged. Flight characteristic, dashing out from prominent perch to catch insect prey, usually returning to same perch. Shows relatively long wings and tail. *Voice:* call sharp 'zit'; song brief sequence of squeaky notes. *Habitat:* woodland clearings, scrub, farmland, parks and gardens with plentiful trees. Widespread.

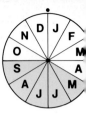

Red-breasted Flycatcher *Ficedula parva* 12cm Tiny, neatly compact flycatcher. Adult and immature dull brown above, with greyish head and nape more prominent in male; whitish eye-ring. Breast orange in summer male; much paler, sometimes almost white, in winter male, female and immature. Tail blackish, flicked frequently, showing diagnostic large white patches at each side of base. Longer-legged and more warbler-like in behaviour than other flycatchers. *Voice:* call trilling twitter; song surprisingly loud, melodious trill. *Habitat:* deciduous woodland and parkland. Locally common.

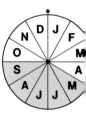

Collared Flycatcher *Ficedula albicollis* 13cm Small flycatcher with pied plumage. Summer adult male largely black above, with bold white wingbars, broad white collar band and conspicuous white forehead. Tail black, white-edged. Western race males usually also show some white on rump. Underparts white. Winter male, female and immature brown above, white below, with buffish shading on breast and flanks, normally indistinguishable from Pied. *Voice:* call harsh 'teck'; song repetitive series of flute-like notes. *Habitat:* open woodland, well-vegetated parks and gardens. Locally common.

Pied Flycatcher *Ficedula hypoleuca* 13cm Small flycatcher with pied plumage. Summer adult male black above (year-old birds may have brownish wings and tail), with bold white wingbars and white patch on forehead. Tail black with white edges, frequently flicked. Underparts white. Winter male, female and immature brown above; white below, with grey-buff shading (*see* Collared). *Voice:* call sharp 'wit'; song unmelodious rattle of notes. *Habitat:* mature woodland, usually deciduous, with scant undergrowth. Locally common.

Spotted Flycatcher

Red-breasted Flycatcher (winter)

Collared Flycatcher ♂ (summer)

Pied Flycatcher ♂ (summer)

Pied Flycatcher ♀

Bearded Tit *Panurus biarmicus* 15cm Small and long-tailed tit. Adult male predominantly chestnut brown above, with distinctive dove grey head. Throat white, with characteristic broad black moustachial streaks. Rest of underparts pale buff. Female and immature brown above, with darker cap; grey-buff below. Tail long and relatively broad. Wings short and rounded; flight feeble. Tends to move in flocks. *Voice:* call distinctive 'ping'; song twittering rattle. *Habitat:* wetlands with extensive *Phragmites* reedbeds. Locally common.

Long-tailed Tit *Aegithalos caudatus* 15cm Tiny but long-tailed tit. Small, rather fluffy body and extremely long white-edged black tail characteristic of adult and immature. Much of upperparts white and brown, tinged pink; head white with dark stripes over eyes (head all-white in northern race). Reddish fleshy wattles over eyes. Beak black, short, stubby. Underparts white, tinged with pale buffish-pink on belly and flanks. Wings short and rounded; flight feeble. Tends to move in noisy flocks. *Voice:* calls repeated, thin 'see' or low 'tupp'; song (rarely heard) varied assemblage of 'see' and 'tsew' notes. *Habitat:* woodland undergrowth, scrub, heathland and farmland hedges. Widespread; often common.

Marsh Tit *Parus palustris* 13cm Small, sombre, brownish tit. Adult and immature uniform brown above, wings and tail slightly darker brown. Crown and nape glossy black, contrasting with whitish cheeks. Underparts largely greyish-buff, with small black bib on throat. *Voice:* call diagnostic, explosive 'pit-chew'; song bell-like note, repeated several times, or sometimes 'pitchaweeoo' variants of the call. *Habitat:* woodland, usually deciduous or mixed, with abundant undergrowth; scrub; park and garden shrubberies. Widespread; rarely numerous.

Willow Tit *Parus montanus* 13cm Small, sombre, brownish tit. Adult and immature uniformly brown above; tail dark brown; wings dark brown, often showing pale central patch. Crown and nape black, contrasting with whitish cheeks (strikingly pure white in northern race). Underparts largely greyish-buff, but black bib appreciably larger than in Marsh. *Voice:* call thin 'dee-dee-dee', 'zee-zee' or occasionally 'tchay'. Song liquid and warbling, but seldom heard. *Habitat:* scrub and shrubby woodland and gardens, often favouring damp areas. Widespread; rarely numerous.

Siberian Tit *Parus cinctus* 14cm Small, dull tit. Adult and immature uniformly pale dull brown above, with richer brown cap (*see* Marsh and Willow) contrasting with white cheeks. Black bib covers much of throat and upper breast, merging gradually to grey-buff on breast and belly. Flanks tinged cinnamon brown. Plumage characteristically loose-feathered and untidy. *Voice:* call long, drawn-out 'zee-zee-zee'; song brief, rarely heard, weak warble. *Habitat:* woodlands of all types. Locally quite common.

Bearded Tit ♂

Long-tailed Tit

Marsh Tit

Willow Tit

Siberian Tit

Crested Tit *Parus cristatus* 12cm Tiny, Europe's only crested tit. Adult and immature uniformly brown above; uniformly pale buff below. Head pattern characteristic: white face with black lines on nape and cheeks; broad black bib; long crest, chequered in black and white. *Voice:* call characteristic purring trill; song high-pitched, repetitive mixture of 'tzee' notes. *Habitat:* mixed or coniferous woodland; ancient pine forest in Britain. Widespread; locally fairly common. ♠♣

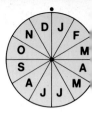

Coal Tit *Parus ater* 12cm Tiny, agile tit. Adult and immature olive-grey above, with glossy black head and bib relieved by contrasting white patches on cheeks and nape. Underparts pale buff, with richer cinnamon tones on flanks. *Voice:* call high-pitched, plaintive 'tseet'; song high-pitched, repetitive 'wheat-see, wheat-see'. *Habitat:* woodland of all types, but favours conifers; gardens and parks. Widespread; often common. ♠♣♠♣

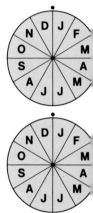

Blue Tit *Parus caeruleus* 12cm Tiny tit. Adult has greenish back and characteristic bright blue wings and tail. Head white, with bright blue crown, black line through eye and black bib. Underparts yellow. Male shows brighter blues than female. Immature less well-marked, with greenish upperparts and lacking blue crown until autumn. *Voice:* varied calls, but 'tsee-tsee-tsee-sit' is often used; song fast trill, opening with series of 'tsee' notes. *Habitat:* catholic - ranging from woodland of all sorts to urban gardens, farmland and even marshland in winter. Widespread; often numerous. ♠♣♠♣♠

Great Tit *Parus major* 15cm Largest of the tits. Adult has greenish back, blue-grey wings with white wingbars, and blackish tail with conspicuous white edges. Crown and nape glossy black, with striking white cheeks and indistinct whitish nape patch. Breast and belly yellow, with central black stripe broader in male than female. Immature duller and greener, with grey-green rather than black markings. Feeds more often on the ground than other tits. *Voice:* calls extremely varied, but 'tchink' common; song characteristically repetitive, ringing 'tea-cher, tea-cher'. *Habitat:* catholic – woodland of all types, farmland, parks and gardens. Widespread; often numerous. ♠♣♠♣♠

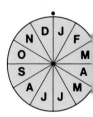

Crested Tit

Coal Tit

lue Tit

Great Tit ♀

Nuthatch *Sitta europaea* 15cm Small and woodpecker-like. Adult, immature distinctive blue-grey above; wings dark grey; white-tipped tail dove grey. Black eye-stripe. Throat white, rest of underparts pale buff, shading to cinnamon on flanks (female) or chestnut (male). Northern race almost white below. Beak long, dagger-like. Moves actively on trunks and branches, head up and head down. *Voice:* call far-carrying, ringing 'chwit'; song 'toowee-toowee'. *Habitat:* deciduous woodland; parkland. Widespread; locally common. ▲♠♣

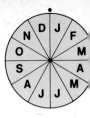

Neumayer's or Rock Nuthatch *Sitta neumayer* 15cm Small and woodpecker-like, except for habitat. Adult and immature similar to Nuthatch, but paler, especially on throat and breast. Lacks white spots on tail. *Voice:* call loud, harsh 'chwit'; song, rattling trill, first accelerating, then slowing. *Habitat:* distinctive: rocky mountain gorges and hillsides. Local; sometimes fairly common. ▲

Wall Creeper *Tichodroma muraria* 16cm Small and woodpecker-like. Summer adult spectacular: grey above and near-black below; wings dark crimson, rounded, showing white spots in flight. Tail grey with white tips to outer feathers, short. Winter adult and immature paler grey above and below, with white throat. Beak long, slender and downcurved. *Voice:* call high-pitched 'pee'; song high-pitched, ascending trill. *Habitat:* rocky gorges and screes, high in mountains. Uncommon and local. ▲

Treecreeper *Certhia familiaris* 12cm Woodpecker-like but tiny. Adult, immature dark brown above, densely streaked white. Whitish eye-stripe over darker brown cheek patch. Underparts whitish, often stained green or brown. Tail brown, long, central feathers pointed. Beak long, pointed, downcurved. Flight undulating, showing multiple wingbars. Creeps mouse-like, head up. *Voice:* call shrill 'tseeu'; song high-pitched, descending with final flourish. *Habitat:* mature woodland, especially conifers. Widespread; rarely numerous. ▲♠♣♣

Short-toed Treecreeper *Certhia brachydactyla* 12cm Woodpecker-like but tiny. Adult, immature dark brown above, streaked white. Whitish eye-stripe over darker brown cheek patch. Underparts whitish, shading to buff on flanks, often stained. Tail, beak as Treecreeper. Shorter hind claw not useful field character: separation from Treecreeper best accomplished by range, habitat and call. *Voice:* call sharp 'zeeet' (*see* Treecreeper); song as Treecreeper, but slower. *Habitat:* mature deciduous woodland. Widespread; rarely numerous. ♠♣♣

Penduline Tit *Remiz pendulinus* 10cm Tiny and tit-like though not member of tit family. Adult back, tail chestnut brown; head and nape pale whitish-grey, contrasting black 'mask' patches around eyes and beak. Underparts buff; some chestnut on breast. Female less well-marked than male. Immature duller; head brownish, lacking mask. *Voice:* call distinctive, lisping 'zee-eeh'; song brief twittering. *Habitat:* reedbeds, marsh and riverside scrubby woodland. Local; sometimes fairly common. ≋

Nuthatch

Neumayer's or Rock Nuthatch

Wall Creeper

Treecreeper

Short-toed Treecreeper

Penduline Tit ♂

Red-backed Shrike *Lanius collurio* 18cm Small, colourful shrike. Adult male back chestnut brown; crown and nape dove grey; rump grey and tail black with white edges. Black patch through eye. Throat white, rest of underparts white, tinged pinkish-buff. Female dull brown above with dark brown eye patch; whitish below, with fine bars. Immature like female, but with heavy, scaly markings. Beak dark, large and conspicuously hooked. *Voice:* call harsh 'chack'; song melodious warble. *Habitat:* dryish, open country with bushes or scrub; heathland. Widespread.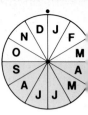

Lesser Grey Shrike *Lanius minor* 20cm Small shrike. Adult pearl grey above; wings black, with white wingbar conspicuous in deeply undulating flight; tail black, white-edged, long; characteristic all-black forehead merges with black eye patches. Throat white, rest of underparts white with pinkish-buff tinge. Immature pale scaly grey-brown above; whitish below. Beak black, hooked. *Voice:* call harsh 'chack'; song subdued, chattering warble. *Habitat:* open country, with scattered bushes and trees; scrub. Locally fairly common.

Great Grey Shrike *Lanius excubitor* 25cm Largest European shrike. Adult back pearl grey; wings black with long white wingbar conspicuous in flight; tail black, white-edged, long. Crown grey, with narrow white band on forehead extending over black eye patch (*see* Lesser Grey). Underparts whitish. Immature similar, but browner and finely barred on underparts. Beak black, hooked. *Voice:* various harsh calls; song jumble of harsh and musical notes. *Habitat:* open, wooded countryside; scrub with taller bushes. Widespread.

Woodchat Shrike *Lanius senator* 18cm Small, colourful shrike. Adult striking, characteristically pied above; back black; rump grey and white; tail black, white-edged; wings black with conspicuous double wing patches; crown and nape reddish-chestnut, richer in male than female. Underparts white. Immature sandy brown, with conspicuous scaly markings. Double pale patches in wings and pale rump conspicuous in flight – useful distinction from immature Red-backed. *Voice:* call harsh 'chack'; sparrow-like chatterings; song varied, mostly musical, extended warble. *Habitat:* dry, open, bushy country with scattered trees. Locally fairly common.

Masked Shrike *Lanius nubicus* 20cm Small, colourful shrike. Adult male blackish above, with white forehead and white edges to distinctively long narrow black tail. Bold white wingpatch visible in closed black wing, but two bars, one less prominent, visible in flight. Underparts white, shading to rich apricot on breast and flanks. Female and immature similarly patterned, but in dark and pale greys. Beak black, hooked. *Voice:* harsh, shrill 'keeer'; song subdued series of scratchy notes. *Habitat:* arid, open country with scattered bushes and trees. Locally common.

Red-backed Shrike ♂

Lesser Grey Shrike

Great Grey Shrike

Woodchat Shrike

Masked Shrike

Jay *Garrulus glandarius* 35cm Medium-sized, brightly coloured crow. Adult and immature rich pinkish-buff above with chestnut shading; white rump and black tail are particularly conspicuous in flight, which is floppy on erratically beating, very rounded, fingered wings. Crown pinkish with black flecks, raised as short crest if excited. Black moustachial stripes. Eye pale pink; beak dark grey, stout. Wings blackish, with bold, white wingbar and bright blue patch conspicuous at 'wrist'. Underparts pale pinkish-buff. *Voice:* noisy: call harsh 'skaark'; song subdued mixture of cackling notes, rarely heard. *Habitat:* woods, farmland and parkland with plentiful trees. Widespread; often quite common.

Siberian Jay *Perisoreus infaustus* 28cm Smallish, dully plumaged crow. Adult and immature dull brown over much of upperparts, but with characteristic chestnut tinge to wings, rump and sides of relatively long, broad tail. Underparts paler, buffish-grey. Beak relatively small and pointed for crow. Often arboreal and agile, usually very tame. *Voice:* call metallic 'pee-aar' or 'kook-kook', and harsh 'chairrr'. *Habitat:* northern coniferous forests. Locally fairly common.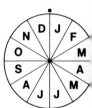

Azure-winged Magpie *Cyanopica cyana* 35cm Medium-sized, small-beaked crow. Adult and immature crown and nape glossy black; back and rump pinkish-brown. Wings and very long wedge-shaped tail striking characteristic blue-grey. Throat white; breast and belly pale pinkish-buff. Beak dark, small and pointed. Gregarious. *Voice:* call metallic 'kree-eek' or trembling 'zhree' on rising note. *Habitat:* open woodland, orchards, parks, olive groves, particularly liking some evergreens to be present. Very local; sometimes quite numerous.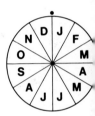

Magpie *Pica pica* 45cm Unmistakable, long-tailed, pied crow. Adult and immature head and nape glossy black; back and upper breast black; belly white; wings black and white; tail black, with purple and green iridescence, long and tapered. Freshly fledged immature duller, with rather shorter tail. Flight direct, but on fluttering, rounded wings. *Voice:* call harsh chatter; song surprisingly musical, quiet collection of piping notes, not often heard. *Habitat:* woodland, parkland, farmland, heath and scrub, mature gardens, even city-centre parks. Widespread; locally numerous.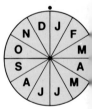

Jay

Siberian Jay

Azure-winged Magpie

Magpie

Nutcracker *Nucifraga caryocatactes* 33cm Medium-sized, brownish crow. In adult and immature most of body is uniform dark greyish-brown, distinctively marked with lines of bold white flecks. Crown blackish-brown; wings blackish. Rump white; tail black with broad white terminal bar, particularly conspicuous in flight, which is direct but floppy. Beak dark, long and dagger-shaped. *Voice:* call raucous growl and Jay-like 'skaark'; song jangle of harsh and mewing notes. *Habitat:* northern and montane coniferous and mixed forests. Locally fairly common; sometimes 'irrupts', migrating west to atypical habitats in winter.

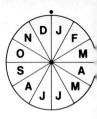

Alpine Chough *Pyrrhocorax graculus* 37cm Medium-sized, slim-beaked crow. Adult male and female plumage wholly black; legs bright coral red; beak yellow, short, relatively slim (*see* Chough). Immature dull sooty grey, with blackish legs. Aerobatic, swooping in air currents on rounded, heavily fingered wings. *Voice:* vocal; calls loud, echoing 'chee-up' or thin 'skree'. *Habitat:* alpine areas at altitudes far greater than Chough, often well above snow-line. Locally common.

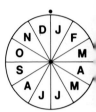

Chough *Pyrrhocorax pyrrhocorax* 37cm Medium-sized, slim-beaked crow. Adult male and female plumage wholly glossy black, with iridescent sheen; legs contrasting deep red; beak crimson, relatively long and slim, down-curved. Immature dull sooty brown, with brown legs and rather shorter orange beak. Aerobatic, swooping about in air currents near cliff faces on rounded, heavily fingered wings. *Voice:* vocal; calls include sharp 'krish' and typical, distinctive 'kee-ow'. *Habitat:* rocky mountainous areas, coastal cliffs and crags. Locally common.

Jackdaw *Corvus monedula* 33cm One of the smaller crows. Adult and immature have most of head and body dull sooty black, with variable amount of grey on crown, nape and upper breast. Beak relatively short, but stout. Eye startlingly white. Flight usually direct, with quicker wingbeats than other crows, and lacking fingered wingtips. Gregarious: often in large flocks with Rooks. *Voice:* vocal; call metallic 'jack'. *Habitat:* open woodland, parkland, farmland and urban areas, often nesting colonially in old trees or ruined buildings. Widespread; often common.

Nutcracker

Alpine Chough

Chough

Jackdaw

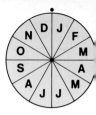

Rook *Corvus frugilegus* 45cm Medium-large crow. Adult male and female plumage wholly glossy black, with iridescent sheen. Feathers of upper leg ('thigh') loose and rough, giving 'baggy-trousered' appearance (*see* Carrion Crow). Beak pale, long, dagger-shaped, running to whitish cheek patches. Immature plumage duller sooty black; beak blackish; lacks cheek patches. Colonial when breeding, and gregarious when feeding, often with Jackdaws. *Voice:* noisy; call raucous 'carr'. *Habitat:* arable farmland, with adjacent woodland or plenty of tall trees. Widespread; often common.

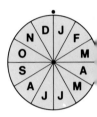

Carrion Crow *Corvus corone corone* 45cm One of the larger crows. Adult and immature wholly black; beak black and stout, with convex upper mandible and black feathers at base (*see* Rook). Feathers of upper leg ('thigh') neatly close-fitting (*see* Rook). Hooded is closely related sub-species: interbreeding occurs where their ranges adjoin and 'intermediate' offspring may have variable amounts of grey in plumage. Only occasionally gregarious. *Voice:* deep, harsh 'caw' or 'corr'. *Habitat:* open countryside of all types with suitable tall trees for nesting; also urban areas, even city centres. Widespread; rarely very numerous.

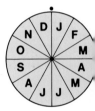

Hooded Crow *Corvus corone cornix* 45cm One of the larger crows. Adult and immature head and throat black; wings and tail black. Typically, back, breast and belly grey, but intermediates occur between this and Carrion, as result of interbreeding where their ranges adjoin; these may have variable amounts of grey on body. Only occasionally gregarious. *Voice:* call deep, harsh 'caw' or 'corr'. *Habitat:* open countryside of all types, including moorland with few trees; sometimes also urban areas. Widespread; rarely very numerous.

Raven *Corvus corax* 63cm Largest of the crow family. Adult and immature wholly black, with iridescent sheen in adult lacking in immature. Wings broad, with heavily fingered tips: often flies aerobatically in upcurrents at cliff faces. Tail relatively long, characteristically wedge-shaped. Head appears heavy, with bristling throat feathers and massive angular beak. Rarely gregarious. *Voice:* call distinctive deep gruff croak or 'gronk'. *Habitat:* rocky coasts, mountain and moorland crags. Widespread; nowhere numerous.

Rook

Carrion Crow

Hooded Crow

Raven

Golden Oriole *Oriolus oriolus* 25cm Small and Starling-like. Adult male unmistakable; rich golden yellow plumage contrasting with black wings (with gold wingbar visible in flight) and black and gold tail. Black patch through eye; beak pink, medium length. Female and immature yellowish olive green above; whitish below, with fine brown streaks on breast and flanks. Secretive. *Voice:* calls harsh and Starling-like; song characteristic, fluting 'too-loo-ee-oo' or 'wheela-whee-oo'. *Habitat:* mature open deciduous woodland, parks, orchards and olive groves. Widespread.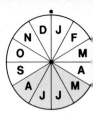

Starling *Sturnus vulgaris* 22cm Small. Summer adult blackish, glossily iridescent at close range, with bright buffish flecks on back. Beak yellow with base blue in male, pink in female; legs pinkish-brown. Winter adult lacks much iridescence and is heavily spotted with white. Immature uniformly drab brown. Gregarious, often in huge flocks. Flight swift and direct, with characteristic triangular wing silhouette. *Voice:* noisy; calls include various harsh shrieks and scolding chattering; song extended and richly varied, including much expert mimicry of other birds, often accompanied by wing-flapping display on perch. *Habitat:* catholic in choice: abundant in most habitats, less so in mountainous regions. Common.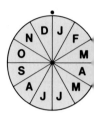

Spotless Starling *Sturnus unicolor* 22cm Small, southern European replacement for Starling, particularly during breeding season. Summer adult blackish, lacking any spotting and only slightly iridescent. Winter adult greyish-black, showing only the faintest of white spots. Immature drab brown; indistinguishable from Starling. Gregarious, though rarely in flocks anywhere near as large as those of Starling. *Voice:* noisy; calls variety of harsh shrieks and chatterings, including loud, whistling 'see-ooo'; song varied and musical, with mimicry. *Habitat:* urban areas, woodlands, cliffs and crags, both inland and coastal. Locally common.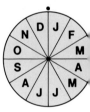

Rose-coloured Starling *Sturnus roseus* 22cm Small. Adult male and female quite unmistakable; crown, short drooping crest, nape and upper breast glossy black, contrasting with strikingly pink back, rump, breast and belly. Wings and tail glossy black. Beak pink in summer, brown in winter; legs pinkish-brown. Immature sandy olive-brown above; paler below, with faint darker streaks on flanks; lacks crest. Wings and tail darker brown; legs brown. Behaviour and flight much as Starling. Gregarious at all times, breeding colonially. *Voice:* raucous shrieks and harsh descending 'tcheeer'; song fast-moving, rather scratchy collection of high-pitched notes. *Habitat:* open country from farmland to rocky mountainsides. Locally common.

Golden Oriole ♂

Starling

Spotless Starling

Rose-coloured Starling

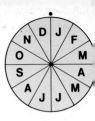

House Sparrow *Passer domesticus* 15cm Small, with triangular beak. Adult male back rich brown, with darker brown streaks; wings brown with double white wingbar. Cheeks whitish; crown grey; nape rich dark chestnut; rump grey-buff. Tail blackish. Throat and upper breast black; rest of underparts whitish. Female, immature sandy brown above, with darker brown markings; clear buff eye-stripe. Underparts pale grey-buff. Beak brownish (female) or blackish (male). Gregarious. *Voice:* noisy; call clear 'chirrup'; song monotonous chirruping notes. *Habitat:* associated with man, particularly farms, towns and cities. Widespread; often numerous.

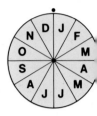

Spanish Sparrow *Passer hispaniolensis* 15cm Small, with triangular beak. Adult male rich mottled brown above, with black streaking. Crown and nape rich chestnut except for short white eye-stripe (*see* House). Throat and upper breast black (far more extensive than in House), contrasting white cheeks; belly whitish, heavily black-streaked on flanks. Female, immature mottled brown above, fawn below; difficult to distinguish from House. Gregarious; often colonial when nesting. *Voice:* call rich 'chirrup'; song monotonous series of chirps. *Habitat:* farmland, woodland, scrub; usually well-removed from habitations. Locally common.

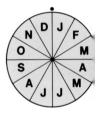

Tree Sparrow *Passer montanus* 13cm Small, with triangular beak. Sexes similar; brown above, mottled with black streaks. Crown and nape chestnut; white cheeks have central black spot. Small black bib; rest of underparts off-white. Immature drabber, less clearly marked. Beak black, stubby. Gregarious. *Voice:* calls short, metallic 'chip' and 'chop', and repeated 'chit-tchup'; distinctive, liquid flight-call 'tek, tek' difficult to describe, but diagnostic once learnt. *Habitat:* woodland, farmland and scrub. Widespread.

Rock Sparrow *Petronia petronia* 15cm Small, with wedge-shaped beak. Sexes similar; sandy brown above, with darker brown mottling. Head pattern distinctive; crown buff, flanked by broad blackish stripes, bordered by whitish stripes over eyes. Underparts pale greyish-fawn, with faint darker streaks; indistinct yellow spot in centre of breast visible only at close range. Wings dark brown; tail dark brown, with characteristic white spots near tips of feathers. *Voice:* chirrups and characteristic, squeaky 'dew-ee'. *Habitat:* barren, rocky areas; rarely near trees or habitation. Local; rarely numerous.

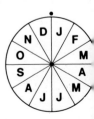

Snow Finch *Montifringilla nivalis* 17cm Small, with triangular beak. Adult male brown above; head and nape smoky grey, slightly darker about cheeks. Wings black, with huge, white patch visible in closed wing; in flight, wings appear strikingly white; wingtips black. Tail black with conspicuous broad white edges. Beak black, small. Underparts off-white, with small black bib. Female, immature duller, lacking bib; beak yellowish. *Voice:* call harsh 'tsweek'; song repetitive, twittering 'sitticher-sitticher'. *Habitat:* bare mountain tops; lower in severe weather. Local; occasionally numerous.

House Sparrow ♂

House Sparrow ♀

Spanish Sparrow ♂

Tree Sparrow

Rock Sparrow

Snow Finch

Chaffinch *Fringilla coelebs* 15cm Small finch. Adult male back rich rufous brown; tail blackish showing conspicuous white outer feathers. Head and nape grey; forehead black. Wings dark brown, with two white wingbars, one especially prominent when perched and both distinctive in deeply undulating flight. Underparts rich pink, shading to white on lower belly. In winter, much of bright plumage subdued by broad buffish feather fringes; black forehead may be scarcely visible. Beak grey, comparatively long. Female, immature brown above; pale fawn below, with white-edged, dark brown tail; wings brownish, showing two distinctive wingbars. Often gregarious in winter. *Voice:* call characteristic, ringing 'pink'; song rich, descending cascade, ending in flourish. *Habitat:* deciduous, mixed, coniferous woodland, especially during summer; farmland, parks, gardens. Widespread; common.

Brambling *Fringilla montifringilla* 15cm Small, colourful finch. Summer adult male head and back largely glossy black, with dark blackish tail and white rump conspicuous in flight. Wings dark brown, with striking orange forewing and white wingbar distinctive in flight. Throat and breast bright orange, shading to white on belly. In winter male, buff scaly markings obscure rich colouration. Female and immature mottled brown and blackish above; pale orange-brown below, but show wingbar and white rump patch conspicuously in flight. Often gregarious in winter. *Voice:* call characteristic, flourishing 'tchway', often given in flight; song repetitive series of 'twee' notes. *Habitat:* in summer, woodland of most types; in winter, woodland margins, farmland and parks. Widespread; variable in numbers.

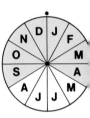

Serin *Serinus serinus* 10cm Tiny finch. Adult male predominantly olive green above, with dark brown streaks. Tail dark brown, contrasting with characteristic yellow rump, distinctive in flight. Wings brown, with double yellow wingbars. Underparts bright yellow, shading to white on lower belly, with dark brown streaks on flanks. Beak small, stubby, triangular (*see* Siskin). Female and immature much duller above; almost white below, but retain distinctive rump patch. *Voice:* call distinctive, musical 'chur-lit'; song extended, musical jingling, often produced in song-flight. *Habitat:* open woodlands, parks and gardens, with plentiful mature trees. Common.

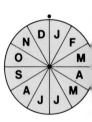

Citril Finch *Serinus citrinella* 10cm Tiny finch. Adult male and female plain yellowish-green above; striking yellowish rump contrasts with dark brown tail. Underparts clear pale yellow, almost white on belly of female. Dark brown wings show narrow double yellow wingbars; their darkness contrasts characteristically in flight with pale body. Immature brownish above; pale buff below, with heavy brown streaks. *Voice:* call plaintive 'sit'; song extended, musical jingle, often produced in song-flight. *Habitat:* alpine or subalpine, open, coniferous woodland. Locally common.

Chaffinch ♂

Chaffinch ♀

Brambling ♂ (winter)

Serin ♂

Citril Finch

Greenfinch *Carduelis chloris* 15cm Small finch with robust beak. Summer adult male olive green above, with grey on nape and cheeks; largely rich yellow below. Wings brown, with bold yellow patches conspicuous in flight; tail brown, with yellow patch on either side of base. Winter male and female brownish-olive, with less dramatic yellow patches in wings and tail. Immature similar, but with narrow brown streaks on back and flanks. Beak comparatively large, pale and triangular. *Voice:* call drawling 'dwee-ee'; song extended, purring trill, often given in butterfly-like display-flight. *Habitat:* open woodland, scrub, farmland, parks and gardens. Widespread; often numerous.

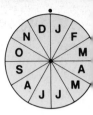

Siskin *Carduelis spinus* 12cm Tiny, dark finch. Adult male greenish above, often heavily streaked with black. Crown and small bib black; underparts yellowish, shading to white on belly; flanks streaked with brown. Wings dark brown, with double yellowish wingbars. Yellow rump and yellow patches at sides of base of dark, deeply forked tail are conspicuous in flight. Female and immature duller and browner, with brown streaking both above and below. Beak dark, relatively long and pointed at tip. *Voice:* call, often given in flight, wheezy 'chwee-oo'; song prolonged twittering. *Habitat:* woodland, including conifers, favouring birch and alder in winter; parks and occasionally gardens. Widespread; sometimes common.

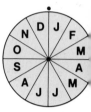

Goldfinch *Carduelis carduelis* 13cm Small, colourful finch. Adult male and female unmistakable, with harlequin plumage. Black crown and nape with red and white face are characteristic. In flight, broad gold wingbars in black wings are distinctive, as is white rump contrasting with black tail. Immature paler and buffer, with plain buff head. Beak whitish with dark tip, relatively long and pointed for finch. *Voice:* call distinctive 'dee-dee-lit'; song prolonged, liquid, warbling twitter. *Habitat:* open woodland, heath, scrub, farmland, parks and gardens. Widespread; locally common.

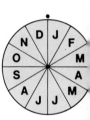

Greenfinch ♂

Greenfinch ♀

Siskin ♂

Goldfinch (adult)

Goldfinch (immature)

Linnet *Carduelis cannabina* 13cm Small brown finch. Summer adult male back rich chestnut, with whitish rump and white-edged black tail. Head and underparts pale fawn, with variable areas of glossy pink on crown and breast. Wings brown, with poorly defined white patch more visible in deeply undulating flight. Winter male, female and immature dull brown, paler below than above, with brown streaks and lacking pink patches. Beak blackish, stubby. Gregarious. *Voice:* call penetrating 'tsweet'; song musical and varied twittering, often given from prominent perch. *Habitat:* heath, scrub and farmland; occasionally parks and gardens. Widespread; locally common.

Twite *Carduelis flavirostris* 13cm Small, the 'mountain Linnet'. Adult male and female dull brown above, with darker streaking; pale buff below, shading to white on belly. In summer, male may show indistinct pinkish rump patch. In winter, beak yellow, not blackish as in otherwise-similar Linnet. Faint wingbar in uniformly dark brown wings. *Voice:* vocal; call characteristic nasal 'tchweet' or 'tchway'; song slow-paced, musical twittering. *Habitat:* breeds on moorland and mountainsides in low scrub. Winters on open ground, usually marshland or farmland, often close to sea. Local; occasionally quite numerous.

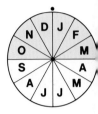

Redpoll *Carduelis flammea* 12cm Small dark finch. Adult male and female brown above, with blackish streaking; buffish below, paling to white on belly. Small black bib; small characteristic red patch on forehead and crown. Male may have pinkish flush on breast in summer. Immature duller, lacking bib and red 'poll'. Several geographical races occur: northern birds tend to be paler and slightly larger than southern ones. *Voice:* call 'chee-chee-chit'; song distinctive, high-pitched, purring trill, often delivered in circling song-flight high above woodland. *Habitat:* mixed woodland, especially where birch is common; farmland and well-treed scrub. Fairly common.

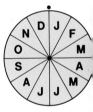

Arctic Redpoll *Carduelis hornemanni* 13cm Small pale finch. Adult male and female pale brown above, with darker brown streaking and characteristically white rump contrasting with dark brown tail (*see* Redpoll). Underparts largely white, often fluffy in appearance; sometimes with pink shading on breast of male. Small black bib; red patch on forehead and crown. Immature duller, lacking bib and red 'poll'. *Voice:* call sharp 'chee-chee-chee'; song purring trill. *Habitat:* breeds on Arctic tundra and in willow scrub. Winters in stunted boreal forests. Locally common; rare outside breeding range.

Linnet ♂ (summer)

Linnet ♀

Twite

Redpoll ♂ (summer)

Arctic Redpoll

SMALLER TRANSATLANTIC VAGRANTS
(see page 26)

Red-eyed Vireo *Vireo olivaceus* 13cm Small and warbler-like. Adult back and tail sandy olive; brownish wings. Crown and nape dove grey; conspicuous black-bordered white eye-stripe. Eye glowing red. Underparts white, shading to buff on flanks. Immature duller, greener, with brown eye; lacks grey crown. *Voice:* call 'tick'; song melodious, phrases clearly separated, often continuing for some minutes. *Habitat:* North American deciduous woodlands. Vagrant. ♣♠♣

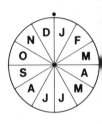

Baltimore Oriole *Icterus galbula* 17cm Brightly coloured and Starling-like icterid. Adult male head and throat glossy black; back black; rump orange; tail black, orange patches either side of tip. Wings black; orange shoulder patches; white wingbar. Underparts orange. Immature, female largely brown above; lack distinctive tail pattern. Throat whitish; other underparts pale orange-buff. Beak grey, relatively long, sharply pointed. *Voice:* call clear whistle; song fluting whistles. *Habitat:* open woodland in North America. Vagrant. ♣♠♣

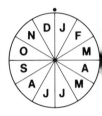

White-throated Sparrow *Zonotrichia albicollis* 15cm Small and sparrow-like. Adult male similar to House, but with black and white striped crown; yellow patch in front of eye; white throat edged by black moustachial streaks. Female and immature resemble female Reed Bunting, but with white throat patch and lacking white outer tail feathers. *Voice:* song high-pitched, repetitive, disyllabic whistle. *Habitat:* dense scrub in North America. Vagrant. ♠♣♠♣▦

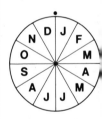

Fox Sparrow *Zonotrichia iliaca* 16cm Small and bunting-like. Adult and immature crown rich brown, streaked black; back greyish, streaked brown; tail rufous brown. Underparts white; brown markings on breast sometimes merge to give moustachial patches or breast band. Beak pale, triangular. Western race darker above, lacking streaking. *Voice:* loud song; bunting-like, slurred opening notes. *Habitat:* North American scrub and woodland undergrowth. Vagrant. ♣♠♣▦

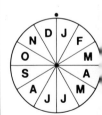

American Redstart *Setophaga ruticilla* 12cm Tiny and warbler-like. Adult male black above; orange patches at sides of base of tail; orange shoulder to wing; broad orange-brown wingbar. Belly white. Female, immature grey-brown above; yellow markings; white eye-ring. Underparts white, tinged yellow on flanks. *Voice:* high-pitched, repetitive notes, finally dropping. *Habitat:* North American woodland undergrowth. Vagrant. ♣

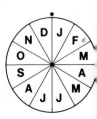

Slate-coloured Junco *Junco hyemalis* 13cm Small and finch-like. Adult has slate grey upperparts and breast; blackish tail shows white outer feathers. Blackish wings. Belly white. Immature similarly-patterned but brown. Beak pinkish-brown, triangular. *Voice:* simple, slow trill. *Habitat:* North American woodland margins, scrub, rough farmland . Vagrant. ♠♣♠♣

Red-eyed Vireo

Baltimore Oriole ♂

White-throated Sparrow ♂

Fox Sparrow

American Redstart ♀

Slate-coloured Junco

Crossbill *Loxia curvirostra* 15cm Small, with heavy, distinctive beak. Adult male predominantly dull reddish or orange; tail blackish, deeply forked; wings blackish, lacking wingbars. Female and immature predominantly yellowish-olive below; appreciably darker greenish-olive above, streaked blackish. Heavy parrot-like beak with crossed tips. Very agile in tree canopy when reaching cones. Often found in small flocks with females/immatures predominating. *Voice:* call characteristic loud, metallic 'jip'; song brief twittering. *Habitat:* coniferous woodland, usually spruce. Locally common; sometimes 'irrupts' in numbers westwards to areas outside normal range. ♠

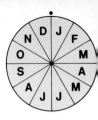

Scottish Crossbill *Loxia scotica* 17cm Small but heavily built crossbill. Adult male predominantly dull reddish or orange; tail blackish, deeply forked; wings blackish, lacking wingbars. Female predominantly yellowish-olive below; darker greenish-olive above, with dark brown streaking. Immature similar, but buffer. Heavier built than Crossbill, with appreciably stouter, parrot-like beak with crossed tips. Probably indistinguishable in the field from Parrot Crossbill, except on geographical distribution. *Voice:* call loud 'jup'; song brief, twittering warble. *Habitat:* restricted to ancient Scottish Caledonian Pine woodland. Locally common. ♠

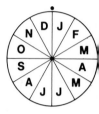

Parrot Crossbill *Loxia pytyopsittacus* 17cm Small but heavily built crossbill. Adult male predominantly dull reddish or orange; tail blackish, deeply forked; wings blackish, lacking wingbars. Female predominantly yellowish-olive below; darker greenish-olive above, with dark brown streaking. Immature similar, but buffer. Heavier built than Crossbill, with appreciably stouter, parrot-like beak with crossed tips. Probably indistinguishable in the field from Scottish Crossbill, except on geographical distribution. *Voice:* call loud 'jup'; song brief, twittering warble. *Habitat:* northern conifer forests, usually of pine. Locally common; may occasionally be driven south or west by food shortage. ♠

Crossbill ♂

Crossbill (immature)

Scottish Crossbill ♀

Parrot Crossbill ♂

Scarlet Grosbeak or Common Rosefinch

Carpodacus erythrinus 15cm Small and finch-like. Adult male predominantly deep pink, rather browner on back, fading to white on belly; tail dark brown; wings dark brown, showing two buffish wingbars, one distinct, one less so. Female and immature streaked brown above, buff below, with brown spotting. Beak black, triangular, but upper mandible rounded like Bullfinch. *Voice:* call soft 'too-eek'; song musical, piping trill. *Habitat:* damp woodland and northern scrub. Locally common.

Pine Grosbeak *Pinicola enucleator* 20cm One of the larger finches. Adult male predominantly dull pink, with darker brown streaking on back, fading to grey on belly. Tail blackish, relatively long. Wings blackish, with two clear white wingbars. Female greenish-olive, immature greyish-buff; both show two characteristic white bars on dark brown wings. Beak black, large even for finch, rounded like Bullfinch. *Voice:* call distinctive, whistling 'see-see-chew'; song loud, melodious warble. *Habitat:* mixed woodland and scrub. Locally common.

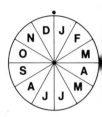

Hawfinch *Coccothraustes coccothraustes* 18cm One of the larger, stouter finches, with massive beak. Adult male and female head chestnut (brighter in male); collar grey; back rich brown; rump brown; tail white-tipped, relatively short, conspicuous in flight. Black facial patch and bib; beak silver grey, diagnostic, huge, triangular. Rest of underparts rich buff. Wings purplish-black, with bold white wingbar very conspicuous in deeply undulating flight. Secretive. *Voice:* call distinctive, explosive 'zik'; song Goldfinch-like, twittering warble, rarely heard. *Habitat:* mature woodland of all types, but particularly deciduous, with hornbeam favoured; plum orchards in winter. Widespread; rarely numerous.

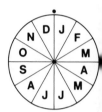

Bullfinch *Pyrrhula pyrrhula* 15cm Small, heavy-headed finch. Adult male has bold black cap, dove grey mantle and back, and striking white rump contrasting with black tail – characteristic in flight. Underparts rich pink to crimson, shading to white on belly. Wings black, with single bold white wingbar. Female has black cap, grey-brown mantle, and back, rump and tail pattern as male. Wing pattern as male. Underparts soft fawn. Immature similar to female, but lacking black cap. Beak black, distinctively rounded. Flight hesitant, deeply undulating. *Voice:* call distinctive, characteristic whistle 'peeu'; song rarely heard, quiet, creaking warble. *Habitat:* deciduous and other woodland, scrub, parks, farmland, including orchards, and gardens. Widespread; rarely numerous.

Scarlet Grosbeak ♂

Pine Grosbeak ♂

Hawfinch

Bullfinch ♂

Bullfinch ♀

Snow Bunting *Plectrophenax nivalis* 17cm Small,
strikingly pale bunting. Male in summer unmistakable;
white with black back, black and white wings and black
centre to tail. Winter male has ginger shading to crown
and nape, and back mottled brown and buff. Female and
immature mottled ginger brown above, with plain brown
cap; fawn below, shaded ginger on flanks and breast. In
flight, black-tipped white wings always characteristic.
Voice: call plaintive 'teeu' or strident 'tsweet'; song rapid,
musical, Skylark-like skirl. *Habitat:* in breeding season,
Arctic tundra and northern alpine zones; in winter, coastal
marshes and beaches. In summer, locally common; in
winter, irregular and rarely numerous.

Lapland Bunting *Calcarius lapponicus* 15cm Small, slim
bunting. Summer adult male mottled black and brown
above, with distinctive chestnut nape and buff eye-stripe;
cheeks, throat and upper breast black. Rest of
underparts white. Tail dark brown, short, with white outer
feathers. Beak yellow, conical. Winter male browner
above, with black feathers masked by buff fringes.
Female and immature mottled brown above, female with
trace of chestnut on nape; buff with brown streaking
below. Spends much time on ground. *Voice:* call
characteristic 'ticky-ticky-tew'; song short, vigorous and
musical. *Habitat:* breeds on Arctic tundra or alpine
moorland. Winters on coastal fields and marshes. In
summer, locally common; in winter, uncommon.

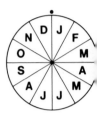

Cirl Bunting *Emberiza cirlus* 15cm Small, relatively long-
billed bunting. Summer adult male back chestnut brown
with darker streaks; characteristic olive brown rump (*see*
Yellowhammer); underparts yellow with chestnut streaks
on flanks. Head pattern distinctive, with black-edged grey
crown, yellow stripe over eye, black stripe through eye,
black-edged yellow cheeks, black bib, and yellow and
olive collar rings. Female and immature closely resemble
Yellowhammer, but retain olive brown, not chestnut, rump.
Voice: call soft 'tsip'; song repetitive series of monotonous,
metallic notes, resembling Lesser Whitethroat but lacking
'tseee' ending. *Habitat:* dry, open country with bushes or
scattered trees; scrub, farmland. Locally quite common.

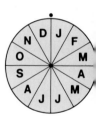

Yellowhammer *Emberiza citrinella* 18cm Small and
yellow. Summer male back, rump and wings rich
chestnut, streaked black and brown. Head and neck
bright yellow, with thin black marks on head. Breast and
belly canary yellow, tinged chestnut on breast and flanks.
Winter male browner; yellow plumage obscured by buff
fringes. Female and immature streaked brown above, but
show characteristic chestnut rump (*see* Cirl). Head
yellowish, with dark streaking; underparts pale yellow,
shading to white on belly, heavily streaked brown on
flanks and breast. Tail dark, with whitish outer feathers,
relatively long. *Voice:* call sharp 'twick'; song repetitive
'zit' notes, usually ending in long drawn-out, wheezy
'zeee'. *Habitat:* heath, scrub and farmland with hedges.
Widespread; often common.

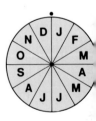

Snow Bunting ♀ (winter)

Snow Bunting ♂ (summer)

Lapland Bunting ♂ (summer)

Cirl Bunting ♀ and ♂ (summer)

Yellowhammer ♂ (summer)

Yellowhammer ♀

Rock Bunting *Emberiza cia* 15cm Small, rufous and grey bunting. Adult male back brown with blackish streaks; rump chestnut and tail white-edged black. Crown and nape grey, with distinctive pattern of black and white stripes on sides of head. Breast pale grey; rest of underparts cinnamon. Female has similar head pattern, but duller and browner. Immature resembles young Yellowhammer, but has distinctive cinnamon tinge to underparts. *Voice:* call sharp 'zeet'; song metallic rattle of high-pitched 'zee' notes. *Habitat:* rocky mountainside scrub; in winter, lower altitudes. Locally fairly common.

Ortolan Bunting *Emberiza hortulana* 15cm Small, rather drab bunting. Adult male back brown with marked black streaking; tail blackish, broadly white-edged; head, nape and breast greyish-olive contrasting with yellow bib and moustachial stripes; whitish eye-ring. Female similar, but drabber. Immature brown above; buff below, heavily streaked; creamy bib and moustachial streaks. All show characteristic pink conical beak. *Voice:* call distinctive 'tlip' or whistling 'chew'; song slow, monotonous rattle of 'zit' notes. *Habitat:* dry, open country with bushes and trees. Widespread.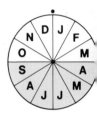

Cretzschmar's Bunting *Emberiza caesia* 16cm Small, similar to Ortolan, but brighter. Adult male back brown, streaked black; tail brown with white outer feathers. Head and breast dove grey (*see* Ortolan), with rich orange-yellow bib and moustachial stripes. Underparts cinnamon. Female similar, but duller and more streaked. Immature very like young Ortolan, but buffer. All show rich pink conical beak. *Voice:* call soft 'chip'; song slow, mono-tonous rattle. *Habitat:* with range, a useful aid in separating from Ortolan; arid, rocky hillsides and near-desert areas with scant vegetation. Locally common.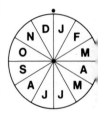

Rustic Bunting *Emberiza rustica* 14cm Small, Reed Bunting-like, but lacking black bib. Summer adult male back rich chestnut, with heavy black streaks; rump chestnut and tail white-edged black. Crown black, with slight crest; striking white eye-stripe over black cheeks. Throat white, collar band chestnut; rest of underparts distinctively white. Female and winter male similar, but with brown in place of black. Immature brown above; greyish-fawn below, heavily streaked. *Voice:* call repeated 'tsip-tsip-tsip'; song soft, but melodious, twittering. *Habitat:* damp scrub; heavy undergrowth in waterside woodland. Only locally fairly common.

Little Bunting *Emberiza pusilla* 13cm Smallest European bunting. Adult male and female brown above, streaked blackish; throat and breast buff, shading to white on belly, with brown streaks on breast and flanks. Head pattern distinctive, with black-edged chestnut crown and cheeks separated by buff outlining stripes. Blackish moustachial streaks on each side of pale buff throat. Immature similar, but dull brown. Secretive. *Voice:* distinctive 'pwick' or brief 'tchick'; song soft, melodious twittering. *Habitat:* tundra and boreal forest margins, birch scrub, often near water. Locally quite common.

Rock Bunting ♂ (summer)

Ortolan Bunting ♂ (summer)

Cretzschmar's Bunting ♂ (summer)

Rustic Bunting ♂ (summer)

Little Bunting ♂ (summer)

Reed Bunting *Emberiza schoeniclus* 15cm Small, well-known bunting. Summer male back rich brown with darker streaks; rump grey-brown; tail blackish with white outer feathers. Head pattern distinctive, with black crown and face, white collar running into white moustachial streaks and whitish underparts; bold black throat and upper breast. In winter, much of this obscured by buff feather fringes. Female and immature brown above; buff below, with dark streaks on back and flanks. Distinctive head pattern of rich brown crown separated from dark cheek patch by buffish eye-stripe, with adjacent whitish and black moustachial streaks. *Voice:* call 'tsee-you'; song short, jangling series of harsh, discordant notes. *Habitat:* marshy areas; often also relatively dry scrub and farmland. Widespread; often common. 🐦🌊

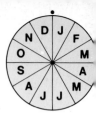

Yellow-breasted Bunting *Emberiza aureola* 14cm Small and strikingly patterned. Summer male back rich brown with black streaking; rump plain chestnut brown; tail blackish with white outer feathers. Head pattern distinctive, with chestnut crown and nape, black face and bib; narrow chestnut breast band separated from black bib by yellow throat. Rest of underparts canary yellow. Winter male has much of this marking obscured by buff feather fringes. Female and immature have dull yellow underparts with streaked flanks, and characteristic striped pattern on crown and cheeks. All show double white wingbar. *Voice:* call 'tick'; song medley of 'zit' notes. *Habitat:* damp scrub and birchwoods. Only locally common. 🌿🌳

Black-headed Bunting *Emberiza melanocephala* 17cm Small bunting. Summer male chestnut above, often only faintly marked; head all-black; tail black, diagnostic, lacking white outer feathers. Underparts canary yellow. Wings brown, with double white wingbar. Winter male has head pattern obscured by buff feather fringes. Female and immature dull brown above; buff below, with darker streaks. Both show characteristic tail and wingbars. *Voice:* call 'zit' or 'chup'; song brief, scratchy warble. *Habitat:* open country with scattered bushes or trees. Locally fairly common. 🐦🌳🏞️

Corn Bunting *Miliaria calandra* 18cm One of the larger and certainly the most nondescript European buntings. Adult and immature relatively plump, dark sandy brown above; paler sandy brown below, paling to white on belly, with copious brown streaks. Tail dark brown, lacking white outer feathers. *Voice:* call short 'tsrip' or disyllabic 'tsip-ip'; song characteristic, unmistakable, harsh, metallic jangling, delivered from prominent song-post. *Habitat:* open, dry farmland, heath and scrub. Widespread; large local variations in numbers. 🐦🏞️

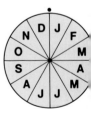

Reed Bunting ♂(summer)

Reed Bunting ♀(summer)

Yellow-breasted Bunting ♂ (summer)

Black-headed Bunting ♂ (summer)

Corn Bunting

PRACTICAL BIRDWATCHING

Every birdwatcher wants to get as close to the species under observation as possible and the best way to do this is to use good, old-fashioned fieldcraft. If wild creatures are not made aware of human presence, they will continue to behave quite naturally, and perhaps pass close by. Fortunately birds (unlike mammals) have little sense of smell, so there are no problems of the wind carrying human scent to them and frightening them. All birds, however, have exceptionally keen eyesight – far better than human vision – a hovering Kestrel can spot a beetle in the grass forty metres below! Birds also have acute hearing and they use all their senses to best effect – their ability to find food and to evade predators depends on this sharpness of their senses

Fieldcraft

What are the rules of good fieldcraft? First, always move quietly; avoid giving birds advance warning of your arrival or they will move away. In woodland, avoid crashing through the undergrowth, snapping twigs underfoot. Pause frequently to listen. If your approach has been quiet, the various songs and calls you hear will tell you which birds you can expect to see. On balance, a great many more birds are heard before they are seen than vice versa. A good knowledge – usually best gained by reference to recordings assisted by long experience in the field – of bird songs and calls is a tremendous asset. Birds have a wide repertoire of calls ranging from contact notes, simply keeping a flock together, through 'come and get it' calls when food is discovered, to various strident and brief alarm calls. Parent birds usually have soft but penetrating instruction calls for their young.

Always walk slowly in good birdwatching habitats. Use the natural cover provided by banks, trees and bushes. As a gap in the vegetation approaches, pause and listen for a few moments, then look around. Occasionally stand (or sit) still for a while, and let nearby birds reveal themselves by moving before you do. Always avoid sudden movements, like pulling out a white hankerchief to blow your nose. Avoid wearing brightly-coloured clothing and noisy plastic Kagouls or anoraks that crackle or scrape against twigs. Choose dull blues, browns and greens.

When preparing for a birdwatching expedition, however modest, it is advisable to use your field guide to establish in advance which species you are likely to see in the chosen habitat, and at that time of year. Take the field guide with you, of course, and provide yourself also with a field notebook. If you are having difficulty with an identification, and for any species with which you are not fully familiar, write down the important characteristics: size, coloration, wing shape, tail shape, type of beak and the shape and extent of any plumage marks – wingbars, eyestripes, etc. Make a note too of the call. Your own phonetic spelling is as good as anyone else's, provided that it reminds you of the sound that you heard. Use the notebook for habitat details and to record the various species that you encountered during the day, and in what numbers.

Information given under the eleven habitat groupings which follow offers further guidance as to how to prepare for different outings.

Cities, Towns and Gardens

Birdwatching, at its most comfortable, can be undertaken just by looking out of your living-room window. From here you can watch feeding and behaviour at close range, on the bird table or at natural nests or nestboxes. Slightly further afield are the opportunities offered by large parks, playing fields, lakes, reservoirs and refuse tips. Each can be rewarding. When visiting a new country anywhere in the world and staying in an unknown city, these are the sites which should be selected for the first few days of birdwatching.

🚜 Farmland

Farmland certainly merits watching regularly throughout the year since natural changes, as birds come and go on migration or as severe weather shrouds the land in snow, coupled with those introduced by the farmer, as the land is ploughed or as crops are harvested, combine to make the pattern of bird life an ever-mobile one. Birdwatching on farmland makes little demand on the observer's energies. Generally farmland is a habitat close at hand and walks need not be long. It is, though, a habitat where a slow approach may be advisable as certainly will the use of hedgerows as a screen to approach feeding birds. The use of a car as a 'mobile hide' can be effective round country lanes, especially during the breeding season. Patience is nowhere better repaid.

🌳 Broad-leaved Woodland

It is all too tempting to consider that summer, with the range of species available and the ability to use your ears to become familiar with bird songs (not just for their intrinsic beauty but also as a major aid to identification), is the only woodland birdwatching season that is worthwhile. However, it is during the winter months that woodlands may be of greatest benefit to their bird population. These months, too, provide good and interesting birdwatching: there is plenty to see, and seeing is easier with the leaves off the trees. It is fascinating to observe how various birds exploit different parts of the tree for food – often feeding as a flock of several species – or which species come to roost: where in the trees and bushes, and at what time? Again, the paramount fieldcraft rules are to move slowly and quietly, pause often, and let your ears do the 'early-warning' work! Ample nest sites should be available in the trees themselves and in the undergrowth: if they are not, and if the undergrowth is sparse, then the wood may not be worth much attention.

🌲 Coniferous Woodland

The fact that there is so little light, and consequently little undergrowth, particularly in conifer plantations, does not mean that there is a paucity of bird life in coniferous woodland. In summer months, tits and chaffinches are extremely active, as are various crossbills. But the best birdwatching occurs in new plantations of conifers during the first ten or fifteen years when the cleared woodland is rich in bird species including finches, thrushes, Wrens, Dunnocks, joined in the summer by whitethroats and warblers. Older, natural conifer forests with widely-spaced trees have a character of their own, be they close to the Mediterranean or in the far north.

🌲🌳 Mixed Woodland

Mixed woodland offers many of the assets of both coniferous and broad-leaved woodlands and can be of particular interest to the birdwatcher where old trees have been allowed to fall and decay. These provide homes for various species from woodpeckers to owls and are worth watching throughout the year.

〜 Wetlands

Upland streams are principally of interest during the summer months, when Dippers and sandpipers will be active. Lowland reedbeds are also predominantly summer birdwatching sites, although winter watching should never be ruled out. Reservoirs and gravel pits can be visited at all seasons of the year. Marshland birdwatching is a wait-and-see occupation: a good sheltered vantage point (not easily achieved) and plenty of quiet patience are even more necessary than usual.

Estuaries

Although estuaries should not be ignored during the summer months by birdwatchers, the best rewards will come from autumn, winter and spring visits, when the range of birds to be seen will be at its greatest. The watching needs careful planning. In an estuary, bird movements are related to tidal cycles, not to day and night, so perhaps several visits will be needed to establish the best viewing points and the best state of the tide. Look out, too, that the viewpoint does not face straight southwards into a low winter sun. Long watches can be chilling, so be prepared with warm clothing and hot drinks. Above all, never venture out onto the mudflats to seek a better view – they are almost always dangerous places – but wait for the tide to bring the birds to you.

Colonies of gulls and terns can be observed throughout the summer. These are spectacular sights, noisy in the extreme, and they make for absorbing detailed study. Viewed from a distance through powerful binoculars or a telescope, the comings and goings in such a crowded avian metropolis are fascinating and give a good insight into the intricacies of bird behaviour, especially how birds conduct between-neighbour squabbles!

Coasts

On most European coasts, a look at a map will indicate promontories and headlands likely to give a good view of passing seabirds, while reference to local bird books or guides will confirm which are the best to visit, and, most important, what weather conditions will bring the birds closest inshore. Once the skill of sea-watching has been acquired – it takes time and practice - this can provide sightings of many seabirds that would otherwise be difficult to encounter. It will also allow views of relatively unusual happenings – for example skuas in piratical pursuit of passing Kittiwakes or terns.

Special plans need to be made for visits to coastal habitats. As these areas are tidal, 'night' and 'day' mean relatively little to the birds – much more important is whether the tide is in, covering their food, or not. At high tide, the ducks may be close to the sea wall (a good 'hide') but the waders will have moved away to high-tide roosting spots, where they will wait until the tide falls. These roosts make excellent watching, but get there well before high tide, and tuck yourself comfortably away in an inconspicuous position. The best time to see ducks and waders feeding in most such habitats is during the couple of hours on either side of high water, when the birds have to be close to you as the water margin approaches. Local tide tables are an invaluable guide.

There are places where birdwatching can be dangerous. Never be tempted to walk out alone over sand or mud at low tide to get a better view of distant birds. Mud and sand can get soft and deep suddenly, and the tide, so far away when you set out, can race in over the flats with frightening speed and potentially lethal effect. Seek a better site, or improve the timing of your visits, or use a telescope. Similarly, always use a telescope or binoculars to get good views of seabirds on cliffs. Never try to climb nearer, as this could be physically dangerous for you, and cause equally dangerous disturbance of the birds.

Because of their need to avoid disturbance, most large seabird colonies are remote from areas of dense human habitation; and to visit them takes more planning than many birdwatching trips. Although some (like the Bass Rock off the south-eastern Scottish coast) can be seen from the mainland, most are best seen from a boat, and some colonies are served in this way by local boatmen. Given fine calm weather, the visual spectacle, the smell and the cacophony of noise will leave a life-long impression.

⛳ Heathland

Heathland is good productive birdwatching habitat right through the year. Choose a still fine day. Remember that heathland vegetation – brambles, gorse and heather in the north, or evergreen scrub in Mediterranean regions – is extremely scratchy, so wear protective clothing. As ever, patience is a virtue. Try making sucking or squeaking noises through pursed lips – often warblers will emerge briefly to see what is going on.

◣ Moorland

In high summer, as any walker will know, the moors are rich in insect life, particularly blood-sucking mosquitoes, midges and horse-flies. But the birds, few and far between, are special enough to make the long days worthwhile. Wear or take adequate protective clothing, and in summer carry some insect repellent to apply to exposed areas. Winter birdwatching can often be less profitable, and the same cautionary notes apply to remote moorland expeditions as much as to mountainous areas.

▲ Mountains

In general, though there can be fine days, mountains are inhospitable habitats for both birds and birdwatchers. Sudden mist, cloud or snow can reduce temperatures and visibility, and in remote areas real caution must be exercised. Maps, a compass and robust footwear are imperative. Travelling alone can be particularly dangerous. If possible, go with a companion, and always leave a note of your route and destination. That said, the rewards in birdwatching terms of venturing into these lonely areas can be considerable.

In remote moorland or mountain areas, remember how easy it is to sprain an ankle and proceed cautiously. Break the rules (only slightly) and take at least one brightly-coloured piece of clothing, in case it is necessary to attract attention in an emergency. In the hills, walking or climbing boots are essential. Elsewhere, short wet walks demand wellington boots; otherwise tough but comfortable footwear should suffice. Particularly in remote areas, but also when you plan to be out all day, have adequate food supplies and wear or carry plenty of warm and waterproof clothing. Weather can change very rapidly – and it is not difficult to shed a layer of sweaters or Kagoul if it gets too warm.

Having concentrated on the human aspects of fieldcraft and safety, and of comfort in the field, it is right to end this section with a cautionary statement about the birds themselves. Always put the birds' interests first. The worst thing for a tired migrant is a closely-pressing throng of birdwatchers – no matter how 'tame' or rare it may be. If you find fledglings out of the nest, leave them where they are. Pathetic and lost they may appear, but nearby there will be an anxious parent much better able to look after them than you. Nesting birds are often specially protected by law from disturbance, but it is common sense not to disturb them and open the way for predators to find their nest. Finally, it is worth remembering that other people may be birdwatching too: when you have finished looking, retreat cautiously, don't just stand up and walk off scaring birds in all directions.

Field Equipment

It is perfectly possible to see – and enjoy – birds without any special equipment but whole new worlds open up to the birdwatcher if binoculars are used. Distant birds cease to be mere dots against an expanse of water or sky, and develop colours and shapes, while close-up views show that feathers have an intrinsic beauty of their own. The use of binoculars also dramatically increases the ability to identify birds correctly, with the added bonus of offering fascinating opportunities to spy on birds going about their daily lives undisturbed.

Because binoculars are so important as a piece of birdwatching equipment, it is worth taking great care in their choice. The first rule is to test them, personally and outdoors. Implicit in this is an avoidance of mail-order offers unless they allow a similar testing opportunity, with easy return and cash refund if the test is unsatisfactory. Check for balance, that they sit easily and comfortably in the hands, with the controls within easy fingertip reach. Do the eyecups keep out stray light? Is the image of good, natural colour, free from 'rainbow' colour fringes or halos (a common fault with cheap lenses). Find and look at a vertical line – a telephone pole will do, it should not seem bent and should be in sharp focus right across the field of view (although a little less detail at the extreme margins may not matter too much).

Choice of magnification depends very much on the sort of birdwatching likely to be undertaken. Good 'all-purpose' magnifications are x7, x8, x9 and x10. Watching to a considerable extent in open habitats, such as coasts, estuaries or the moors, demands rather higher power, at least x9 and preferably x10 or x12, but such binoculars are normally comparatively large and carry a weight penalty. In contrast, woodland watching benefits from a lower magnification, say x7 or x8, coupled with lenses designed to give a wide field of view, useful when locating birds up in the tree canopy; wide-field binoculars may also be comparatively bulky. High magnification binoculars normally have smaller fields of view and may let in less light and be less suitable for evening work.

Binoculars are normally marked with two figures (eg 8 x 30): the first figure is the magnification, the second the diameter (in mm) of the larger lenses. Divide the second figure by the first ($30 \div 8 = 3.75$, or for 10 x 50, $50 \div 10 = 5.0$) to obtain a rough guide to their poor-light suitability. A factor of 5 means better light transmission (and thus better evening viewing) than 3.75. Expensive binoculars may not necessarily be the best birdwatching value – there are many excellent, reasonably-priced binoculars available. Beware of gimmicks – very high magnifications and low-cost zoom lenses for example – neither is likely to give a good optical performance.

For long-distance work – on the shore, over large lakes and reservoirs or for detailed observation of groups offering considerable identification challenges, like the waders – a telescope (and a rigid tripod to support it) is a thoroughly worthwhile investment. Most modern telescopes are compact, with much better light transmission than their forebears. They have viable magnification which allows the target bird to be located (not always easy) on low-magnification/wide field, and, once centred in the field of view, then studied in detail on high magnification, with its inevitably smaller field of view. Once again, personal testing in the field is a 'must' before a final choice is made. Other birdwatchers will happily let you try their favourites and this is by far the best way of gaining experience.

Conservation

In recent years, concern for the environment has become an issue prompting ever-widening public support. There is no doubt that our wildlife is endangered by a number of factors. Destruction of habitats is one major threat and the widespread use of fertilizers and pesticides is another practice with far-reaching and sometimes unpredictable long-term effects. The dumping of industrial waste and sewage sludge around our coasts and chemical seepage into inland waterways are further causes for anxiety.

But before condemning out of hand the activities of farmers and developers, it is as well to admit to our own vested interests. Farmers do use fertilizers and pesticides, but the public expect to buy produce that is uniform in size and colour and totally blemish-free. With every kilometre of new motorway, many thousands of habitats are destroyed, but motorists like to reach their destinations quickly and industrialists and householders alike expect the swift delivery of goods and services. The answer is for conservationists and developers to work ever more closely together and to pool their resources of expert knowledge so that serious mistakes are avoided in the future. The extraction of oil from the North Sea is a case in point. It took the political pressure of concerned people as well as the knowledge of seabird watchers to ensure that proper precautions were taken to protect the fragile marine environment.

How can we, as individuals, help to protect our bird life? Firstly we can give financial support by joining such bodies as the National Trust and the Royal Society for the Protection of Birds, thus adding numerical strength to their voice in countryside matters – a voice that is increasingly being heard. We can also participate more actively by offering our time to the British Trust for Ornithology, or to local ornithological societies. Assisting with the compilation of data banks of bird numbers, movements, habitat usage etc provides the birdwatcher with a valuable, perhaps vital role which makes the birdwatching even more satisfying.

Birdwatchers should also be aware of the law as it relates to birds. In Britain all birds and their eggs are protected under the Wildlife and Countryside Acts, except for gamebirds, including certain species of duck and wader, which may be taken outside the breeding season. Certain pest species may be killed by an authorized person. The gamebirds and pest species are listed in schedules at the end of the Acts. There are additional penalties for harming specially endangered species, when wilful disturbance or even approaching the nest may constitute an offence. We should be careful at all times to put the birds' interests first: to disturb them as little as possible, particularly in the breeding season, on migration and in exposed habitats, and ensure that other birdwatchers behave equally responsibly.

Finally, and perhaps to state the obvious, we should never litter the birds' environment with our own superfluous belongings. Plastic wrappings are not just aesthetically displeasing – they can also be lethal. Always take your rubbish home with you and dispose of it safely.

Clubs and Societies

In Britain three major voluntary bodies share the bulk of the provision of nature reserves with one government body, **The Nature Conservancy Council**. **The National Trust** has under its protection, as well as the better-known stately homes, large areas of the countryside and coast, some of it as nature reserves. **The Wildfowl and Wetland Trust** has a number of wildfowl refuges in various parts of Britain and, incidentally, keeps wildfowl collections which are well worth seeing to gain familiarity with this group of birds. **The Royal Society for the Protection of Birds (RSPB)** also maintains and wardens many reserves in all types of habitat in Britain and Northern Ireland. Besides acting as the birdwatcher's chief 'watchdog' in protecting rare birds and their eggs and habitats, the RSPB is Britain's most powerful bird life conservation lobby because of its membership, in excess of half a million. Members have privileges when it comes to visiting the reserves, and the Society has a range of film and educational services, with a well-organized junior wing, the Young Ornithologists' Club.

On a more local level, most British counties have a **County Naturalists' Trust** which manages a variety of reserves (not all for birds). Most counties, too, will have an Ornithological Society, as will some major towns and cities and many towns also have an RSPB members' group. These provide meetings and outings to good birdwatching locations which can be invaluable to the beginner, and to the newcomer to the area alike. Many, particularly the County Trusts, offer the opportunity to become practically involved in the hard work of reserve creation and maintenance.

On a national level, the **British Trust for Ornithology (BTO)** was founded by birdwatchers to co-ordinate their field-work activities. The BTO organizes the bird ringing scheme, and at any one time will have several censuses, surveys and other projects under way. Involvement can be as intensive or as casual as the individual birdwatcher desires, but one thing is certain: your birdwatching will be richer, more meaningful, more useful – and no less enjoyable – for your involvement.

British Committee for the Prevention of Mass Destruction of Migratory Birds
c/o The Lodge, Sandy, Beds SG19 2DL

British Ornithologists' Club (BOC)
c/o British Ornithologists' Union,
Zoological Society of London,
Regent's Park, London NW1 4RY

British Ornithologists' Union (BOU)
c/o Zoological Society of London,
Regent's Park, London NW1 4RY

British Trust for Ornithology (BTO)
Beech Grove, Station Road, Tring, Herts HP23 5NR

British Waterfowl Association
6 Caldicott Close, Over, Windsford, Cheshire CW7 1LW

Hawk Trust
c/o Birds of Prey Section, Zoological Society of London,
Regent's Park, London NW1 4RY

International Council for Bird Preservation (ICBP)
32 Cambridge Road, Girton, Cambridge CB3 OPJ

National Birds of Prey Centre
Bousldon House, Newent, Glos GL18 1JJ

National Trust
36 Queen Anne's Gate, London SW1H 9AS

National Trust for Scotland
5 Charlotte Square, Edinburgh EH2 4DU

Nature Conservancy Council (NCC)
Northminster House, Northminster Road,
Peterborough, Cambs PE1 1UA

North Sea Bird Club (NSBC)
c/o Phillips Petroleum Co E-A,
The Adelphi, John Adam Street,
London WC2N 6BW

Royal Society for the Protection of Birds (RSPB)
The Lodge, Sandy, Beds SG19 2DL

Scottish Ornithologists' Club
21 Regent Terrace, Edinburgh EH7 5BT

Seabird Group
c/o The Lodge, Sandy, Beds SG19 2DL

Wildfowl and Wetland Trust
Gatehouse, Slimbridge, Glos GL2 7BT

World Pheasant Association
PO Box 5, Lower Basildon, Reading, Berks RG8 9PF

The addresses of County Naturalists' Trusts and local ornithological societies can be obtained from local libraries.

BIBLIOGRAPHY

Of the vast number of bird books available, the following is a small but representative – and useful – cross-section.

Campbell, B and Lack, E (Eds.), *A Dictionary of Birds.* T. & A.D. Poyser, Calton, 1985

Cramp, S. and Simmonds, K.E.L. (Eds.), *Handbook of the Birds of Europe, the Middle East and North Africa.* Oxford University Press, Oxford, 1977 – (vols. I-V published to date)

Fisher, J. and Flegg, J., *Watching Birds.* Penguin Books, Harmondsworth, 1978

Flegg, J., *In Search of Birds; Their Haunts and Habitats.* Blandford Press, Poole, 1983

Flegg, J., *Birdlife.* Pelham Books, London, 1986

Harrison, P., *Seabirds – an Identification Guide.* Croom Helm, London, 1985

Hayman, P., Marchant, J. and Prater, T., *Shorebirds – an Identification Guide.* Croom Helm, London 1986

Jellis, R., *Bird Sounds and Their Meaning.* BBC Publications, London 1977

Lack, D., *Population Studies of Birds.* Oxford University Press, Oxford, 1966

Lack, D., *Ecological Adaptations for Breeding in Birds.* Methuen, London, 1968

Lack, P., (Ed.), *The Atlas of Wintering Birds in Britain and Ireland.* T. & A.D. Poyser, Calton, 1986

Madge, S., *Wildfowl: An Identification Guide to the Ducks, Geese and Swans of the World.* Christopher Helm, London, 1988

Mead, C., *Bird Migration.* Country Life Books, London, 1983

Mikkola, H., *Owls of Europe.* T. & A.D. Poyser, Calton, 1983

Moreau, R.E., *The Palaearctic-African Bird Migration Systems.* Academic Press, London, 1972

Ogilvie, M.A., *Wildfowl of Britain and Europe.* Oxford University Press, Oxford, 1982

Porter, R.F., Willis, I., Christiansen, S. and Nielsen, B.P., *Flight Identification of European Raptors.* T. & A.D. Poyser, Berkhamsted, 1974

Sharrock, J.T.R. (Ed.), *The Atlas of Breeding Birds in Britain and Ireland.* T.& A.D. Poyser, Berkhamsted, 1976

INDEX

Common Names

INDEX

Scientific Names